MAKE IT NEW
ESSAYS BY EZRA POUND

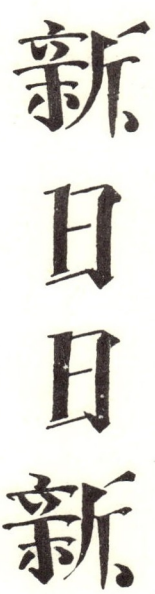

1935
NEW HAVEN · YALE UNIVERSITY PRESS

Republished 1971
Scholarly Press, Inc., 22929 Industrial Drive East
St. Clair Shores, Michigan 48080

Copyright, 1935, by Ezra Pound
Printed in the United States of America
All rights reserved. This book may not be reproduced, in whole or in part, in any form (except by reviewers for the public press), without written permission from the publishers.

Six of the following essays have been published in *Pavannes and Divisions* (Knopf, 1918) and *Instigations* (Boni and Liveright, 1920).
Library of Congress Catalog Card Number: 71-145243
ISBN 0-403-01158-2

BY THE SAME AUTHOR
A B C OF READING

Published on the
Mary Cady Tew Memorial Fund

CONTENTS

DATE LINE — *page* 3

I. TROUBADOURS: THEIR SORTS AND CONDITIONS—*about* 1912 — 23

II. ARNAUT DANIEL—1920 — 43

III. NOTES ON ELIZABETHAN CLASSICISTS—*before* 1918 — 95

IV. TRANSLATORS OF GREEK—*before* 1918 — 125

V. FRENCH POETS—*February* 1918 — 159

VI. HENRY JAMES AND REMY DE GOURMONT—*August* 1918 *and February* 1919 — 251

A STRAY DOCUMENT — 335

VII. CAVALCANTI—1910/1931 — 345

DATE LINE

DATE LINE

Rapallo Jan. 28th, anno XII

I

Criticism has at least the following categories, differing greatly in the volume of their verbal manifestation, and not equally zoned.

1. Criticism by discussion, extending from mere yatter, logic-chopping, and description of tendencies up to the clearly defined record of procedures and an attempt to formulate more or less general principles.

Aristotle being neither poet nor complete imbecile contented himself with trying to formulate some of the general interior and exterior relations of work already extant.

He has presumably the largest bastard family of any philosopher. Ninkus, Pinkus and Swinky all try to say what the next writer must do.

Dante who was capable of executing the work and of holding general ideas, set down a partial record of procedures.

2. Criticism by translation.

3. Criticism by exercise in the style of a given period.

As you would not seriously consider a man's knowledge of tennis until he either could make or had made some sort of show in a tournament, so we can assume that until a man can actually control a given set of procedures there must be many elements in them of which he has but an imperfect knowledge.

DATE LINE

This introduces almost a personal note, or at least a long-delayed reply to carpers who objected to my spending three days in translating Fontenelle on the grounds that I should have been "doing original work and not wasting my energies in translation". They took the *Divagation* as a proof that I was merely gathering daisies.

4. Criticism via music, meaning definitely the setting of a poet's words; e.g. in *Le Testament*, Villon's words, and in *Cavalcanti*, I have set Guido's and Sordello's. In the famous caricature of Edward and Alfonso, seated on a bench in the Bois, the elder monarch remarks to the younger: "A votre âge j'étais seulement Prince de Galles, c'est le seul moyen de bien connaître Paris".

This is the most intense form of criticism save:

5. Criticism in new composition.

For example the criticism of Seneca in Mr Eliot's *Agon* is infinitely more alive, more vigorous than in his essay on Seneca.

Years ago I made the mistake of publishing a volume (*Instigations*) without blatantly telling the reader that the book had a design. Coming after an era of gross confusion and irrelevance, wherein malicious camouflage is infinitely more general than any sort of coherence whatsoever, such violent rupture with the general public habit is perfectly useless, and may, for all I know, be unfair to those readers who inhabit a middle zone between effulgent intellect and *les cuistres*.

There would have been no point in asking indulgence as long as the appearances were so greatly against one, I mean so long as the appearance of mere haphazard gave ground for argument, and the reader of ill-will had ample basis for hostile demonstration.

DATE LINE

II

Criticism so far as I have discovered has two functions:

1. Theoretically it tries to forerun composition, to serve as gun-sight, though there is, I believe, no recorded instance of this foresight having EVER been of the slightest use save to actual composers. I mean the man who formulates any forward reach of co-ordinating principle is the man who produces the demonstration.

The others who use the principle learn usually from the example, and in most cases merely dim and dilute it.

I think it will usually be found that the work outruns the formulated or at any rate the published equation, or at most they proceed as two feet of one biped.

2. Excernment. The general ordering and weeding out of what has actually been performed. The elimination of repetitions. The work analogous to that which a good hanging committee or a curator would perform in a National Gallery or in a biological museum;

The ordering of knowledge so that the next man (or generation) can most readily find the live part of it, and waste the least possible time among obsolete issues.

"Admitted that it had nothing to do with life but said that it couldn't be changed, therefore I did not take the course." (Letter from Cambridge student, Nov. 1933. The letter referred to economics and not to literature, but it is too good an example of the academic, of the, alas, "university" spirit to leave unused.)

It is impossible to deal with the whole question of education, "culture", *paideuma*, in one volume of literary criticism. What Mr Eliot calls "Para something or other" need not for a few hundred pages concern us, save to say that Univer-

sity education during my time failed from lack of attention to its circle of reference:
   (*a*) Society in general.
   (*b*) The general intellectual life of the nation.
   I take it this was equally true of England, the U.S.A. and several other nations with which I have had less painful experience.

We have passed from the time wherein it was possible to illude oneself by a "glittering" or other generality. The contemporary philosopher on the Greek model with one profound (? if any) central (more or less) intuition and a lot of unverified hypotheses, analogies, uninspected detail, no longer inveigles serious attention. Philosophy since Leibnitz (at least since Leibnitz) has been a weak trailer after material science, engaging men of tertiary importance.

It is not to be expected that the knowledge of the human consciousness, or its most efficient registering material, language, can dispense with progress in method at least par with that of the particular sciences, nor that any one individual can escape all the limitations of his confrères. No biologist expects to formulate a WHOLE NEW biology. At best he expects to explore a limited field, to improve the knowledge of certain details and, if lucky, to clarify the relations of that field, both in regard to the field itself, and to its exterior reference.

You don't necessarily expect the bacilli in one test tube to "lead to" those in another by a mere logical or syllogistic line. The good scientist now and then discovers similarities, he discovers family groups, similar behaviour in presence of like reagents, etc. Mark Carleton "the great" improved American wheat by a series of searches. I see no reason why a similar seriousness should be alien to the critic of letters.

Language is not a mere cabinet curio or museum exhibit. It does definitely function in all human life from the tribal state onward. You cannot govern without it, you cannot make laws without it. That is you make laws, and they become mere mare's nests for graft and discussion. "The meaning has to be determined", etc.

There are other means of direct human communication but they are all narrowly zoned to their *specific* departments, plastic directness, mathematical relations (in music, or engineering), and in borderline territory where a little very clear language has to be used along with the "technical" expression. (Even if it be only to label the photograph or the slide.) However much you accept of Frobenius' theory of *paideuma* as general and overreaching, overstretching the single man, whether you take this as literal fact, or as convenient modus of correlation, the spoken idiom is not only a prime factor, but certainly one of the most potent, progressively so as any modality of civilization ages. Printed word or drum telegraph are neither without bearing on the aggregate life of the folk. As language becomes the most powerful instrument of perfidy, so language alone can riddle and cut through the meshes. Used to conceal meaning, used to blur meaning, to produce the complete and utter inferno of the past century... discussion of which would lead me out of the bounds of this volume... against which, SOLELY a care for language, for accurate registration by language avails. And if men too long neglect it their children will find themselves begging and their offspring betrayed. Summaries of my conclusions after thirty years' search are now available (*How to Read, ABC of Reading*).

The present volume is a collection of reports (in the biologists' sense) on specific bodies of writing, undertaken in the hope, or with the aims, of criticism and in accordance with the ideogrammic method, approached in my very early *Serious Artist*, and there exemplified in at least one case; seriously indicated in Ernest Fenollosa's *The Chinese Written Character*, there dealt with narratively rather than formulated as a method *to be used*. This method is too necessary a conclusion from all the more intelligent activity of many decades for there to be the least question of its belonging to anyone in particular.

Fenollosa's work was given me in manuscript when I was ready for it. It saved me a great deal of time. It saved probably less time to a limited number of writers who noticed it promptly but who didn't live with it as closely as I did. Fenollosa died in 1908. I began an examination of comparative European literature in or about 1901; with the definite intention of finding out what had been written, and how. The motives I presumed to differ with the individual writers.

Rodolf Agricola had centuries before indicated at least three main groups of literary purpose:

"Ut doceat, ut moveat, ut delectet",

which divisions had, I suppose, come down from antiquity. Over and above any such great general zones, we now discern beyond and instead of simple process or "technique" in the single work of a given time, the modalities, the general congeries of equations implied in "style of a period". That is a mode of writing which implies a very considerable basis of agreement between writer and reader, between writer and an order of existence, together with a comparatively low percentage of difference.

"*Toutes mes choses datent de quinze ans*", says Brancusi. There is nothing very new in this section of preface, I am only trying to save the reader's time by condensing, instead of republishing, a considerable amount of printed matter, the initial purposes of which have already been served.

DATE LINE

III

THE PARABLE OF THE HORSE AND THE WATER

You can take a man to Perugia or to Borgo San Sepolcro but you can't make him prefer one kind of painting to another. All you can do is to prevent his supposing that there is only one kind of painting, or writing, or only two or three or a limited gamut.

When you broach such matters with a confrère, you listen to his account of things you yourself do not know from experience, you tell him what he doesn't know, and you discuss, or confer on things which both have seen.

In aiming at a new *paideuma*, whatever use my criticism may be found, in the long run, to have, it has been for some years the attempt to ascertain the relations of at least a certain number of literary phenomena (blocks of verbal manifestation) without which any opinion on writing as such, is bound to be incompetent, defective to a degree that will either cause "pain" proportionate to the sensibility of the auditor, or excite his risible faculty.

English and American criticism of the generation preceding mine, and the completely contemptible and damnable activity of the literary bureaucracy in power (materially in power in the editorial offices, publishing houses, etc.) has been occupied chiefly with the inane assertion of the non-existence of the giraffe, and *magari* not of the giraffe alone, but of whole tribes of animals, the puma, the panther, the well-known Indian buffalo. Sheep and gelded oxen they had seen, but no W. H. Hudson was to be let back from the Andes with reports of birds "antient upon the Earth", no Beebe was to go down with a patent appliance and get any more kinds of fish out of the sea depth. The largest of all beasts was the horned moose of the Dominion, and so forth. The concept of fauna was to be kept within bounds. And so forth.

That these *cuistres* have been shown up for fools time and again, has as yet had almost no effect on the book trade. One piece of evidence against the whole cockeyed system is the signal incapacity of the "ploot" to do anything for the enlivenment of letters. Seven blind men to pick the company's rifleshot. Sterile incompetents charged to spend the income of millions no longer even in monuments, where the facts are comparatively easy to discover, but *magari* in CHOOSING the paladins of tomorrow, in PICKING the rising talent, which is so subtile a process that even the best player attempts it with diffidence.

Demonstration has not availed. Capacity to pick the winner has, most signally, NOT affected these domains of material action. Men who have been wrong steadily decade after decade, who have persistently at intervals of five years, or ten years or even less than five, printed vast blurbs about authors now relegated to desuetude, still decree what books shall be printed, what books the vast congeries of American Carnegie libraries shall purchase. No "regular and established publisher" has yet printed a new author's book or indeed any book on my recommendation (unless a couple of anthologies are to be counted). An analogous condition of affairs would doubtless be comic in the higher intellectual circles of pugilism or greyhound racing, but so is it gravely and solemnly on...well I suppose they aren't the slopes of Parnassus....The mountain is still intact, the spring water still excellent. The Palux Laerna has always existed.

My present publishers or at least one member of the firm suggested including my early reviews of authors of my own generation. I don't see the use of it. This book ought to be printed to read, each page ought to convey at least a little to the reader. We are not here to pass a state examination. A board of auditors wanting to verify the accounts of past literary transactions can still find at least an adequate amount of the data in the British Museum, and there must be a few copies of out-of-print volumes of mine still unpurloined from the New York and Brooklyn public libraries.

Let it stand that the function of criticism is to efface itself when it has established its dissociations. Let it stand that from 1912 onward for a decade and more I was instrumental in forcing into print, and *secondarily* in commenting on, certain work now recognized as valid by all competent readers, the dates of various reviews, anthologies, etc., are ascertainable. René Taupin took the trouble to look up a good many that I had forgotten. Careless statement, due either to laziness (in fact more probably to general mental slovenliness than to any one cause) or to local pride and prejudice, or disposition to remain in comfortable inherited preconceptions invalidates a certain amount of writing in popular editions intended to be "informative".

I think there is only one largish current error of this sort, namely that in America, the stay-at-home, local congeries did ANYTHING toward the *stil' nuovo* or the awakening. Robinson is still old style, Lindsey did have a rayon of his own, the rest trundled along AFTER the hypodermic injection had been effected via London. Even Frost the prize autochthonous specimen made his début in London, and was forced into the local New England bucolic recognition from Kensington, W. 8. The *pièces justificatives* are the back files of *Poetry* and the *Egoist* from October 1912 onward. The *Little Review*, 1917–19, as monthly, with the later quarterly issues.

The gall and wormwood to the *tribus cimicium* was that but for the present execrated writer a number of troublesome fellows could have been left unnoticed, and that oblivion would have been much less disturbing to the lethargy, sloth, etc. All of which has (and always had) a humorous side, now increasingly apparent to the dispassionate regarder of human turmoil.

DATE LINE

Emerging from cenacles; from scattered appearances in unknown periodicals, the following dates can function in place of more extensive reprint: *Catholic Anthology*, 1915, for the sake of printing sixteen pages of Eliot (poems later printed in *Prufrock*). Criticism of Joyce's *Dubliners*, in *Egoist*, 1916, and the series of notes on Joyce's work, from then on. Instrumentality in causing Joyce to be published serially and in volume form, *Egoist*, *Little Review*, culminating with the criticism of *Ulysses* in the *Mercure de France*, June 1922. This was, I believe, the first serious French criticism of Mr Joyce (that is to say it was in "French" of a sort, but at any rate comprehensible).

It might here be noted that the *Mercure* was founded on decent principles, impersonal, franco-centric but with the belief in facts, and in open discussion. Having been *the* great European review of letters for more decades than we can remember, the decline of the *Mercure* is merely the natural fatigue of men who have grown old, and outlasted their strength. It is not a voluntary stultification or a refusal of information.

Valette's reply to my comment on the deficiencies of the *Mercure*'s American notes, was to offer me the rubric...at a time when I couldn't undertake it. Any contemporary English or American old-established literary review of his time would have tried to protect some form of ignorance or incompetence.

Perhaps my criticism of Mr Lewis was primarily for his power in organization of forms, but apart from Blast, and Gaudier's sculpture, *Tarr* was serialized in the *Egoist* and the foreign editorship of the *Little Review* was undertaken "in order that the work of Joyce, Lewis, Eliot and myself might appear promptly and regularly and in one place, without inane and idiotic delay" (*Lit. Rev.* May 1917). As well as *Ulysses* (until publicly banned by 100 per cent. subjects of Woodie Wilson the damned), and poems of Eliot's second phase, the review published a number of Mr Lewis' most active short stories. I think we were suppressed for *Cantleman's Spring Mate* before we were suppressed for Bloom's deshabille.

The decision against *Ulysses* has been revoked, as I suppose the world at large knows, but the baboon law is part of the American statute. The legal machinery for future imbecility on the lines of the suppression of *Ulysses* is still there and it would take only a slip back into the era of Andy Mellon to produce another and similar grin through the eternal horse collar of the Anglo-Saxon community.

The fact that certain authors now tempt the avarice of Tauchnitz and similars seems to me to eliminate the need of repeating or reinspecting the arguments used years ago to draw unwilling attention.

In another thirty years perhaps the gross idiocy of two decades of publishers will also be more apparent. I mean their short-sightedness; and particularly their policy of debasing the literary coin to a point where it no longer deceives even the gulls. Trade bad save in inferior imitations of Edgar Wallace, because greed of immediate profit blinded them to the necessity of keeping alive just a wee bit of inventiveness, of fostering just enough good seed corn for new crop, of cherishing just that little bit of extra perception, just that bit of unwanted honesty that divides say McAlmon from Sinclair Lewis, and makes the latter so acceptable to the boob whose recognized limitations he portrays, without pulling the gaff on something that affects personal vanity.

New York the eternal goat! Year after year, decade after decade the same sort of obtuseness. America is now teeming with printed books written by imitators of McAlmon, inferior to the original. So far as I know no volume by McAlmon has yet been printed in his own country.

Antheil once gave me a list of forgotten musical composers going back to the 1860's who had, at successive intervals, been hailed as the great real thing in America to the delay or detriment of remembered composers.

It is not the *vox populi*. One is inclined to talk of popular taste, when one should hunt for the chaps working the oracle.

It becomes at this point increasingly difficult to keep economic discussion out of the narrative. Or say that lacking any decent organization, lacking any sense of responsibility toward letters, lacking men having any such sense and at the same time any power or energy, the economic factors (trade control, etc.) became increasingly capable of forcing the degradation of books. Culmination perhaps in withdrawal of overdrafts of London publishers who didn't behave.

At any rate from 1917 to 1919 the more active British product appeared in New York. New York had the chance of taking over the leadership in publishing and was too hog-stupid to grasp it. The chance lay there unnoticed for a decade, and is, I should think, by now lost.

For the post-war years up till 1924 or 1925 the activity of both America and England was perhaps more apparent in Paris than anywhere else.

The new lot of American *émigrés* were anything but the Passionate Pilgrims of James' day or the enquirers of my own. *We* came to find something, to learn, possibly to conserve, but this new lot came in disgust, harbingers, I think the term is, of an era of filth and degradation at "home" which will, I think, be increasingly apparent as just that. From Harding to Hoover, no clean thing in power. And heaven knows Wilson's stink was sufficient.

In 1933 we see the States with no contemporary daily news bulletin, the situation summed up by one experienced syndicate journalist: "Of course the revolution has occurred but the press hasn't been told yet".

IV

With the dawn of the year XII of the present era, the chronicler's old sap moves again; for the first time since we were that way ourselves, I am ready to take rash chances, to put my money on this year's colts.

That, however, is not yet chronicle and does not enter this book.

In the year XII where are we? We are in the epoch of Stalin, Gesell, C. H. Douglas and of Il Duce, with Mr Roosevelt still a more or less nebulous figure, a little here, a little there, a little to the fellow who's got the silver (without, however, "ladling it out" to the owners of foreign idem), a little to the naval gun-smiths, a little discreet hope and family rumour that F.D. understands this and that, the great master of carom shot. (To-day January 28.)

What I wrote in last February he by March had admitted the half of, leaving the rest in the fog. *Und so weiter*. Mussolini a male of the species, and the author of this year's *consegna*.

"Gli uomini vivono in pochi". Frobenius very much on the job, Cocteau "fragile ma non debole".

To come to my table of contents:

An examination
   OF speech in relation to music. Sections I, II.
   OF speech   III, IV, V.

VI. General summary of state of human consciousness in decades immediately before my own, the H. James and De Gourmont compendium.

VII. Cavalcanti, as bringing together all of these strands, the consciousness, depth of same almost untouched in writing between his time and that of Ibsen and James; meaning if you come at it not as platonic formulation of philosophy but as psychology.

VIII. A final segment, deferred to another volume, was retrospect to a more immediate past. After that section I have submitted to guidance. I had intended to provide the book derisively with an appendix, vermiform. Papa Flaubert compiled a *sottisier*, I also compiled a *sottisier*. I do not yield a jot in my belief that such compilations are useful, I concede that there may be no need of reprinting mine at this moment. At any rate the snippets are there on file. You can't know an era merely by knowing its best. Gourmont and James weren't the whole of the latter half of a century. There are all strata down to the bottom, the very.

You get the Middle Ages from Mussato, in a way you do not, I think, get them from Dante without Mussato; and Mussato is again a summit.

The contention that my *sottisier*, compiled fifteen years ago, could be equalled in the current press, doesn't seem to me relevant. But for a few lines by Milord Rochester one might think certain inanities were wholly Victorian and not *of* the laced Restoration.

I admit, without being asked, that the *sottisier* would have displayed nothing appertaining to the "best that has been known and thought". It might, *anzi*, help toward evaluation. However there is no hurry about it, the careful historian of the 1910's is not yet busy in numbers.

The rest of the items are I think either self-explanatory, or better indicated in immediate notes.

J'Y TIENS

There is no use my moderator's suggesting that in my notes on Monro and Housman in the *Criterion* I have in a general way indicated the state of English culture in 1910–30 or 1933. I am not specifically concerned with the state of enlightenment among a few hundred very refined persons with an abnormal or super-medium interest in *belles lettres*. I distinctly assert that I made the *sottisier*, that I definitely examined

DATE LINE

symptoms which the visiting anthropologist or student of Kulturmorphologie would have noticed as "customs of the tribus Britannicus", the material which the average man would have found easy to hand as printed matter in the city of London about 1918–19.

That constitutes a definite dimension, its examination a species of measurement of *mœurs contemporaines*. To be used as "off set" against any other more special conditions.

As to enlightened opinion: By 1920 or whatever date more precise, enlightened opinion had digested Fabre and Frazer, at least to the extent shown by the Gourmont citations.

By somewhere about 1750 "enlightened opinion" was digesting the disposition of Fontenelle toward the cosmos. The modality of such statement has an effect on the "literal meaning".

By 1934 Frazer is sufficiently digested for us to know that opposing systems of European morality go back to the opposed temperaments of those who thought copulation was good for the crops, and the opposed faction who thought it was bad for the crops (the scarcity economists of prehistory). That ought to simplify a good deal of argument. The Christian in being Christian might at least decide whether he is for Adonis or Atys, or whether he is Mediterranean. The exact use of dyeing Europe with a mythology elucubrated to explain the thoroughly undesirable climate of Arabia Petraea is in some reaches obscure.

Further attempt to answer Mr Eliot's indirect query as to "What Mr P. believes", would be perhaps out of place at this juncture. The peculiar frenzies of the Atys cult seem unadapted to the pleasanter parts of the Mediterranean basin. I have, I think, at no time attempted to conceal my beliefs from my so eminent colleague, but I have at all times desired to know the demarcation between what I know and what I do not know, as perhaps even the partial reprint of my *Cavalcanti* will help to convince the reader (if not, he can consult the Genova edition, with plates and further apparatus, if same be in the Museum Britannicum).

This difference between what is known, and what is merely faked or surmised has at all times seemed to me worth discovering. Obviously the more limited the field the more detailed can the demarcation become.

It is, I feel, obvious that only a limited number of authors are worth the attention there (*Rime*, Marsano edition) demonstrably given to Guido, it is I think arguable whether, even there, such attention would have been wisely spent *had I not* later set a good deal of him to music, or had I not wanted the edition to serve as a model for editions of a very limited number of authors.

(Again on the principle of getting the factors of main importance clearly detached from the rest... in this case very much a matter of photos and typography.)

It seems to me desirable to establish demarcation between the known and the unknown, in at least a few specimen areas.

Until one has taken the trouble to do so I don't see how one is to escape a certain gross clumsiness in the general Anschauung.

I mean for example, as I have said in a much shorter book (*à propos* Donne in the *ABC of Reading*) that it is perfectly ascertainable that a number of men in succeeding epochs have managed to be intelligible to each other concerning a gamut of perceptions which other bodies of men wholly deny.

It would seem to me rather unscientific to deny their existence at least as perceptions, at least as a correlatable congeries of communicable data, even though you quite obviously cannot discuss them profitably with nine-tenths of your acquaintance, though you occasionally can with quite simple unfeigning people.

As to what I believe:

        I believe the *Ta Hio*.

DATE LINE

When a dozen people have convinced me that they understand that so lucid work, I may see reason for attempting a more elaborate exposition. Until then the case seems rather to resemble that of my last four pages on "great bass", I don't know anyone save Antheil and Tibor Serly, and possibly two other composers who could make any use of those pages. The American composer John Becker tried vainly to get them printed in several musical periodicals, they serve just as well in carbon copies and in conversation as they now could in print.

An epic is a poem including history. I don't see that anyone save a sap-head can now think he knows any history until he understands economics. Whether he propose to do anything, or to incite anyone else to action, he manifestly cannot understand Gibbon or Gatti's *Dazj e Monti* or any other collection of data and documents touching the workings, without Ariadne's thread—the proof being that generations of so-called historians just haven't. Wherever you find a Medici you find a loan at low interest, often at half that of their contemporaries'.

I thought in my jactancy that I had performed a *tour de force* when I reduced a contemporary economic equation to what the benevolent consider verse, within 24 hours (twenty-four hours) I came on Dante inveighing against Philippe le Bel for debasing the currency (*Paradiso* XIX, 118).

I am leaving my remark on *anagke* in the H. James notes, but the Act of God alters with time. The wreck of a fifteenth-century vessel might be an Act of God, whereas disaster in storm of like dimensions would to-day be due to gross carelessness either in construction, navigation or in care of the machines. Some infamies in the year XII are as needless as death by thirst in the city of London. There is a TIME in these things.

It is quite obvious that we do not all of us inhabit the same time.

I

TROUBADOURS*
THEIR SORTS AND
CONDITIONS

The argument whether or no the troubadours are a subject worthy of study is an old and respectable one. If Guillaume, Count of Peiteus, grandfather of King Richard Cœur de Lion, had not been a man of many energies, there might have been little food for this discussion. He was, as the old book says of him, "of the greatest counts in the world, and he had his way with women". He made songs for either them or himself or for his more ribald companions. They say that his wife was Countess of Dia, "fair lady and righteous", who fell in love with Raimbaut d'Aurenga and made him many a song. Count Guillaume brought composition in verse into court fashions, and gave it a social prestige which it held till the crusade of 1208 against the Albigenses. The mirth of Provençal song is at times anything but sunburnt, and the mood is often anything but idle. De Born advises the barons to pawn their castles before making war, thus if they won they could redeem them, if they lost the loss fell on the holder of the mortgage.

The forms of this poetry are highly artificial, and as artifice they have still for the serious craftsman an interest, less indeed

* The *Quarterly Review*, 1913.

than they had for Dante, but by no means inconsiderable. No student of the period can doubt that the involved forms, and the veiled meanings in the "trobar clus", grew out of living conditions, and that these songs played a very real part in love intrigue and in the intrigue preceding warfare. The time had no press and no theatre. If you wish to make love to women in public, and out loud, you must resort to subterfuge: and Guillaume St Leider even went so far as to get the husband of his lady to do the seductive singing.

If a man of our time be so crotchety as to wish emotional, as well as intellectual, acquaintance with an age so out of fashion as the twelfth century, he may try in several ways to attain it. He may read the songs themselves from the old books—from the illuminated vellum—and he will learn what the troubadours meant to the folk of the century just after their own. He will learn a little about their costume from the illuminated capitals. Or he may try listening to the words with the music, for, thanks to Jean Beck and others,* it is now possible to hear the old tunes. They are perhaps a little Oriental in feeling, and it is likely that the spirit of Sufism is not wholly absent from their content. Or, again, a man may walk the hill roads and river roads from Limoges and Charente to Dordogne and Narbonne and learn a little, or more than a little, of what the country meant to the wandering singers. He may learn, or think he learns, why so many canzos open with speech of the weather; or why such a man made war on such and such castles. Or he may learn the outlines of these events from the "razos", or prose paragraphs of introduction, which are sometimes called "lives of the troubadours". And, if he have mind for these latter, he will find in the Bibliothèque Nationale at Paris the manuscript of Miquel de la Tour, written perhaps in the

* Walter Morse Rummel's *Neuf Chansons de Troubadours*, pub. Augener, Ltd., etc.; also the settings by Aubry.

author's own handwriting; at least we read "I Miquel de la Tour, scryven, do ye to wit".

Miquel gives us to know that such and such ladies were courted with greater or less good fortune by such and such minstrels of various degree, for one man was a poor vavassour, and another was King Amfos of Aragon; and another, Vidal, was son of a furrier, and sang better than any man in the world; and Raimon de Miraval was a poor knight that had but part of a castle; and Uc Brunecs was a clerk, and he had an understanding with a *borgesa* who had no mind to love him or to keep him, and who became mistress to the Count of Rodez. "Voila l'estat divers d'entre eulx."

The monk, Gaubertz de Poicebot, "was a man of birth; he was of the bishopric of Limozin, son of the castellan of Poicebot. And he was made monk when he was a child in a monastery, which is called Sain Leonart. And he knew well letters, and well to sing, and well *trobar*.* And for desire of woman he went forth from the monastery. And he came thence to the man to whom came all who for courtesy wished honour and good deeds—to Sir Savaric de Malleon—and this man gave him the harness of a joglar and a horse and clothing; and then he went through the courts and composed and made good canzos. And he set his heart upon a donzella gentle and fair and made his songs of her, and she did not wish to love him unless he should get himself made a knight and take her to wife. And he told En Savaric how the girl had refused him, wherefore En Savaric made him a knight and gave him land and the income from it. And he married the girl and held her in great honour. And it happened that he went into Spain, leaving her behind him. And a knight out of England set his mind upon her and did so much and said so much that he led her with him, and he kept her long time his mistress and then let her go

---

* Poetical composition, literally "to find".

to the dogs (*malamen anar*). And En Gaubertz returned from Spain, and lodged himself one night in the city where she was. And he went out for desire of woman, and he entered the *alberc* of a poor woman; for they told him there was a fine woman within. And he found his wife. And when he saw her, and she him, great was the grief between them and great shame. And he stopped the night with her, and on the morrow he went forth with her and took her to a nunnery where he had her enter. And for this grief he ceased to sing and to compose". If you are minded, as Browning was in his *One Word More*, you may search out the song that En Gaubertz made, riding down the second time from Malleon, flushed with the unexpected knighthood.

"Per amor del belh temps suau
E quar fin amor men somo."*

"For love of the sweet time and soft" he beseeches this "lady in whom joy and worth have shut themselves and all good in its completeness" to give him grace and the kisses due to him a year since. And he ends in envoi to Savaric.

"Senher savaric larc e bo
Vos troba hom tota fazo
Quel vostre ric fag son prezan
El dig cortes e benestan."†

La Tour has given us seed of drama in the passage above rendered. He has left us also an epic in his straightforward prose. "Piere de Maensac was of Alverne (Auvergne) a poor knight, and he had a brother named Austors de Maensac,

* "For love of the fair time and soft,
  And because fine love calleth me to it."
† "Milord Savaric, generous
  To thy last bond, men find thee thus,
  That thy rich acts are food for praise
  And courtly are thy words and days."

TROUBADOURS—THEIR SORTS AND CONDITIONS

and they both were troubadours and they both were in concord that one should take the castle and the other the *trobar*." And presumably they tossed up a *marabotin* or some such obsolete coin, for we read, "And the castle went to Austors and the poetry to Piere, and he sang of the wife of Bernart de Tierci. So much he sang of her and so much he honoured her that it befell that the lady let herself go (*furar a del*). And he took her to the castle of the Dalfin of Auvergne, and the husband, in the manner of the golden Menelaus, demanded her much, with the church to back him and with the great war that they made. But the Dalfin maintained him (Piere) so that he never gave her up. He (Piere) was a straight man (*dreitz om*) and good company, and he made charming songs, tunes and the words, and good coblas of pleasure". And among them is one beginning

> "Longa saison ai estat vas amor
> Humils e francs, y ai faich son coman".*

Dante and Browning have created so much interest in Sordello that it may not be amiss to give the brief account of him as it stands in a manuscript in the Ambrosian library at Milan. "Lo Sordels *si fo di Mantovana*. Sordello was of Mantuan territory of Sirier (this would hardly seem to be Goito), son of a poor cavalier who had name Sier Escort (Browning's El Corte), and he delighted himself in chançons, to learn and to make them. And he mingled with the good men of the court. And he learned all that he could and he made coblas and sirventes. And he came thence to the court of the Count of St Bonifaci, and the Count honoured him much. And he fell in love with the wife of the Count, in the form of pleasure (*a forma de solatz*), and she with him. (The Palma of Browning's poem and the Cunizza of Dante's.) And it befell that the Count stood ill with her brothers. And

---

* "For a long time have I stood toward Love
  Humble and frank, and have done his commands."

TROUBADOURS—THEIR SORTS AND CONDITIONS

thus he estranged himself from her, and from Sier Sceillme and Sier Albrics. Thus her brothers caused her to be stolen from the Count by Sier Sordello and the latter came to stop with them. And he (Sordello) stayed a long time with them in great happiness, and then he went into Proenssa where he received great honours from all the good men and from the Count and from the Countess who gave him a good castle and a wife of gentle birth." (Browning with perfect right alters this ending to suit his own purpose.)

The luck of the troubadours was as different as their ranks, and they were drawn from all social orders. We are led far from polite and polished society when we come to take note of that Gringoire, Guillem Figiera, "son of a tailor; and he was a tailor; and when the French got hold of Toulouse he departed into Lombardy. And he knew well *trobar* and to sing, and he made himself *joglar* among the townsfolk (*ciutadins*). He was not a man who knew how to carry himself among the barons or among the better class, but much he got himself welcomed among harlots and slatterns and by inn-keepers and taverners. And if he saw coming a good man of the court, there where he was, he was sorry and grieved at it, and he nearly split himself to take him down a peg (*et ades percussava de lui abaissar*)".

For one razo that shows an unusual character there are a dozen that say simply that such or such a man was of Manes, or of Cataloigna by Rossilon, or of elsewhere, "a poor cavalier".* They made their way by favour at times, or by singing, or by some other form of utility. Ademar of Gauvedan "was of the castle Marvois, son of a poor knight. He was knighted by the lord of Marvois. He was a brave man but could not keep up his estate as knight, and he became jongleur and was respected by all the best people. And later he went into orders at Gran Mon". Elias Cairels "was

* For example, Peire Bermon and Palazol.

of Sarlat; ill he sang, ill he composed, ill he played the fiddle and worse he spoke, but he was good at writing out words and tunes. And he was a long time wandering, and when he quitted it, he returned to Sarlat and died there". Perdigo was the son of a fisherman and made his fortune by his art. Peirol was a poor knight who was fitted out by the Dalfin of Auvergne and made love to Sail de Claustra; and all we know of Cercamon is that he made *vers* and *pastorelas* in the old way and that "he went everywhere he could get to". Pistoleta "was a singer for Arnaut of Marvoil, and later he took to *trobar* and made songs with pleasing tunes and he was well received by the best people, although a man of little comfort and of poor endowment and of little stamina. And he took a wife at Marseilles and became a merchant and became rich and ceased going about the courts". Guillems the skinny was a joglar of Manes, and the capital letter shows him throwing 3, 5, and 4, on a red dice board. "Never had he on harness, and what he gained he lost *malamen*, to the taverns and the women. And he ended in a hospital in Spain."

The razos have in them the seeds of literary criticism. The speech is, however, laconic. Aimar lo Ners was a gentleman. "He made such songs as he knew how to." Aimeric de Sarlat, a joglar, became a troubadour, "and yet he made but one song". Piere Guillem of Toulouse "Made good coblas, but he made too many". Daude of Pradas made canzos "per sen de trobar", which I think we may translate "from a mental grasp of the craft". "But they did not move from love, wherefore they had not favour among folk. They were not sung." We find also that the labour and skill were divided. One man played the viol most excellently, and another sang, and another spoke his songs to music,* and another, Jaufre Rudel, Brebezieu's father-in-law, made "good tunes with poor words to go with them".

* Richard of Brebezieu (disia sons).

TROUBADOURS—THEIR SORTS AND CONDITIONS

The troubadour's person comes in for as much free criticism as his performance. Elias fons Salada was "a fair man verily, as to feature, a joglar, no good troubadour".* But Faidit, a joglar of Uzerche, "was exceedingly greedy both to drink and to eat, and he became fat beyond measure. And he took to wife a public woman; very fair and well taught she was, but she became as big and fat as he was. And she was from a rich town Alest of the Mark of Provenca from the seignory of En Bernart d'Andussa".

One of the noblest figures of the time, if we are to believe the chronicle, was Savaric de Mauleon, the rich baron of Peitieu, mentioned above, son of Sir Reios de Malleon; "lord was he of Malleon and of Talarnom and of Fontenai, and of castle Aillon and of Boet and of Benaon and of St Miquel en Letz and of the isle of Ners and of the isle of Mues and of Nestrine and of Engollius and of many other good places". As one may read in the continuation of this notice and verify from the razos of the other troubadours, "he was of the most open-handed men in the world". He seems to have left little verse save the tenzon with Faidit.

"Behold divers estate between them all!" Yet, despite the difference in conditions of life between the twelfth century and our own, these few citations should be enough to prove that the people were much the same, and if the preceding notes do not do this, there is one tale left that should succeed.

"The Vicomte of St Antoni was of the bishopric of Caortz (Cahors), Lord and Vicomte of St Antoni; and he loved a noble lady who was wife of the seignor of Pena Dalbeges, of a rich castle and a strong. The lady was gentle and fair and valiant and highly prized and much honoured; and he very valiant and well trained and good at arms and charming,

---

* The "joglar" was the player and singer, the "troubadour" the "finder" or composer of songs and words.

and a good trobaire, and had name Raimons Jordans; and the lady was called the Vicomtesse de Pena; and the love of these two was beyond all measure. And it befell that the Viscount went into a land of his enemies and was grievous wounded, so that report held him for dead. And at the news she in great grief went and gave candles at church for his recovery. And he recovered. And at this news also she had great grief." And she fell a-moping, and that was the end of the affair with St Antoni, and "thus was there more than one in deep distress". "Wherefore" Elis of Montfort, wife of William à-Gordon, daughter of the Viscount of Trozena, the glass of fashion and the mould of form, the pride of "youth, beauty, courtesy", and presumably of justice, mercy, long-suffering, and so forth, made him overtures, and successfully. And the rest is a matter much as usual.

If humanity was much the same, it is equally certain that individuals were not any more like one another; and this may be better shown in the uncommunicative *canzoni* than in the razos. Thus we have a pastoral from the sensitive and little known Joios of Tolosa:

"Lautrier el dous temps de pascor
En una ribeira",

which runs thus:

"The other day, in the sweet time of Easter, I went across a flat land of rivers hunting for new flowers, walking by the side of the path, and for delight in the greenness of things and because of the complete good faith and love which I bear for her who inspires me, I felt a melting about my heart and at the first flower I found, I burst into tears.

"And I wept until, in a shady place, my eyes fell upon a shepherdess. Fresh was her colour, and she was white as a snow-drift, and she had doves' eyes,"....

TROUBADOURS—THEIR SORTS AND CONDITIONS

In very different key we find the sardonic Count of Foix, in a song which begins mildly enough for a spring song:

"Mas qui a flor si vol mesclar",

and turns swiftly enough to a livelier measure:

"Ben deu gardar lo sieu baston
Car frances sabon grans colps dar
Et albirar ab lor bordon
E nous fizes in carcasses
Ni en genes ni en gascon".

"Let no man lounge amid the flowers
Without a stout club of some kind.
Know ye the French are stiff in stour
And sing not all they have in mind,
So trust ye not in Carcason,
In Genovese, nor in Gascon."

My purpose in all this is to suggest to the casual reader that the Middle Ages did not exist in tapestry alone, nor in the fourteenth-century romances, but that there was a life like our own, no mere sequence of citherns and citoles, nor a continuous stalking about in sendal and diaspre. Men were pressed for money. There was unspeakable boredom in the castles. The chivalric singing was devised to lighten the boredom; and this very singing became itself in due time, in the manner of all things, an ennui.

There has been so much written about the poetry of the best Provençal period, to wit the end of the twelfth century, that I shall say nothing of it here, but shall confine the latter part of this essay to a mention of three efforts, or three sorts of effort which were made to keep poetry alive after the crusade of 1208.

Any study of European poetry is unsound if it does not commence with a study of that art in Provence. The art of quantitative verse had been lost. This loss was due more to ignorance than to actual changes of language, from Latin, that is, into the younger tongues. It is open to doubt whether the Aeolic singing was ever comprehended fully even in Rome. When men began to write on tablets and ceased singing to the *barbitos*, a loss of some sort was unavoidable. Propertius may be cited as an exception, but Propertius writes only one metre. In any case the classic culture of the Renaissance was grafted on to mediaeval culture, a process which is excellently illustrated by Andreas Divus Iustinopolitanus' translation of the *Odyssey* into Latin. It is true that each century after the Renaissance has tried in its own way to come nearer the classic, but, if we are to understand that part of our civilization which is the art of verse, we must begin at the root, and that root is mediaeval. The poetic art of Provence paved the way for the poetic art of Tuscany; and to this Dante bears sufficient witness in the *De Vulgari Eloquio*. The heritage of art is one thing to the public and quite another to the succeeding artists. The artist's inheritance from other artists can be little more than certain enthusiasms, which usually spoil his first work; and a definite knowledge of the modes of expression, which knowledge contributes to perfecting his more mature performance. This is a matter of technique.

After the compositions of Vidal, Rudel, Ventadour, of Bornelh and Bertrans de Born and Arnaut Daniel, there seemed little chance of doing distinctive work in the "canzon de l'amour courtois". There was no way, or at least there was no man in Provence capable of finding a new way of saying in six closely rhymed strophes that a certain girl, matron or widow was like a certain set of things, and that the troubadour's virtues were like another set, and that all this was very sorrowful or otherwise, and that there was but one obvious remedy. Richard of Brebezieu had done his best for tired ears; he had made similes of beasts and of the stars which got him a passing favour. He had compared himself to the fallen elephant and to the self-piercing pelican, and no one could go any further. Novelty is reasonably rare even in modes of decadence and revival. The three devices tried for poetic restoration in the early thirteenth century were the three usual devices. Certain men turned to talking art and aesthetics and attempted to dress up the folk-song. Certain men tried to make verse more engaging by stuffing it with an intellectual and argumentative content. Certain men turned to social satire. Roughly, we may divide the interesting work of the later Provençal period into these three divisions. As all of these men had progeny in Tuscany, they are, from the historical point of view, worth a few moments' attention.

The first school is best represented in the work of Giraut Riquier of Narbonne. His most notable feat was the revival of the *Pastorela*. The Pastorela is a poem in which a knight tells of having met with a shepherdess or some woman of that class, and of what fortune and conversation befell him. The form had been used long before by Marcabrun, and is familiar to us in such poems as Guido Cavalcanti's *In un boschetto trovai pastorella*, or in Swinburne's *An Interlude*. Guido, who did all things well, whenever the fancy took him, has raised this form to a surpassing excellence in his poem *Era in pensier d'Amor, quand' io trovai*. Riquier is most amusing in his account of the inn-mistress at Sant Pos de Tomeiras, but even there he is less amusing than was Marcabrun when he sang of the shepherdess in *L'autrier iost' una sebissa*. Riquier has, however, his place in the apostolic succession; and there is no reason why Cavalcanti and Riquier should not have met while the former was on his journey to Campostella, although Riquier may as easily have been in Spain at the time. At any rate the Florentine noble would have heard the *pastorelas* of Giraut; and this may have set him to his *ballate*, which seem to date from the time of his meeting with Mandetta in Toulouse. Or it may have done nothing of the kind. The only more or less settled fact is that Riquier was then the best-known living troubadour and near the end of his course.

The second, and to us the dullest of the schools, set to explaining the nature of love and its effects. The normal modern will probably slake all his curiosity for this sort of work in reading one such poem as the King of Navarre's *De Fine amour vient science e beautez*. "Ingenium nobis ipsa puella facit", as Propertius put it, or *anglice*:

"Knowledge and beauty from true love are wrought,
And likewise love is born from this same pair;
These three are one to whoso hath true thought", etc.

There might be less strain if one sang it. This peculiar variety of flame was carried to the altars of Bologna, whence Guinicello sang:

"Al cor gentil ripara sempre amore,
Come l'augello in selva alla verdura".

And Cavalcanti wrote: "A lady asks me, wherefore I wish to speak of an accident* which is often cruel", and Dante, following in his elders' footsteps, the *Convito*.

The third school is the school of satire, and is the only one which gives us a contact with the normal life of the time. There had been Provençal satire before Piere Cardinal; but the sirventes of Sordello and De Born were directed for the most part against persons, while the Canon of Clermont drives rather against conditions. In so far as Dante is critic of morals, Cardinal must be held as his forerunner. Miquel writes of him as follows:

"Peire Cardinal was of Veillac of the city Pui Ma Donna, and he was of honourable lineage, son of a knight and a

* *Accidente*, used as a purely technical term of his scholastic philosophy.

lady. And when he was little his father put him for canon in the *canonica major* of Puy; and he learnt letters, and he knew well how to read and to sing; and when he was come to man's estate he had high knowledge of the vanity of this world, for he felt himself gay and fair and young. And he made many fair arguments and fair songs. And he made canzos, but he made only a few of these, and sirventes; and he did best in the said sirventes where he set forth many fine arguments and fair examples for those who understand them; for much he rebuked the folly of this world and much he reproved the false clerks, as his sirventes show. And he went through the courts of kings and of noble barons and took with him his joglar who sang the sirventes. And much was he honoured and welcomed by my lord the good king of Aragon and by honourable barons. And I, master Miquel de la Tour, escriuan (scribe), do ye to wit that N. Peire Cardinal when he passed from this life was nearly a hundred. And I, the aforesaid Miquel, have written these sirventes in the city of Nemze (Nîmes) and here are written some of his sirventes".

If the Vicomtesse de Pena reminds us of certain ladies with whom we have met, these sirventes of Cardinal may well remind us that thoughtful men have in every age found almost the same set of things or at least the same sort of things to protest against; if it be not a corrupt press or some monopoly, it is always some sort of equivalent, some conspiracy of ignorance and interest. And thus he says, "Li clerc si fan pastor". The clerks pretend to be shepherds, but they are wolfish at heart.

If he can find a straight man, it is truly matter for song; and so we hear him say of the Duke of Narbonne, who was, apparently, making a fight for honest administration:

"Coms raymon duc de Narbona
 Marques de proensa

> Vostra valors es tan bona
> Que tot lo mon gensa,
> Quar de la mar de bayona
> En tro a valenca
> Agra gent falsae fellona
> Lai ab vil temensa,
> Mas vos tenetz vil lor
> Q'n frances bevedor
> Plus qua* perditz austor
> No vos fan temensa".

"Now is come from France what one did not ask for"—he is addressing the man who is standing against the North—

> "Count Raymon, Duke of Narbonne,
> Marquis of Provence,
> Your valour is sound enough
> To make up for the cowardice of
> All the rest of the gentry.
> For from the sea at Bayonne,
> Even to Valence,
> Folk would have given in (sold out),
> But you hold them in scorn,
> [Or, reading 'l'aur', 'scorn the gold'.]
> So that the drunken French
> Alarm you no more
> Than a partridge frightens a hawk".

Cardinal is not content to spend himself in mere abuse, like the little tailor Figeira, who rhymes Christ's "mortal pena" with

> "Car voletz totzjors portar la borsa plena",

* Here lies the difficulty of all this sort of scholarship! Is this "qua" or "que"? The change of the letter will shift us into irony.

which is one way of saying "Judas!" to the priests. He, Cardinal, sees that the technique of honesty is not always utterly simple.

> "Li postilh, legat elh cardinal
> Fa cordon tug, y an fag establir
> Que qui nos pot de traisson esdir",

which may mean, "The pope and the legate and the cardinal have twisted such a cord that they have brought things to such a pass that no one can escape committing treachery". As for the rich:

> "Li ric home an pietat tan gran
> Del autre gen quon ac caym da bel.
> Que mais volon tolre q̄ lop no fan
> E mais mentir que tozas de bordelh".

"The rich men have such pity
For other folk—about as much as Cain had for Abel.
For they would like to leave less than the wolves do,
And to lie more than girls in a brothel."

Of the clergy, "A tantas vey baylia", "So much the more do I see clerks coming into power that all the world will be theirs, whoever objects. For they'll have it with taking or with giving" (i.e. by granting land, belonging to one man, to someone else who will pay allegiance for it, as in the case of De Montfort), "or with pardon or with hypocrisy; or by assault or by drinking and eating; or by prayers or by praising the worse; or with God or with devilry". We find him putting the age-long query about profit in the following:

> "He may have enough harness
> And sorrel horses and bays;
> Tower, wall, and palace,
> May he have
> —The rich man denying his God".

The stanza runs very smoothly to the end
> "Si mortz no fos
> Elh valgra per un cen".
> "A hundred men he would be worth
> Were there no death".

The modern Provençal enthusiast in raptures at the idea of chivalric love (a term which he usually misunderstands), and little concerned with the art of verse, has often failed to notice how finely the sound of Cardinal's poems is matched with their meaning. There is a lash and sting in his timbre and in his movement. Yet the old man is not always bitter; or, if he is bitter, it is with the bitterness of a torn heart and not of a hard one. It is so we find him in the sirvente beginning:
> "As a man weepeth for his son or for his father,
> Or for his friend when death has taken him,
> So do I mourn for the living who do their own ill,
> False, disloyal, felon, and full of ill-fare,
> Deceitful, breakers-of-pact,
> Cowards, complainers,
> Highwaymen, thieves-by-stealth, turn-coats,
> Betrayers, and full of treachery,
> Here where the devil reigns
> And teaches them to act thus".

He is almost the only singer of his time to protest against the follies of war. As here:
> "Ready for war, as night is to follow the sun,
> Readier for it than is the fool to be cuckold
> When he has first plagued his wife!
> And war is an ill thing to look upon,
> And I know that there is not one man drawn into it
> But his child, or his cousin or someone akin to him
> Prays God that it be given over".

TROUBADOURS—THEIR SORTS AND CONDITIONS

He says plainly, in another place, that the barons make war for their own profit, regardless of the peasants. "Fai mal senher vas los sieu." His sobriety is not to be fooled with sentiment either martial or otherwise. There is in him little of the fashion of feminolatry, and the gentle reader in search of trunk-hose and the light guitar had better go elsewhere. As for women: "L'una fai drut".

"One turns leman for the sake of great possessions;
And another because poverty is killing her,
And one hasn't even a shift of coarse linen;
And another has two and does likewise.
And one gets an old man—and she is a young wench,
And the old woman gives the man an elixir."

As for justice, there is little now: "If a rich man steal by chicanery, he will have right before Constantine (i.e. by legal circumambience), but the poor thief may go hang". And after this there is a passage of pity and of irony fine-drawn as much of his work is, for he keeps the very formula that De Born had used in his praise of battle, "Belh mes quan vey"; and, perhaps, in Sir Bertrans' time even the Provençal wars may have seemed more like a game, and may have appeared to have some element of sport and chance in them. But the twelfth century had gone, and the spirit of the people was weary, and the old canon's passage may well serve as a final epitaph on all that remained of silk thread and *cisclatons*, of viol and *gai saber*.

"Never again shall we see the Easter come in so fairly,
That was wont to come in with pleasure and with song.
No! but we see it arrayed with alarms and excursions,
Arrayed with war and dismay and fear,
Arrayed with troops and with cavalcades,
Oh, yes, it's a fine sight to see holder and shepherd
Going so wretched that they know not where they are."

2

ARNAUT DANIEL

RAZO

En Ar. Daniel was of Ribeyrac in Périgord, under Lemosi, near to Hautefort, and he was the best fashioner of songs in the Provençal, as Dante has said of him in his *Purgatorio* (XXVI, 140), and Tasso says it was he who wrote *Lancillotto*, but this is not known for certain, but Dante says only "proze di romanzi". Nor is it known if Benvenuto da Imola speaks for certain when he says En Arnaut went in his age to a monastery and sent a poem to the princes, nor if he wrote a satire on Boniface Castillane; but here are some of his canzos, the best that are left us; and he was very cunning in his imitation of birds, as in the poem *Autet*, where he stops in the middle of his singing, crying: "Cadahus, en son us", as a bird cries, and rhyming on it cleverly, with no room to turn about on the words, "Mas pel us, estauc clus", and in the other versets. And in *L'aura amara*, he cries as the birds in the autumn, and there is some of this also in his best poem, *Doutz brais e critz*.

And in *Breu brisaral*, he imitates, maybe, the rough singing of the *joglar engles*, from whom he learnt *Ac et no l'ac*; and though some read this *escomes*, not *engles*, it is likely enough that in the court of En Richart there might have been an English joglar, for En Bertrans calls Richart's brother "joven re Engles", so why should there not be a joglar of the same, knowing alliterations? And he may, in the ending "piula",

ARNAUT DANIEL

have had in mind some sort of Arabic singing; for he knew well letters, in Langue d'Oc and in Latin, and he knew Ovid, of whom he takes Atalanta; and may be Virgil; and he talks of the Palux Lerna, though most copiers have writ this "Uzerna", not knowing the place he spoke of. So it is as like as not he knew Arabic music, and perhaps had heard, if he understood not the meaning, some song in rough Saxon letters.

And by making song in *rimas escarsas* he let into Provençal poetry many words that are not found elsewhere and maybe some words half Latin, and he uses many more sounds on the rhyme, for, as Canello or Lavaud has written, he uses ninety-eight rhyme sounds in seventeen canzos, and Peire Vidal makes use of but fifty-eight in fifty-four canzos and Folquet of thirty-three in twenty-two poems, and Raimbaut Orenga uses 129 rhymes in thirty-four poems, a lower proportion than Arnaut's. And the songs of En Arnaut are in some versets wholly free and uneven the whole length of the verset, then the other five versets follow in the track of the first, for the same tune must be sung in them all, or sung with very slight or orderly changes. But after the earlier poems he does not rhyme often inside the stanza. And in all he is very cunning, and has many uneven and beautiful rhythms, so that if a man try to read him like English iambic he will very often go wrong; though En Arnaut made the first piece of "blank verse" in the seven opening lines of the *Sols sui*; and he, maybe, in thinning out the rhymes and having but six repetitions to a canzone, made way for Dante who sang his long poem in threes. But this much is certain, he does not use the rhyme -*atage* and many other common rhymes of the Provençal, whereby so many canzos are all made alike and monotonous on one sound or two sounds to the end from the beginning.

Nor is there much gap from *Lancan vei fueill'* or *D'autra guiza* to the form of the sonnet, or to the receipt for the

Italian strophes of canzoni, for we have both the repetition and the unrepeating sound in the verset. And in two versets the rhymes run *abab cde abab cde*; in one, and in the other *abba cde abba cde*; while in sonnets the rhymes run *abab abab cde cde*; or *abba abba cde cde*. And this is no very great difference. A sonetto would be the third of a *son*.

And I do not give *Ac et no l'ac*, for it is plainly told us that he learnt this song from a jongleur, and he says as much in his coda:

"Miells-de-ben ren
Sit pren
Chanssos grazida
C'Arnautz non oblida".

"Give thanks my song, to Miells-de-ben that Arnaut has not forgotten thee." And the matter went as a joke, and the song was given to Arnaut to sing in his repertoire "E fo donatz lo cantar an Ar Daniel, qui et aysi trobaretz en sa obra". And I do not give the tenzon with Trucs Malecs for reasons clear to all who have read it; nor do I translate the sestina, for it is a poor one, but maybe it is interesting to think if the music will not go through its permutation as the end words change their places in order, though the first line has only eight syllables.

And En Arnaut was the best artist among the Provençals, trying the speech in new fashions, and bringing new words into writing, and making new blendings of words, so that he taught much to Messire Dante Alighieri as you will see if you study En Arnaut and the *De Vulgari Eloquio*; and when Dante was older and had well thought the thing over he said simply, "il miglior fabbro". And long before Francesco Petrarca, he, Arnaut, had thought of the catch about "*Laura*, laura, l'aura", and the rest of it, which is no great thing to his credit. But no man in Provençal has written as he writes in *Doutz brais*: "E quel remir" and the rest of it, though Ovid, where he recounts Atalanta's flight from Hippomenes in the tenth book, had written:

"cum super atria velum
Candida purpureum simulatas inficit umbras".

And in Dante we have much in the style of:

"Que jes Rozers per aiga que l'engrois".

And Dante learned much from his rhyming, and follows him in *agro* and *Meleagro*, but more in a comprehension, and Dante has learned also of Ovid: "in Metamorphoseos":

"Velut ales, ab alto
Quae teneram prolem produxit in aera nido",

although he talks so much of Virgil.

I had thought once of the mantle of indigo as of a thing seen in a vision, but I have now only fancy to support this. It is like that men slandered Arnaut for Dante's putting him in his *Purgatorio*, but the Trucs Malecs poem is against this.

En Arnaut often ends a canzone with a verset in different tone from the rest, as markedly in *Si fos Amors*. In *Breu brisaral* the music is very curious, but is lost for us, for there are only two pieces of his music, and those in Milan, at the Ambrosiana (in R 71 superiore).

And at the end of *Doutz brais*, is a verset like the verset of a sirvente, and this is what he wrote as a message, not making a whole sirvente, nor, so far as we know, dabbling in politics or writing of it, as Bertrans de Born has; only in this one place is all that is left us. And he was a joglar, perhaps for his living, and only composed when he would, and could not to order, as is shown in the story of his remembering the joglar's canzone when he had laid a wager to make one of his own.

Can chai la fueilla is more like a sea song or an *estampida*, though the editors call it a canzone, and *Amors e jois*, and some others were so little thought of, that only two writers have copied them out in the manuscripts; and the songs are all different one from another, and their value nothing like even. Dante took note of the best ones, omitting *Doutz brais*, which is for us perhaps the finest of all, though having some lines out of strict pertinence. But *Can chai la fueilla* is very cleverly made with five, six, and four and seven. And in *Sols sui* and in other canzos verse is syllabic, and made on the number of syllables, not by stresses, and the making by syllables cannot be understood by those of Petramala, who imagine the language they speak was that spoken by Adam, and that one system of metric was made in the world's beginning, and has since existed without change. And some think if the stress fall not on every second beat, or the third, that they must have right before Constantine. And the art of En Ar. Daniel is not literature but the art of fitting words well with music, wellnigh a lost art, and if one will look to the music of *Chansson doil motz*, or to the movement of *Can chai la fueilla*, one will see part of that which I mean, and if one will look to the falling of the rhymes in other poems, and the blending and lengthening of the sounds, and their sequence, one will learn more of this. And En Arnaut wrote between 1180 and 1200 of the era, as nearly as we can make out, when the Provençal was growing weary, and it was to be seen if it could last, and he tried to make almost a new language, or at least to enlarge the Langue d'Oc, and make new things possible. And this scarcely happened till Guinicello, and Guido Cavalcanti and Dante; Peire Cardinal went to realism and made satirical poems. But the art of singing to music went wellnigh out of the words, for Metastasio has left a few catches, and so has Lorenzo di Medici, but in Bel Canto in the times of Durante, and Piccini, Paradeis, Vivaldi, Caldara and Benedetto Marcello, the music turns the words out of doors and strews them and distorts them to the tune, out of all recognition; and the philosophic canzoni of Dante and his timesmen are not understandable if they are sung, and in their time music and poetry parted company; the canzone's tune becoming a sonata without singing. And the ballad is a shorter form, and the Elizabethan lyrics are but scraps and bits of canzoni much as in the "nineties" men wrote scraps of Swinburne.

Charles d'Orléans made good roundels and songs, as in *Dieu qui la fait* and in *Quand j'oie la tambourine*, as did also Jean Froissart before him in:

> "Reviens, ami; trop longue est ta demeure:
> Elle me fait avoir peine et doulour.
> Mon esperit te demande à toute heure.
> Reviens, ami; trop longue est ta demeure.
>
> Car il n'est nul, fors toi, qui me sequerre,
> Ne secourra, jusques à ton retour.
> Reviens, ami; trop longue est ta demeure:
> Elle me fait avoir peine et doulour".

And in:

> "Le corps s'en va, mais le cœur vous demeure".

And in:

> "On doit le temps ainsi prendre qu'il vient:
> Tout dit que pas ne dure la fortune.
> Un temps se part, et puis l'autre revient:
> On doit le temps ainsi prendre qu'il vient.
>
> Je me comforte en ce qu'il me souvient
> Que tous les mois avons nouvelle lune:
> On doit le temps ainsi prendre qu'il vient:
> Tout dit que pas ne dure la fortune".

Which is much what Bernart de Ventadour has sung:

> "Per dieu, dona, pauc esplecham d'amor
> Va sen lo temps e perdem lo melhor".

ARNAUT DANIEL

And Campion was the last, but in none of the later men is there the care and thought of En Arnaut Daniel for the blending of words sung out; and none of them all succeeded, as indeed he had not succeeded in reviving and making permanent a poetry that could be sung. But none of them all had thought so of the sound of the words with the music, all in sequence and set together as had En Arnaut of Ribeyrac, nor had, I think, even Dante Alighieri when he wrote *De Eloquio.*

And we find in Provence beautiful poems, as by Vidal when he sings:

"Ab l'alen tir vas me l'aire".

And by the Viscount of St Antoni:

"Lo clar temps vei brunezir
E'ls auzeletz esperdutz,
Que'l fregz ten destregz e mutz
E ses conort de jauzir.
Donc eu que de cor sospir
Per la gensor re qu'anc fos,
    Tan joios
  Son, qu'ades m'es vis
Que folh' e flor s'espandis.
D'amor son tug miei cossir..."

and by Bertrans de Born in *Dompna puois di me*, but these people sang not so many diverse kinds of music as En Arnaut, nor made so many good poems in different fashions, nor thought them so carefully, though En Bertrans sings with more vigour, it may be, and in the others, in Cerclamon, Arnaut of Marvoil, in De Ventadour, there are beautiful passages. And if the art, now in France, of saying a song—*disia sons*, we find written of more than one troubadour—is like the art of En Arnaut, it has no such care for the words, nor such ear for hearing their consonance.

ARNAUT DANIEL

Nor among the Provençals was there any one, nor had Dante thought out an aesthetic of sound; of clear sounds and opaque sounds, such as in *Sols sui*, an opaque sound like Swinburne at his best; and in *Doutz brais* and in *L'aura amara* a clear sound, with staccato; and of heavy beats and of running and light beats, as very heavy in *Can chai la fueilla*. Nor do we enough notice how with his drollery he is in places nearer to Chaucer than to the Italians, and indeed the Provençal is usually nearer the English in sound and in feeling, than it is to the Italian, having a softer humour, not a bitter tongue, as have the Italians in ridicule.

Nor have any yet among students taken note enough of the terms, both of love terms, and of terms of the singing; though theology was precise in its terms, and we should see clearly enough in Dante's treatise when he uses such words as *pexa, hirsuta, lubrica,* combed, and shaggy and oily to put his words into categories, that he is thinking exactly. Would the Age of Aquinas have been content with anything less? And so with the love terms, and so, as I have said in my Guido, with metaphors and the exposition of passion. Cossir, solatz, plazers, have in them the beginning of the Italian philosophic precisions, and *amors qu'inz el cor mi plou* is not a vague decoration. By the time of Petrarca the analysis had come to an end, only the vague decorations were left. And if Arnaut is long before Cavalcanti,

"Pensar de lieis m'es repaus
E traigom ams los huoills crancs,
S'a lieis vezer nols estuich",

leads toward *E gli occhi orbati fa vedere scorto*, though the music in Arnaut is not, in this place, quickly apprehended. And those who fear to take a bold line in their interpretation of *Cill de Doma*, might do worse than re-read:

"Una figura de la donna mia"

and what follows it. And for the rest any man who would read Arnaut and the troubadours owes great thanks to Emil Levy of Freiburg i/B for his long work and his little dictionary (*Petit Dictionnaire Provençal-Français*, Karl Winter's Universitätsbuchhandlung, Heidelberg), and to U. A. Canello, the first editor of Arnaut, who has shown, I think, great profundity in his arrangement of the poems in their order, and has really hit upon their sequence of composition, and the developments of En Arnaut's trobar; and lastly to René Lavaud for his new Tolosan edition.

II

The twenty-three students of Provençal and the seven people seriously interested in the technic and aesthetic of verse may communicate with me in person. I give here only enough to illustrate the points of the razo, that is to say, as much as, and probably more than, the general reader can be bothered with. The translations are a makeshift; it is not to be expected that I can do in ten years what it took two hundred troubadours a century and a half to accomplish; for the full understanding of Arnaut's system of echoes and blending there is no substitute for the original; but in extenuation of the language of my verses, I would point out that the Provençals were not constrained by the modern literary sense. Their restraints were the tune and rhyme-scheme, they were not constrained by a need for certain qualities of writing, without which no modern poem is complete or satisfactory. They were not competing with De Maupassant's prose. Their triumph is, as I have said, in an art between literature and music; if I have succeeded in indicating some of the properties of the latter I have also let the former go by the board. It is quite possible that if the troubadours had been bothered about "style", they would not have brought their blend of word and tune to so elaborate a completion.

ARNAUT DANIEL

Can chai la fueilla is interesting for its rhythm, for the sea-chantey swing produced by the simple device of caesurae. The poem does not keep the same rhyme throughout, and the only reason for giving the whole of it in my English dither is that one can *not* get the effect of the thumping and iterate foot-beat from one or two strophes alone.

CAN CHAI LA FUEILLA

When sere leaf falleth
        from the high forkèd tips,
And cold appalleth
        dry osier, haws and hips,
Coppice he strips
        of bird, that now none calleth.
Fordel* my lips
        in love have, though he galleth.

Though all things freeze here,
        I can naught feel the cold,
For new love sees, here
        my heart's new leaf unfold;
So am I rolled
        and lapped against the breeze here:
Love who doth mould
        my force, force guarantees here.

Aye, life's a high thing,
        where joy's his maintenance,
Who cries 'tis wry thing
        hath danced never my dance,
I can advance
        no blame against fate's tithing
For lot and chance
        have deemed the best thing my thing.

* Pre-eminence.

ARNAUT DANIEL

CAN CHAI
Can chai la fueilla
        dels ausors entrecims,
El freitz s'ergueilla
        don sechal vais' el vims,
Dels dous refrims
        vei sordezir la brueilla;
Mas ieu soi prims
        d'amor, qui que s'en tueilla.

Tot quant es gela
        mas ieu non puesc frezir,
C'amors novela
        mi fal cor reverdir;
Non dei fremir
        c'Amors mi cuebr' em cela
Em fai tenir
        ma valor em cabdela.

Bona es vida
        pos joia la mante,
Que tals n'escrida
        cui ges no vai tan be;
No sai de re
        coreillar m'escarida,
Que per ma fe
        del miells ai ma partida.

ARNAUT DANIEL

Of love's wayfaring
        I know no part to blame,
All other pairing,
        compared, is put to shame,
Man can acclaim
        no second for comparing
With her, no dame
        but hath the meaner bearing.

I'ld ne'er entangle
        my heart with other fere,
Although I mangle
        my joy by staying here
I have no fear
        that ever at Pontrangle
You'll find her peer
        or one that's worth a wrangle.

She'd ne'er destroy
        her man with cruelty
'Twixt here 'n' Savoy
        there feeds no fairer she,
Than pleaseth me
        till Paris had ne'er joy
In such degree
        from Helena in Troy.

She's so the rarest
        who holdeth me thus gay,
The thirty fairest
        can not contest her sway;

ARNAUT DANIEL

De drudaria
    nom sai de re blasmar,
C'autrui paria
    torn ieu en reirazar*;
Ges ab sa par
    no sai doblar m'amia,
C'una non par
    que segonda noill sia.

No vueill s'asemble
    mos cors ab autr' amor
Si qu'eu jail m'emble
    ni volval cap aillor;
Non ai paor
    que ja cel de Pontremble
N'aia gensor
    de lieis ni que la semble.

Ges non es croia
    cella cui soi amis;
De sai Savoia
    plus bella nos noiris;
Tals m'abelis
    don ieu plus ai de joia
Non ac Paris
    d'Elena, cel de Troia.

Tan pareis genta
    cella quem te joios
Las gensors trenta
    vens de belas faisos;

 * Call for second throw of the dice.

ARNAUT DANIEL

'Tis right, par fay,
      thou know, O song that wearest
Such bright array,
      whose quality thou sharest.

Chançon, nor stay
      till to her thou declarest:
"Arnaut would say
      me not, wert thou not fairest".

Lancan son passat shows the simple and presumably early style of Arnaut, with the kind of reversal from more or less trochaic to more or less iambic movement in fifth and eighth lines, a *kind* of rhythm taken over by Elizabethan lyricists. Terms trochaic and iambic are, however, utterly inaccurate when applied to syllabic metres set to a particular melody.

LANCAN SON PASSAT LI GIURE

When the frosts are gone and over,
And are stripped from hill and hollow,
When in close the blossom blinketh
From the spray where the fruit cometh,
    The flower and song and the clarion
Of the gay season and merry
Bid me with high joy to bear me
    Through days while April's coming on.

Though joy's right hard to discover,
Such sly ways doth false Love follow,
Only sure he never drinketh
At the fount where true faith hometh;
    A thousand girls, but two or one
Of her falsehoods over chary,
Stabbing whom vows make unwary
    Their tenderness is vilely done.

ARNAUT DANIEL

Ben es razos
        doncas que mos chans senta,
Quar es tan pros
        e de ric pretz manenta.
Vai t'en chansos
        denan lieis ti prezenta;
Que s'ill no fos
        noi meir'* Arnautz s'ententa.

LANCAN SON PASSAT

Lancan son passat li giure
E noi reman puois ni comba,
Et el verdier la flors trembla
Sus el entrecim on poma,
    La flor e li chan eil clar quil
Ab la sazon doussa e coigna
M'enseignon c'ab joi m'apoigna,
    Sai al temps de l'intran d'april,

Ben greu trob' om joi desliure,
C'a tantas partz volv e tomba
Fals' Amors, que no s'asembla
Lai on leiautatz asoma;
    Qu'ieu non trob jes doas en mil
Ses falsa paraulla loigna,
E puois c'a travers non poigna
    E no torne sa cartat vil.

       * Lavaud: *metr'*.

ARNAUT DANIEL

The most wise runs drunkest lover,
Sans pint-pot or wine to swallow,
If a whim her locks unlinketh,
One stray hair his noose becometh.
    When evasion's fairest shown,
Then the sly puss purrs most near ye.
Innocents at heart beware ye,
    When she seems colder than a nun.

See, I thought so highly of her!
Trusted, but the game is hollow,
Not one won piece soundly clinketh;
All the cardinals that Rome hath,
    Yea, they all were put upon.
Her device is "Slyly Wary".
Cunning are the snares they carry,
    Yet while they watched they'd be undone.

Whom Love makes so mad a rover,
'Ll take a cuckoo for a swallow,
If she say so, sooth! he thinketh
There's a plain where Puy-de-Dôme is.
    Till his eyes and nails are gone,
He'll throw dice and follow fairly
—Sure as old tales never vary—
    For his fond heart he is foredone.

Well I know, sans writing's cover,
What a plain is, what's a hollow.
I know well whose honour sinketh,
And who 'tis that shame consumeth.
    They meet. I lose reception.
'Gainst this cheating I'd not parry
Nor amid such false speech tarry,
    But from her lordship will be gone.

ARNAUT DANIEL

Tuich li plus savi en vant hiure
Ses muiol e ses retomba,
Cui il gignosetz esclemba
La crin queil pend a la coma;
   E plus pres li brui de l'auzil
On plus gentet s'en desloigna;
Et fols cre miells d'una moigna
   Car a simple cor e gentil.

Ses fals' Amor cuidiei viure,
Mas ben vei c'un dat mi plomba
Quand ieu mieills vei qu'il m'o embla;
Car tuich li legat de Roma
   No son jes de sen tant sotil,
Que na devisa "Messoigna",
Que tant soaument caloigna,
   Mens poiria falsar un fil.

Qui Amor sec, per tals liure:
Cogul tenga per colomba,
S'il l'o ditz ni ver li sembla
Fassaill plan del Puoi de Doma;
   Quan d'ei plus prop es tant s'apil
Si col proverbis s'acoigna;
Sil trai l'uoill, el puois loil oigna,
   Sofra e sega ab cor humil.

Ben conosc ses art d'escriure
Que es plan o que es comba,
Qu'ieu sai drut que si assembla
Don blasm' a leis, el col groma;
   Qu'ieu n'ai ja perdut ric cortil
Car non vuoill gabs ab vergoigna
Ni blasme ab honor loigna
   Per que ieu loing son seignoril.

ARNAUT DANIEL

Coda

<blockquote>
Sir Bertran,* sure no pleasure's won
Like this freedom naught so merry
Twixt Nile 'n' where the suns miscarry
To where the rain falls from the sun.
</blockquote>

The fifth poem in Canello's arrangement, *Lanquan vei fueill' e flor e frug*, has strophes in the form:

<blockquote>
"When I see leaf, and flower and fruit
Come forth upon light lynd and bough,
And hear the frogs in rillet bruit,
And birds quhitter in forest now,
Love inkirlie doth leaf and flower and bear,
And trick my night from me, and stealing waste it,
Whilst other wight in rest and sleep sojourneth".
</blockquote>

The sixth is in the following pattern, and the third strophe translates:

<blockquote>
"Hath a man rights at love? No grain.
Yet gowks think they've some legal lien.
But she'll blame you with heart serene
That ships for Bari sink, mid-main,
Or 'cause the French don't come from Gascony
And for such crimes I am nigh in my shroud,
Since, by the Christ, I do such crimes or none".
</blockquote>

Autet e bas is interesting for the way in which Arnaut breaks the flow of the poem to imitate the bird call in *Cadahus en son us*, and the repetitions of this sound in the succeeding strophes, highly treble, presumably, "Neis Jhezus, Mas pel us", etc.

* Presumably De Born

ARNAUT DANIEL

Bertran, non cre de sai lo Nil
Mais tant de fin joi m'apoigna
Tro lai on lo soleills poigna,
    Tro lai on lo soleills plovil.

"Lanquan vei fueill' e flor e frug
    Parer dels albres eill ramel,
Et aug lo chan que faun el brug
    Ranas el riu, el bosc l'auzel,
Doncs mi fueilla em floris em fruch' Amors
El cor tan gen que la nueit me retsida
Quant autra gens dorm e pauz' e sojorna."

ARNAUT DANIEL

AUTET E BAS ENTRELS PRIMS FUOILLS

Now high and low, where leaves renew,
Come buds on bough and spalliard pleach
And no beak nor throat is muted;
Auzel each in tune contrasted
Letteth loose
Wriblis* spruce.
Joy for them and spring would set
Song on me, but Love assaileth
Me and sets my words t' his dancing.

I thank my God and mine eyes too,
Since through them the perceptions reach,
Porters of joys that have refuted
Every ache and shame I've tasted;
They reduce
Pains, and noose
Me in Amor's corded net.
Her beauty in me prevaileth
Till bonds seem but joy's advancing.

My thanks, Amor, that I win through;
Thy long delays I naught impeach;
Though flame's in my marrow rooted
I'd not quench it, well 't hath lasted,
Burns profuse,
Held recluse
Lest knaves know our hearts are met,
Murrain on the mouth that aileth,
So he finds her not entrancing.

* Wriblis = warblings.

AUTET

Autet e bas entrels prims fuoills
Son nou de flors li ram eil renc
E noi ten mut bec ni gola
Nuills auzels, anz braia e chanta
Cadahus
En son us;
Per joi qu'ai d'els e del tems
Chant, mas amors mi asauta
Quils motz ab lo son acorda.

Dieu o grazisc e a mos huoills,
Que per lor conoissensam venc.
Jois, qu'adreich auci e fola
L'ira qu'ieu n'agui e l'anta,
Er va sus
Qui qu'en mus,
D'Amor don sui fis e frems;
C'ab lieis c'al cor m'azauta
Sui liatz ab ferma corda.

Merces, Amors, c'aras m'acuoills!
Tart mi fo, mas en grat m'o prenc,
Car si m'art dinz la meola
Lo fuocs non vuoill que s'escanta;
Mas pel us
Estauc clus
Que d'autrui joi fant greus gems
E pustell ai' en sa gauta
Cel c'ab lieis si desacorda.

ARNAUT DANIEL

He doth in Love's book misconstrue,
And from that book none can him teach,
Who saith ne'er's in speech recruited
Aught, whereby the heart is dasted.
Word's abuse
Doth traduce
Worth, but I run no such debt.
Right 'tis if man over-raileth
He tear tongue on tooth mischancing.*

That I love her, is pride, is true,
But my fast secret knows no breach.
Since Paul's writ was executed
Or the forty days first fasted,
Not Cristus
Could produce
Her similar, where one can get
Charms total, for no charm faileth
Her who's memory's enhancing.

Grace and valour, the keep of you
She is, who holds me, each to each,
She sole, I sole, so fast suited,
Other women's lures are wasted,
And no truce
But misuse
Have I for them, they're not let
To my heart, where she regaleth
Me with delights I'm not chancing.

Arnaut loves, and ne'er will fret
Love with o'er-speech, his throat quaileth,
Braggart voust's not to his fancying.

* This is nearly as bad in the original.

ARNAUT DANIEL

De bon' amor falsa l'escuoills,
E drutz es tornatz en fadenc,
Qui di qu'el parla noil cola
Nuilla res quel cor creanta
De pretz l'us;
Car enfrus
Es d'aco qu'eu mout ai crems;
E qui de parlar trassauta
Dreitz es qu'en la lengais morda.

Vers es qu'ieu l'am et es orguoills,
Mas ab jauzir cela loi tenc;
Qu'anc pos Sainz Pauls fetz pistola
Ni nuills hom dejus caranta,
Non poc plus,
Neis Jhesus,
Far de tals, car totz absems
Als bos aips don es plus auta
Cella c'om per pros recorda.

Pretz e Valors, vostre capduoills
Es la bella c'ab sim retenc,
Qui m'a sol et ieu liei sola,
C'autra el mon nom atalanta;
Anz sui brus
Et estrus
Als autras el cor teing prems,
Mas pel sieu joi trepa e sauta
No vuoill c' autra m'o comorda.

Arnautz ama e no di nems,
C'Amors l'afrena la gauta
Que fols gabs no laill comorda.

ARNAUT DANIEL

In the next poem we have the chatter of birds in autumn, the onomatopoeia obviously depends upon the "*-utz, -etz, -encs* and *-ortz*" of the rhyme-scheme, seventeen of the sixty-eight syllables of each strophe therein included. I was able to keep the English in the same sound as the *Cadahus*, but I have not been able to make more than a map of the relative positions in this canzo.

I

The bitter air
Strips panoply
From trees
Where softer winds set leaves,
The glad
Beaks
Now in brakes are coy,
Scarce peep the wee
Mates
And un-mates.
   What gaud's the work?
   What good the glees?
What curse
I strive to shake!
Me hath she cast from high,
In fell disease
I lie, and deathly fearing.

II

So clear the flare
That first lit me
To seize
Her whom my soul believes;
If cad
Sneaks,

ARNAUT DANIEL

L'AURA AMARA

I

L'aura amara
Fals bruoills brancutz
Clarzir
Quel doutz espeissa ab fuoills,
Els letz
Becs
Dels auzels ramencs
Ten balps e mutz,
Pars
E non-pars;
Per qu'eu m'esfortz
De far e dir
Plazers
A mains per liei
Que m'a virat bas d'aut,
Don tem morir
Sils afans no m'asoma.

II

Tant fo clara
Ma prima lutz
D'eslir
Lieis don crel cors los huoills,
Non pretz
Necs

ARNAUT DANIEL

Blabs, slanders, my joy
Counts little fee
Baits
And their hates.
   I scorn their perk
    And preen, at ease.
Disburse
Can she, and wake
Such firm delights, that I
Am hers, froth, lees
Bigod! from toe to earring.

III

Amor, look yare!
Know certainly
The keys;
How she thy suit receives;
Nor add
Piques,
'Twere folly to annoy.
I'm true, so dree
Fates;
No debates
   Shake me, nor jerk.
   My verities
Turn terse,
And yet I ache.
Her lips, not snows that fly
Have potencies
To slake, to cool my searing.

Mans dos aigonencs*;
D'autra s'esdutz
Rars
Mos preiars,
Pero deportz
M'es adauzir
Volers,
Bos motz ses grei
De liei don tant m'azaut
Qu'al sieu servir
Sui del pe tro c'al coma.

III

Amors, gara,
Sui ben vengutz
C'auzir
Tem far sim desacuoills
Tals detz
Pecs
Que t'es miells quet trencs;
Qu'ieu soi fis drutz
Cars
E non vars,
Mal cors ferms fortz
Mi fai cobrir
Mains vers;
Cab tot lo nei
M'agr' ops us bais al chaut
Cor refrezir
Que noi val autra goma.

* Lavaud: *angovencs*. Most probable meaning an angevin, small coin of Anjou, with argot diminutive ending.

ARNAUT DANIEL

IV

Behold my prayer,
(Or company
Of these)
Seeks whom such height achieves;
Well clad
Seeks
Her, and would not cloy.
Heart apertly
States
Thought. Hope waits
  'Gainst death to irk:
  False brevities
And worse!
To her I raik.*
Sole her; all others' dry
Felicities
I count not worth the leering.

V

Ah, fair face, where
Each quality
But frees
One pride-shaft more, that cleaves
Me; mad frieks
(O' thy beck) destroy,
And mockery
Baits
Me, and rates.
  Yet I not shirk
  Thy velleities,
Averse
Me not, nor slake
Desire. God draws not nigh

   * Raik = haste precipitate.

IV

Si m'ampara
Cill cuim trahutz
D'aizir,
Si qu'es de pretz capduoills,
Dels quetz
Precs
C'ai dedinz a rencs,
L'er fors rendutz
Clars
Mos pensars;
Qu'eu fora mortz
Mas fam sofrir
L'espers
Queill prec quem brei,
C'aisson ten let e baut;
Que d'als jauzir
Nom val jois una poma.

V

Doussa car', a
Totz aips volgutz,
Sofrir
M'er per vos mainz orguoills,
Car etz
Decs
De totz mos fadencs,
Don ai mainz brutz
Pars
E gabars;
De vos nom tortz,
Nim fai partir
Avers,
C'anc non amei
Ren tan ab meins d'ufaut,

ARNAUT DANIEL

To Dome,* with pleas
Wherein's so little veering.

VI

Now chant prepare,
And melody
To please
The king, who'll judge thy sheaves.
Worth, sad,
Sneaks
Here; double employ
Hath there. Get thee
Plates
Full, and cates,
    Gifts, go! Nor lurk
    Here till decrees
Reverse,
And ring thou take.
Straight t' Arago I'd ply
Cross the wide seas
But "Rome" disturbs my hearing.

Coda

At midnight mirk,
In secrecies
I nurse
My served make †
In heart; nor try
My melodies
At other's door nor mearing. ‡

* Our Lady of Puy-de-Dôme? No definite solution of this reference yet found.
  † Make = mate, fere, companion.
  ‡ Dante cites this poem in the second book of *De Vulgari Eloquio* with poems of his own, De Born's, and Cino Pistoija's.

Anz vos desir
Plus que Dieus cill de Doma.

VI

Erat para
Chans e condutz,
Formir
Al rei qui t'er escuoills;
Car pretz
Secs
Sai, lai es doblencs,
E mantengutz
Dars
E manjars:
De joi lat portz,
Son anel mir,
Sil ders,
C'anc non estei
Jorn d'Aragon quel saut
Noi volgues ir,
Mas sai m'an clamat Roma.

Coda

Faitz es l'acortz
Qu'el cor remir
Totz sers
Licis cui domnei
Ses parsonier Arnaut;
Qu'en autr' albir
N'es fort m'ententa soma.

The onomatopoeia giving sound of angry twitter of birds in autumn.

ARNAUT DANIEL

The eleventh canzo is mainly interesting for the opening bass onomatopoeia of the wind rowting in the autumn branches. Arnaut may have caught his alliteration from the *joglar engles*, a possible hrimm-hramm-hruffer, though the device dates at least from Naevius.

> "En breu brisaral temps braus,
> Eill bisa busina els brancs
> Qui s'entreseignon trastuich
> De sobreclaus rams de fuoilla;
> Car noi chanta auzels ni piula
> M' enseign' Amors qu'ieu fassa adonc
> Chan que non er segons ni tertz
> Ans prims d'afrancar cor agre."

The rhythm is too tricky to be caught at the first reading,
or even at the fifth reading; there is only part of it in my copy.
"Briefly bursteth season brisk,
Blasty north breeze racketh branch,
Branches rasp each branch on each
Tearing twig and tearing leafage,
   Chirms now no bird nor cries querulous;
So Love demands I make outright
A song that no song shall surpass
For freeing the heart of sorrow.

Love is glory's garden close,
And is a pool of prowess staunch
Whence get ye many a goodly fruit
If true man come but to gather.
   Dies none frost bit nor yet snowily,
For true sap keepeth off the blight
Unless knave or dolt there pass...."

The second point of interest is the lengthening out of the rhyme in *piula, niula,* etc. In the fourth strophe we find:
"The gracious thinking and the frank
Clear and quick perceiving heart
Have led me to the fort of love.
Finer she is, and I more loyal
Than were Atalanta and Meleager".

Then the quiet conclusion, after the noise of the opening, "Pensar de lieis m'es repaus":
"To think of her is my rest
And both of my eyes are strained wry
When she stands not in their sight,
Believe not the heart turns from her,
   For nor prayers nor games nor violing
Can move me from her a reed's-breadth".

ARNAUT DANIEL

The most beautiful passages of Arnaut are in the canzo beginning: "Doutz brais e critz".

GLAMOUR AND INDIGO

Sweet cries and cracks
        and lays and chants inflected
By auzels who, in their Latin belikes,
Chirm each to each, even as you and I
Pipe toward those girls on whom our thoughts attract;
Are but more cause that I, whose overweening
Search is toward the Noblest, set in cluster
Lines where no word pulls wry, no rhyme breaks gauges.

No culs de sacs
        nor false ways me deflected
When first I pierced her fort within its dykes,
Hers, for whom my hungry insistency
Passes the gnaw whereby was Vivien wracked;*
Day-long I stretch, all times, like a bird preening,
And yawn for her, who hath o'er others thrust her
As high as true joy is o'er ire and rages.

Welcome not lax,
        and my words were protected
Not blabbed to other, when I set my likes
On her. Not brass but gold was 'neath the die.
That day we kissed, and after it she flacked
O'er me her cloak of indigo, for screening
Me from all culvertz' eyes, whose blathered bluster
Can set such spites abroad; win jibes for wages.

   * Vivien, strophe 2, nebotz Sain Guillem, an allusion to the romance *Enfances Vivien*.

ARNAUT DANIEL

DOUTZ BRAIS E CRITZ

Doutz brais e critz,
Lais e cantars e voutas
Aug del auzels qu'en lor latins fant precs
Quecs ab sa par, atressi cum nos fam
A las amigas en cui entendem;
E doncas ieu qu'en la genssor entendi
Dei far chansson sobre totz de bell' obra
Que noi aia mot fals ni rima estrampa.

Non fui marritz
Ni non presi destoutas
Al prim qu'intriei el chastel dinz lo decs,
Lai on estai midonz, don ai gran fam
C'anc non l'ac tal lo nebotz Sain Guillem;
Mil vetz lo jorn en badaill em n'estendi
Per la bella que totas autras sobra
Tant cant val mais fis gaugz qu'ira ni rampa.

Ben fui grazitz
E mas paraulas coutas,
Per so que jes al chausir no fui pecs,
Anz volgui mais prendre fin aur que ram,
Lo jorn quez ieu e midonz nos baizem
Em fetz escut de son bel mantel endi
Que lausengier fals, lenga de colobra,
Non o visson, don tan mals motz escampa.

ARNAUT DANIEL

God, who did tax
                not Longus' sin,* respected
That blind centurion beneath the spikes
And him forgave, grant that we two shall lie
Within one room, and seal therein our pact,
Yes, that she kiss me in the half-light, leaning
To me, and laugh and strip and stand forth in the lustre
Where lamp-light with light limb but half engages.

The flowers wax
                with buds but half perfected;
Tremble on twig that shakes where the bird strikes—
But not more fresh than she! No empery,
Though Rome and Palestine were one compact,
Would lure me from her; and with hands convening
I give me to her. But if kings could muster
In homage similar, you'd count them sages.

Mouth, now what knacks!
                What folly hath infected
Thee? Gifts, that th' Emperor of the Salonikes
Or Lord of Rome were greatly honoured by,
Or Syria's lord, thou dost from me distract;
O fool I am! to hope for intervening
From Love that shields not love! Yea, it were juster
To call him mad, who 'gainst his joy engages.

                Political Postscript
The slimy jacks
                with adders' tongues bisected,
I fear no whit, nor have; and if these tykes
Have led Galicia's king to villeiny—†

    * Longus, centurion in the crucifixion legend.
    † King of the Galicians, Ferdinand II, King of Galicia, 1157–88, son of Berangere, sister of Raimon Berenger IV ("quattro figlie ebbe", etc.) of Aragon, Count of Barcelona.

ARNAUT DANIEL

Dieus lo chauzitz
Per cui foron assoutas
Las faillidas que fetz Longis lo cecs,
Voilla, sil platz, qu'ieu e midonz jassam
En la chambra on amdui nos mandem
Uns rics convens don tan gran joi atendi,
Quel seu bel cors baisan rizen descobra
E quel remir contral lum de la lampa.

Ges rams floritz
De floretas envoutas
Cui fan tremblar auzelhon ab lurs becs
Non es plus frescs, per qu'ieu no volh Roam
Aver ses lieis ni tot Jherusalem;
Pero totz fis mas juntas a lim rendi,
Qu'en liei amar, agr' ondral reis de Dobra
O celh cui es l'Estel e Luna-pampa.

Bocca, que ditz?
Qu'eu crei quem auras toutas
Tals promessas don l'emperaire grecs
En for' onratz ol senher de Roam
Ol reis que ten Sur e Jherusalem;
Doncs ben sui fols que queir tan quem rependi
Ni eu d'Amor non ai poder quem cobra,
Ni saveis es nuls om que joi acampa.

Los deschauzitz
Ab las lengas esmoutas
Non dubt' ieu jes, sil seignor dels Galecs
An fag faillir, perqu'es dreitz s'o blasmam,

ARNAUT DANIEL

His cousin in pilgrimage hath he attacked—
We know—Raimon the Count's son*—my meaning
Stands without screen. The royal filibuster
Redeems not honour till he unbar the cages.

Coda

I should have seen it, but I was on such affair,
Seeing the true king crown'd here in Estampa.†

Arnaut's tendency to lengthen the latter lines of the strophe after the diesis shows in: *Er vei vermeils, vertz, blaus, blancs, gruocs,* the strophe form being:

"Vermeil, green, blue, peirs, white, cobalt,
Close orchards, hewis, holts, hows, vales,
And the bird-song that whirls and turns
Morning and late with sweet accord,
Bestir my heart to put my song in sheen
T'equal that flower which hath such properties,
It seeds in joy, bears love, and pain ameises".

The last cryptic allusion is to the quasi-allegorical descriptions of the tree of love in some long poem like the *Romaunt of the Rose.*

Dante takes the next poem as a model of canzo construction; and he learned much from its melody. We note the soft suave sound as against the staccato of *L'aura amara.*

* His second son, Lieutenant of Provence, 1168.
† King crowned at Etampes, Philippe Auguste, crowned May 29, 1180, at age of sixteen. This poem might date Arnaut's birth as early as 1150.

ARNAUT DANIEL

Que son paren pres romieu, so sabem,
Raimon lo filh al comte, et aprendi
Que greu faral reis Ferrans de pretz cobra
Si mantenen nol solv e nol escampa.

Eu l'agra vist, mas estei per tal obra,
C'al coronar fui del bon rei d'estampa.

(Mos sobrecors, si tot grans sens lo sobra,
Tenga que ten, si non gaire nois ampa.)

"Er vei vermeils, vertz, blaus, blancs, gruocs
    Vergiers, plans, plais, tertres e vaus;
Eil votz del auzels sona e tint
    Ab doutz acort maitin e tart.
Som met en cor qu'ieu colore mon chan
D'un' aital flor don lo friutz sia amors,
E jois lo grans, e l'olors d'enoi gandres."

ARNAUT DANIEL

Canzon.

I only, and who elrische pain support,
Know out love's heart o'er borne by overlove,
For my desire that is so firm and straight
And unchanged since I found her in my sight
And unturned since she came within my glance,
That far from her my speech springs up aflame;
Near her comes not. So press the words to arrest it.

I am blind to others, and their retort
I hear not. In her alone, I see, move,
Wonder.... And jest not. And the words dilate
Not truth; but mouth speaks not the heart outright:
I could not walk roads, flats, dales, hills, by chance,
To find charm's sum within one single frame
As God hath set in her t'assay and test it.

And I have passed in many a goodly court
To find in hers more charm than rumour thereof....
In solely hers. Measure and sense to mate,
Youth and beauty learnèd in all delight,
Gentrice did nurse her up, and so advance
Her fair beyond all reach of evil name,
To clear her worth, no shadow hath oppresst it.

Her contact flats not out, falls not off short...
Let her, I pray, guess out the sense hereof
For never will it stand in open prate
Until my inner heart stand in daylight,
So that heart pools him when her eyes entrance,
As never doth the Rhone, fulled and untame,
Pool, where the freshets tumult hurl to crest it.

Flimsy another's joy, false and distort,
No paregale that she springs not above...
Her love-touch by none other mensurate.

ARNAUT DANIEL
SOLS SUI

Sols sui qui sai lo sobrafan quem sortz
Al cor d'amor sofren per sobramar,
Car mos volers es tant ferms et entiers
C'anc no s'esduis de celliei ni s'estors
Cui encubric al prim vezer e puois:
Qu'ades ses lieis dic a lieis cochos motz,
Pois quan la vei non sai, tant l'ai, que dire.

D'autras vezer sui secs e d'auzir sortz,
Qu'en sola lieis vei et aug et esgar;
E jes d'aisso noill sui fals plazentiers
Que mais la vol non ditz la bocal cors;
Qu'eu no vau tant chams, vauz ni plans ni puois
Qu'en un sol cors trob aissi bos aips totz:
Qu'en lieis los volc Dieus triar et assire.

Ben ai estat a maintas bonas cortz,
Mas sai ab lieis trob pro mais que lauzar
Mesura e sen et autres bos mestiers,
Beutat, joven, bos faitz e bels demors.
Gen l'enseignet Cortesia e la duois,
Tant a de si totz faitz desplazens rotz
De lieie no cre rens de ben si' a dire.

Nuills jauzimens nom fora breus ni cortz
De lieis cui prec qu'o vuoilla devinar,
Que ja per mi non o sabra estiers
Sil cors ses dirs nos presenta de fors;
Que jes Rozers per aiga que l'engrois
Non a tal briu c'al cor plus larga dotz
Nom fassa estanc d'amor, quand la remire.

Jois e solatz d'autram par fals e bortz,
C'una de pretz ab lieis nois pot egar,
Quel sieus solatz es dels autres sobriers.

ARNAUT DANIEL

To have it not? Alas! Though the pains bite
Deep, torture is but galzeardy and dance,
For in my thought my lust hath touched his aim.
God! Shall I get no more! No fact to best it!

No delight I, from now, in dance or sport,
Nor will these toys a tinkle of pleasure prove,
Compared to her, whom no loud profligate
Shall leak abroad how much she makes my right.
Is this too much? If she count not mischance
What I have said, then no. But if she blame,
Then tear ye out the tongue that hath expresst it.

The song begs you: Count not this speech ill chance,
But if you count the song worth your acclaim,
Arnaut cares lyt who praise or who contest it.

The XVIth canto goes on with the much discussed and much too emphasized cryptogram of the ox and the hare. I am content with the reading which gives us a classic allusion in the palux Laerna. The lengthening of the verse in the last three lines of the strophe is, I think, typically Arnaut's. I leave the translation solely for the sake of one strophe.

"Ere the winter recommences
And from bough the leaf be wrested,
On Love's mandate will I render
A brief end to long prolusion:
So well have I been taught his steps and paces
That I can stop the tidal-sea's inflowing.
My stot outruns the hare; his speed amazes.

Me he bade without pretences
That I go not, though requested;
That I make no whit surrender

ARNAUT DANIEL

Ai si no l'ai! las! Tant mal m'a comors!
Pero l'afans m'es deportz, ris e jois
Car en pensan sui de lieis lecs e glotz:
Ai Dieus, si ja'n serai estiers jauzire!

Anc mais, sous pliu, nom plac tant treps ni bortz
Ni res al cor tant de joi nom poc dar
Cum fetz aquel don anc feinz lausengiers
No s'esbrugic qu'a mi solses tresors...
Dic trop? Eu non, sol lieis non sia enois.
Bella, per dieu, lo parlar e la votz
Vuoill perdre enans que diga ren queus tire.

Ma chansos prec que nous sia enois
Car si voletz grazir lo son els motz
Pauc preza Arnautz cui que plassa o que tire.

ERE THE WINTER

"Ans quel cim reston de branchas
Sec ni despoillat de fuoilla
Farai, c'Amors m'o comanda,
Breu chansson de razon loigna.
Que gen m'a duoich de las artz de s'escola;
Tant sai quel cors fatz restar de suberna
E mos bous es pro correns que lebres.

Ab razos coindas e franchas
M'a mandat qu'ieu no m'en tuoilla
Ni non serva autra ni' n blanda,

ARNAUT DANIEL

Nor abandon our seclusion:
'Differ from violets, whose fear effaces
Their hue ere winter; behold the glowing
Laurel stays, stay thou. Year long the genet blazes.'

'You who commit no offences
'Gainst constancy; have not quested;
Assent not! Though a maid send her
Suit to thee. Think you confusion
Will come to her who shall track out your traces?
And give your enemies a chance for boasts and crowing?
No! After God, see that she have your praises.'

Coward, shall I trust not defences!
Faint ere the suit be tested?
Follow! till she extend her
Favour. Keep on, try conclusion
For if I get in this naught but disgraces,
Then must I pilgrimage past Ebro's flowing
And seek for luck amid the Lernian mazes.

If I've passed bridge-rails and fences,
Think you then that I am bested?
No, for with no food or slender
Ration, I'd have joy's profusion
To hold her kissed, and there are never spaces
Wide to keep me from her, but she'd be showing
In my heart, and stand forth before his gazes.

Lovelier maid from Nile to Sences
Neither robed is, nor divested,
So great is her body's splendour
That you would think it illusion.
Amor, if she but hold me in her embraces,
I should not feel hail cold, nor winter's blowing,
Nor break for all the pain in fever's dazes.

ARNAUT DANIEL

Puois tant fai c'ab si m'acoigna;
Em di que flors noil semble de viola
Quis camja leu sitot nonca s'inverna,
Ans per s'amor sia laurs o genebres.

Dis: tu, c'aillors non t'estranchas
Per autra quit deing nit vuoilla,
Totz plaitz esquiva e desmanda
Sai e lai qui quet somoigna;
Gran son dan fai qui se meteus afola,
E tu no far failla don hom t'esquerna,
Mas apres Dieu lieis honors e celebres.

E tu, coartz, non t'afranchas
Per respeich c'amar not vuoilla;
Sec, s'il te fuig nit fai ganda,
Que greu er c'om noi apoigna
Qui s'afortis de preiar e no cola.
Qu'ieu passera part la palutz de Lerna
Com peregrins o lai per on cor Ebres.

S'ieu n'ai passatz pons ni planchas
Per lieis, cuidatz qu'ieu m'en duoilla?
Non eu, c'ab joi ses vianda
M'en sap far meizina coigna
Baisan tenen; el cors, sitot si vola,
Nois part de lieis quel capdella el governa.
Cors, on qu'ieu an, de lieis not loinz ni sebres!

De part Nil entro c'a Sanchas
Gensser nois viest nis despuoilla,
Car sa beutatz es tant granda
Que semblariaus messoigna.
Bem vai d'amor, qu'elam baisa e m'acola,
E nom frezis freitz ni gels ni buerna,
Nim fai dolor mals ni gota ni febres.

ARNAUT DANIEL

Arnaut hers from foot to face is,
He would not have Lucerne, without her, owing
Him, nor lord the land whereon the Ebro grazes."

The feminine rhyming throughout and the shorter opening lines keep the strophe much lighter and more melodic than that of the canzo which Canello prints last of all.

SIM FOS AMORS DE JOI DONAR TANT LARGA

"Ingenium nobis ipsa puella facit."
PROPERTIUS II, I.

Had Love as little need to be exhorted
To give me joy, as I to keep a frank
And ready heart toward her, never he'd blast
My hope, whose very height hath high exalted,
And cast me down...to think on my default,
And her great worth; yet thinking what I dare,
More love myself, and know my heart and sense
Shall lead me to high conquest, unmolested.

I am, spite long delay, pooled and contorted
And whirled with all my streams 'neath such a bank
Of promise, that her fair words hold me fast
In joy, and will, until in tomb I am halted.
As I'm not one to change hard gold for spalt,
And no alloy's in her, that debonaire
Shall hold my faith and mine obedience
Till, by her accolade, I am invested.

Long waiting hath brought in and hath extorted
The fragrance of desire; throat and flank
The longing takes me...and with pain surpassed
By her great beauty. Seemeth it hath vaulted
O'er all the rest...them doth it set in fault
So that whoever sees her anywhere

ARNAUT DANIEL

Sieus es Arnautz del cim tro en la sola
E senes lieis no vol aver Lucerna
Nil senhoriu del reion que cor Ebres."

SIM FOS AMORS

Sim fos Amors de joi donar tant larga
Cum ieu vas lieis d'aver fin cor e franc,
Ja per gran ben nom calgra far embarc,
Qu'er am tant aut quel pes mi poia em plomba;
Mas quand m'albir cum es de pretz al som
Mout m'en am mais car anc l'ausiei voler,
C'aras sai ieu que mos cors e mos sens
Mi farant far, lor grat, rica conquesta.

Pero s'ieu fatz lonc esper no m'embarga,
Qu'en tant ric luoc me sui mes e m'estanc
C'ab sos bels digz mi tengra de joi larc,
E segrai tant qu'om mi port a la tomba,
Qu'ieu non sui ges cel que lais aur per plom;
E pois en lieis nos taing c'om ren esmer
Tant li serai fis et obediens
Tro de s'amor, s'il platz, baisan m'envesta.

Us bons respietz mi reven em descarga
D'un doutz desir don mi dolen li flanc,
Car en patz prenc l'atan el sofr' el parc
Pois de beutat son las autras en comba,
Que la genser par c'aia pres un tom
Plus bas de liei, qui la ve, et es ver;

ARNAUT DANIEL

Must see how charm and every excellence
Hold sway in her, untaint, and uncontested.

Since she is such: longing no wise detorted
Is in me...and plays not the mountebank,
For all my sense is her, and is compassed
Solely in her; and no man is assaulted
(By God his dove!) by such desires as vault
In me, to have great excellence. My care
On her so stark, I can show tolerance
To jacks whose joy's to see fine loves uncrested.

Miels-de-Ben, have not your heart distorted
Against me now; your love has left me blank,
Void, empty of power or will to turn or cast
Desire from me...not brittle,* nor defaulted.
Asleep, awake, to thee do I exalt
And offer me. No less, when I lie bare
Or wake, my will to thee, think not turns thence,
For breast and throat and head hath it attested.

Pouch-mouthed blubberers, culrouns and aborted,
May flame bite in your gullets, sore eyes and rank
T' the lot of you, you've got my horse, my last
Shilling, too; and you'd see love dried and salted.
God blast you all that you can't call a halt!
God's itch to you, chit-cracks that overbear
And spoil good men, ill luck your impotence!!
More told, the more you've wits smeared and congested.

Coda

Arnaut has borne delay and long defence
And will wait long to see his hopes well nested.

* "Brighter than glass, and yet as glass is, brittle." The comparisons to glass went out of poetry when glass ceased to be a rare, precious substance. (Cf. *Passionate Pilgrim*, III.)

Que tuig bon aip, pretz e sabers e sens
Reingnon ab liei, c'us non es meins ni'n resta.

E pois tant val, nous cujetz que s'esparga
Mos ferms volers ni qu'eisforc ni qu'eisbranc,
Car eu no sui sieus ni mieus si m'en parc,
Per cel Seignor queis mostret en colomba:
Qu'el mon non ha home de negun nom
Tant desires gran benanansa aver
Cum ieu fatz lieis, e tenc a noncalens
Los enoios cui dans d'Amor es festa.

Na Miells-de-ben, ja nom siatz avarga
Qu'en vostr' amor me trobaretz tot blanc,*
Qu'ieu non ai cor ni poder quem descarc
Del ferm voler que non hieis de retomba;
Que quand m'esveill ni clau lo huoills de som
A vos m'autrei, quan leu ni vau jazer;
E nous cujetz queis merme mos talens,
Non fara jes, qu'aral sent en la testa.

Fals lausengier, fuocs las lengas vos arga
E que perdatz ams los huoill de mal cranc,
Que per vos son estraich caval e marc,
Amor toletz c'ab pauc del tot non tomba;
Confondaus Dieus que ja non sapchatz com,
Queus fatz als drutz maldire e vil tener;
Malastres es queus ten, desconoissens,
Que peior etz qui plus vos amonesta.

Arnautz a faitz e fara loncs atens,
Qu'atenden fai pros hom rica conquesta.

* Cf. *Donna mi prega*, strophe v, l. 8.

ARNAUT DANIEL

[In *De Vulgari Eloquio* II, 13, Dante calls for freedom in the rhyme order within the strophe, and cites this canzo of Arnaut's as an example of poem where there is no rhyme within the single strophe. Dante's "Rithimorum quoque relationi vacemus" implies no carelessness concerning the blending of rhyme sounds, for we find him at the end of the chapter "et tertio rithimorum asperitas, nisi forte sit lenitati permista: nam lenium asperorumque rithimorum mixtura ipsa tragoedia nitescit", as he had before demanded a mixture of shaggy and harsh words with the softer words of a poem. "Nimo scilicet eiusdem rithimi repercussio, nisi forte novum aliquid atque intentatum artis hoc sibi praeroget." The *De Eloquio* is ever excellent testimony of the way in which a great artist approaches the detail of métier.]

3

NOTES ON ELIZABETHAN CLASSICISTS*

I

The reactions and "movements" of literature are scarcely, if ever, movements against good work or good custom. Dryden and the precursors of Dryden did not react against *Hamlet*. If the eighteenth-century movement toward regularity is among those least sympathetic to the public of our moment, it is "historically justifiable", even though the katachrestical vigours of Marlowe's *Hero and Leander* may not be enough to "explain" the existence of Pope. A single faulty work showing great powers would hardly be enough to start a "reaction"; only the mediocrity of a given time can drive the more intelligent men of that time to "break with tradition".

I take it that the phrase "break with tradition" is currently used to mean "desert the more obvious imbecilities of one's immediate elders"; at least, it has had that meaning in the periodical mouth for some years. Only the careful and critical mind will seek to know how much tradition inhered in the immediate elders.

Vaguely in some course of literature we heard of "the old fourteeners", vulgariter, the metre of the *Battle of Ivry*.

* *Egoist*, 1915-16 or thereabouts.

NOTES ON ELIZABETHAN CLASSICISTS

Hamlet could not have been written in this pleasing and popular measure. The "classics", however, appeared in it. For Court ladies and cosmopolitan heroes it is perhaps a little bewildering, but in the mouth of Oenone:

The Heroycal Epistles of the learned Poet Publius Ovidius Naso. In English verse: set out and translated by George Tuberuile. 1567. London: Henry Denham.

OENONE TO PARIS

To Paris that was once her owne
  though now it be not so,
From Ida, Oenon greeting sendes
  as these hir letters show,
May not thy nouel wife endure
  that thou my Pissle reade.
That they with Grecian fist were wrought
  thou needste not stand in dreade.

Pegasian nymph renounde in Troie,
  Oenone hight by name,
Of thee (of thee that were mine owne), complaine
  if thou permit the same,
What froward god doth seeke to barre
  Oenone to be thine?
Or by what guilt have I deserude
  that Paris should decline?
Take paciently deserude woe
  and never grutch at all:
But undeserued wrongs will grieve
  a woman at the gall.

Scarce were thou of so noble fame,
  as platly doth appeare:
When I (the offspring of a floud)
  did choose the for my feere.

And thou, who now art Priams sonne
  (all reuerence layde apart)
Were tho a Hyard to beholde
  when first thou wanste my heart.
How oft have we in shaddow laine
  whylst hungrie flocks have fedde?
How oft have we of grasse and greanes
  preparde a homely bedde?
How oft on simple stacks of strawe
  and bennet did we rest?
How oft the dew and foggie mist
  our lodging hath opprest?
Who first discouerde thee the holtes
  and Lawndes of lurcking game?
Who first displaid thee where the whelps
  lay sucking of their Dame?
I sundrie tymes have holpe to pitch
  thy toyles for want of ayde:
And forst thy Hounds to climbe the hilles
  that gladly would have stayde.

One boysterous Beech Oenone's name
  in outward barke doth beare:
And with thy caruing knife is cut
  OENON, every wheare.
And as the trees in tyme doe ware
  so doth encrease my name:
Go to, grow on, erect your selves
  helpe to aduance my fame.

There growes (I minde it uerie well)
  upon a banck, a tree
Whereon ther doth a fresh recorde
  and will remaine of mee,

NOTES ON ELIZABETHAN CLASSICISTS

> Live long thou happie tree, I say,
>   that on the brinck doth stande;
> And hast ingraued in thy barke
>   these wordes, with Paris hande:
>
> "When Pastor Paris shall reuolte,
>   and Oenon's love forgoe:
> Than Xanthus waters shall recoyle,
>   and to their Fountaines floe."
> Now Ryuer backward bend thy course,
>   let Xanthus streame retier:
> For Paris hath renounst the Nymph
>   and prooude himself a lier.
> That cursed day bred all my doole,
>   the winter of my joy,
> With cloudes of froward fortune fraught
>   procurde me this annoy;
>
> When cankred crafte Iuno came
>   with Venus (Nurce of Love)
> And Pallas eke, that warlike wench,
>   their beauties pride to proue.

. . . . . .

The pastoral note is at least not unpleasing, and the story more real than in the mouths of the later poets, who enliven us with the couplet to the tune:

> "Or Paris, who, to steal that daintie piece,
>   Traveled as far as 'twas 'twixt Troy and Greece".

The old versions of Ovid are worth more than a week's random reading. Turning from the *Heroides* I find this in a little booklet said to have been "printed abroad". It is undated, and bears "C. Marlow" on the title-page.

NOTES ON ELIZABETHAN CLASSICISTS

AMORUM*

Now on the sea from her olde loue comes shee
That drawes the day from heaven's cold axle-tree,
Aurora whither slidest thou down againe,
And byrdes from Memnon yeerly shall be slaine.
Now in her tender arms I sweetlie bide,
If euer, now well lies she by my side,
The ayre is colde, and sleep is sweetest now,
And byrdes send foorth shril notes from every bow.
Whither runst thou, that men and women loue not,
Holde in thy rosie horses that they moue not.
Ere thou rise stars teach seamen where to saile,
But when thou comest, they of their course faile.
Poore trauailers though tired, rise at thy sight,
The painful Hinde by thee to fild is sent,
Slow oxen early in the yoke are pent.
Thou cousnest boyes of sleep, and dost betray them
To Pedants that with cruel lashes pay them.

. . . .

Any fault is more pleasing than the current fault of the many. One should read a few bad poets of every era, as one should read a little trash of every contemporary nation, if one would know the worth of the good in either.

Turning from translations, for a moment, to *The Shepherdes Starre* (1591), for the abandonment of syntax and sense, for an interesting experiment in metric, for beautiful lines astray in a maze of unsense, I find the incoherent conclusion of much incoherence, where Amaryllis says: "In the meane while let this my Roundilay end my follie"; and tilts at the age-old bogie of "Sapphics", Aeolium Carmen, which perhaps Catullus alone of imitators has imitated with success.

* *Amorum*, lib. I, elegia 13.

NOTES ON ELIZABETHAN CLASSICISTS

THE SHEPHERDES STARRE, 1591

Amaryllis. In the meane while let this my Roundilay end my follie:

    Sith the nymphs are thought to be happie creatures,
    For that at faier *Helicon* a Fountaine,
    Where all use like white Ritch iuorie foreheads
        Daily to sprinckle,

    Sith the quire of Muses atend *Diana,*
    Ever use to bathe heauie thoughts refyning,
    With the Silver skinne, Civet and Mir using
        For their adornment,

    Sith my sacred Nymphs priuiledge abateth,
    Cause *Dianas* grace did elect the *Myrtle,*
    To be pride of every branch in order
        last of her handmaides;

    Should then I thus liue to behold euerted
    Skies, with impure eyes in a fountaine harboured
    Where *Titans* honour seated is as under
        All the beholders?

    Helpe wofull *Ecco,* reabound relenting,
    That *Dianas* grace on her helpe recalling,
    May well heare thy voice to bewaile, reanswere
        Faire *Amaryllis.*

    Fairer in deede then *Galatea,* fairest
    Of *Dianas* troope to bewitch the wisest,
    With amasing eye to abandon humours
        of any gallants,

    Shee *Thetis* faier, *Galataea* modest,
    —Albeit some say in a Chrystal often,
    Tis a rule, there lurketh a deadly poyson,
        Tis but a false rule.

> For what Yse is hid in a Diamond Ring,
> Where the wise beholder hath eyes refusing,
> Allabasters vaines to no workman hidden,
>   Gold to no Touchstone.
>
> There bedeckes fairest *Rosamond* the fountaine,
> Where resorts those greene *Driades* the waterie
> Nimphs, of olive plants recreat by *Phaebus*
>   Till they be maried.
>
> So beginning ends the report of her fame,
> Whose report passing any pennes relation,
> Doth entreat her loue, by reinspiration
> To dull heads yeelding faer eies reflection,
>   Still to be present.

Surely among poems containing a considerable amount of beauty, this is one of the worst ever written. Patient endeavour will reveal to the reader a little more coherence and syntax than is at first glance apparent, but from this I draw no moral conclusion.

For all half-forgotten writing there is, to my mind, little criticism save selection. "Those greene Driades"; Oenone, "offspring of a floud"; the music of the Elegy must make their own argument.

II

A great age of literature is perhaps always a great age of translations; or follows it. The Victorians in lesser degree had Fitzgerald, and Swinburne's Villon, and Rossetti. One is at first a little surprised at the importance which historians of Spanish poetry give to Boscan, but our histories give our own translators too little. And worse, we have long since fallen under the blight of the Miltonic or noise tradition, to a stilted dialect in translating the classics, a dialect which

NOTES ON ELIZABETHAN CLASSICISTS

imitates the idiom of the ancients rather than seeking their meaning, a state of mind which aims at "teaching the boy his Latin" or Greek or whatever it may be, but has long since ceased to care for the beauty of the original; or which perhaps thinks "appreciation" obligatory, and the meaning and content mere accessories.

Golding was no inconsiderable poet, and the Marlow of the translations has beauties no whit inferior to the Marlowe of original composition. In fact, the skill of the translations forbids one to balk at the terminal *e*. We conclude the identity without seeking through works of reference.

Compare (pardon the professional tone whereof I seem unable to divest myself in discussing these matters), compare the anonymous rather unskilled work in the translation of *Sixe Idillia*, with Marlow's version of *Amorum*, lib. III, 13.

THE XVIII JDILLION

HELLENS EPITHALAMION*

In Sparta long agoe, where Menelaus wore the crowne,
Twelve noble Virgins, daughters to the greatest in the towne,
All dight upon their haire in Crowtoe garlands fresh and greene,
Danst at the chamber doore of Helena the Queene,
What time this Menelay, the younger Sonne of Atreus,
Did marry with this louely daughter of Prince Tyndarus.
And therewithal at eue, a wedding song they jointly sung,
With such a shuffling of their feete, that all the Pallace rung.

. . . . .

* *Sixe Idillia*, published by Joseph Barnes, Oxford, 1588; one hundred copies reprinted by H. Daniel, Oxford, 1883.

NOTES ON ELIZABETHAN CLASSICISTS

THE IX JDILLION

CYCLOPS TO GALATEA THE WATER-NYMPH

. . . . . .

O Apple, sweet, of thee, and of myself I use to sing,
And that at midnight oft, for thee, aleavne faunes up I bring,
All great with young, and foure beares whelps, I nourish up
    for thee.
But come thou hither first, and thou shalt have them all of me.
And let the blewish colorde Sea beat on the shore so nie.
The night with me in cave, thou shalt consume more
    pleasantlie.
There are the shadie Baies, and there tall Cypres-trees doe
    sprout,
And there is Ivie blacke, and fertill Vines are al about.
Coole water there I haue, distilled of the whitest snowe,
A drinke divine, which out of wooddy Aetna mount doth
    flowe.
In these respects, who in the Sea and waues would rather be?
But if I seem as yet, too rough and sauage unto thee,
Great store of Oken woode I have, and never quenched fire;
And I can well endure my soul to burn with thy desire,
With this my onely eie, then which I nothing think more
    trimme.
Now woe is me, my mother bore not me with finns to
    swimme,
That I might dive to thee.

. . . . . .

The "shuffling of their feete" is pleasing, but the Cyclops speaks perhaps too much in his own vein. Marlow is much more dexterous.

NOTES ON ELIZABETHAN CLASSICISTS

AMORUM*

Ad amicam si pecatura est, ut occulte peccat

Seeing thou are faire, I bar not thy false playing,
But let not me poore soule wit of thy straying.
Nor do I give thee counsaile to liue chast
But that thou wouldst dissemble when 'tis past.
She hath not trod awry that doth deny it,
Such as confesse haue lost their good names by it.
What madness ist to tell night sports by day,
Or hidden secrets openly to bewray,
The strumpet with the stranger will not do,
Before the room be cleare, and dore put too.
Will you make shipwracke of your honest name
And let the world be witnesse of the same?
Be more aduisde, walke as a puritaine,
And I shall think you chast do what you can.
Slippe still, onely deny it when tis done,
And before people immodest speeches shun,
The bed is for lasciuious toyings meete,
There use all toyes, and treade shame under feete,
When you are up and drest, be sage and graue,
And in the bed hide all the faults you haue.
Be not a shamed to strippe you being there,
And mingle thighes, mine ever yours to beare,
There in your rosie lips my tongue intomb,
Practise a thousand sports when there you come,
Forbare no wanton words you there would speake,
And with your pastime let the bedsted creake.

* *Amorum*, lib. III, elegia 13. These translations are reprinted in the Clarendon Press edition of Marlowe's Works, 1910.

NOTES ON ELIZABETHAN CLASSICISTS

But with your robes, put on an honest face,
And blush and seeme as you were full of grace.
Deceiue all, let me erre, and think I am right
And like a wittal, thinke thee uoide of slight.

The reader, if he can divert his thought from matter to manner, may well wonder how much the eighteenth-century authors have added, or if they added anything save a sort of faculty for systematization of product, a power to repeat certain effects regularly and at will.

But Golding's book published before all these others will give us more matter for reverie. One wonders, in reading it, how much more of the Middle Ages was Ovid. We know well enough that they read him and loved him more than the more Tennysonian Virgil.

Yet how great was Chaucer's debt to the Doctor Amoris? That we will never know. Was Chaucer's delectable style simply the first Ovid in English? Or, as likely, is Golding's Ovid a mirror of Chaucer? Or is a fine poet ever translated until another his equal invents a new style in a later language? Can we, for our part, know our Ovid until we find him in Golding? Is there one of us so good at his Latin, and so ready in imagination that Golding will not throw upon his mind shades and glamours inherent in the original text which had for all that escaped him? Is any foreign speech ever our own, ever so full of beauty as our *lingua materna* (whatever *lingua materna* that may be)? Or is not a new beauty created, an old beauty doubled when the overchange is well done?

Will

"...cum super atria velum
Candida purpureum simulatas inficit umbras"

quite give us the "scarlet curtain" of the simile in the *Flight from Hippomenes*? Perhaps all these things are personal matters, and not matter for criticism or discussion. But it is certain that "we" have forgotten our Ovid, "we" being the reading public, the readers of English poetry, have forgotten our Ovid since Golding went out of print.

METAMORPHOSES*

While in this garden Proserpine was taking hir pastime,
In gathering eyther Violets blew, or Lillies white as Lime,
And while of Maidenly desire she fillde hir Haund and Lap,
Endeauoring to outgather hir companions there. By hap
Dis spide her: lovde her: caught her up: and all at once
    well nere.
So hastie, hote, and swift a thing is Loue as may appeare.
The Ladie with a wailing voyce afright did often call
Hir mother and hir waiting Maides, but Mother most of all.

. . . . . .

ATALANTA†

And from the Citie of Tegea there came the Paragone
Of Lycey forrest, Atalant, a goodly Ladie, one
Of Schoenyes daughters, then a Maide. The garment she did
    weare
A brayded button fastned at hir gorget. All hir heare
Untrimmed in one only knot was trussed. From hir left
Side hanging on hir shoulder was an Ivorie quiuer deft:
Which being full of arrowes, made a clattering as she went.
And in hir right hand she did beare a bow already bent.
Hir furniture was such as this. Hir countnance and hir grace
Was such as in a Boy might well be cald a Wenches face.

. . . . . .

  * *Metamorphoses*, by Arthur Golding, 1567. The Fyft booke. Reprint of 300 copies by De la More Press, in folio
  † *Atalanta*. The Eight booke.

NOTES ON ELIZABETHAN CLASSICISTS

THE HUNTING

Assoone as that the men came there, some pitched the toyles,
Some tooke the couples from the Dogs, and some pursude the foyles
In places where the swine had tract: desiring for to spie
Their owne destruction. Now there was a hollow bottom by,
To which the watershots of raine from all the high grounds drew.
Within the compasse of this pond great store of Oysyers grew:
And Sallowes lithe, and flackring flags, and moorish Rushes eke,
And lazie Reedes on little shankes, and other baggage like.
From hence the Bore was rowzed out, and fiersly forth he flies
Among the thickest of his foes as thunder from the Skies.

FLIGHT FROM HIPPOMENES

. . . Now while Hippomenes
Debates theis things within himself and other like to these,
The Damzell ronnes as if her feete were wings. And though that shee
Did fly as swift as arrow from a Turkye bowe: yit hee
More woondred at hir beawtye than at swiftnesse of her pace,
Her ronning greatly did augment her beawtye and her grace.
The wynd ay whisking from her feete the labells of her socks
Uppon her back as whyght as snowe did tosse her golden locks,
And eke thembroydred garters that were tyde beneathe her ham.
A redness mixt with whyght uppon her tender body cam,
As when a scarlet curtaine streynd ageinst a playstred wall
Dooth cast like shadowe, making it seeme ruddye therewith all.

NOTES ON ELIZABETHAN CLASSICISTS

Reality and particularization! The Elizabethans themselves began the long series of sins against them. In Ovid at least they are not divorced from sweeping imagination as in the *Fasti* (v. 222):

"Unius tellus ante coloris erat";

or in the opening of the *Metamorphoses*, as by Golding:

"Which Chaos hight, a huge rude heape and nothing else but even
A heavie lump and clottred clod of seedes.
. . . . . .

Nor yet the earth amiddes the ayre did hang by wondrous slight
Just peysed by hir proper weight. Nor winding in and out
Did Amphitrytee with her armes embrace the earth about,
For where was earth, was sea and ayre, so was the earth unstable.
The ayre all darke, the sea likewise to beare a ship unable.
. . . . . .

The suttle ayre to flickring fowles and birdes he hath assignde".

I throw in the last line for the quality of one adjective, and close this section of excerpts with a bit of fun anent Bacchus.

ADDRESS TO BACCHUS. IV

Thou into Sea didst send
The Tyrrhene shipmen. Thou with bittes the sturdy neckes dost bend
Of spotted Lynxes: throngs of Fownes and Satyres on thee tend,

And that old Hag that with a staff his staggering limmes
   doth stay
Scarce able on his Asse to sit for reeling every way.
Thou comest not in any place but that is hearde the noyse
Of gagling womens tatling tongues and showting out of
   boyes.
With sound of Timbrels, Tabors, Pipes, and Brazen pannes
   and pots
Confusedly among the rout that in thine Orgies trots.

III

The sin or error of Milton—let me leave off vague expressions of a personal active dislike, and make my yearlong diatribes more coherent. Honour where it is due! Milton undoubtedly built up the sonority of the blank verse paragraph in our language. But he did this at the cost of his idiom. He tried to turn English into Latin; to use an uninflected language as if it were an inflected one, neglecting the genius of English, distorting its fibrous manner, making schoolboy translations of Latin phrases: "Him who disobeys me disobeys".

I am leaving apart all my disgust with what he has to say, his asinine bigotry, his beastly hebraism, the coarseness of his mentality, I am dealing with a technical matter. All this clause structure modelled on Latin rhetoric, borrowed and thrust into sonorities which are sometimes most enviable.

The sin of vague pompous words is neither his own sin nor original. Euphues and Gongora were before him. The Elizabethan audience was interested in large speech. "Multitudinous seas incarnadine" caused as much thrill as any epigram in *Lady Windermere's Fan* or *The Importance of Being Earnest*. The dramatists had started this manner, Milton but continued in their wake, adding to their high-soundingness his passion for latinization, the latinization of a language peculiarly unfitted for his sort of latinization. Golding in the ninth year of Elizabeth can talk of "Charles his wane" in translating Ovid, but Milton's fields are "irriguous", and worse, and much more notably displeasing, his clause structure is a matter of "quem's", "cui's", and "quomodo's".

Another point in defence of Golding: his constant use of "did go", "did say", etc., is not fustian and mannerism; it was contemporary speech, though in a present-day poet it is impotent affectation and definite lack of technique. I am not saying "Golding is a greater poet than Milton";[*] these quantitative comparisons are in odium. Milton is the most unpleasant of English poets, and he has certain definite and analysable defects. His unpleasantness is a matter of personal taste. His faults of language are subject to argument just as are the faults of any other poet's language. His popularity has been largely due to his bigotry, but there is no reason why that popular quality should be for ever a shield against criticism. His real place is nearer to Drummond of Hawthornden than to "Shakespear" and "Dante" whereto the stupidity of our forbears tried to exalt him.

His short poems are his defenders' best stronghold, and it will take some effort to show that they are better than Drummond's *Phoebus Arise*. In all this I am not insisting on "Charles his wane" as the sole mode of translation. I point out that Golding was endeavouring to convey the sense of the original to his readers. He names the thing of his original author, by the name most germane, familiar, homely, to his hearers. He is intent on conveying a meaning, and not on bemusing them with a rumble. And I hold that the real poet is sufficiently absorbed in his content to care more for the content than the rumble; and also that Chaucer and Golding are more likely to find the *mot juste* (whether or no

[*] 1929. His *Metamorphoses* form possibly the most beautiful book in our language.

they held any theories there-anent) than were for some centuries their successors, saving the author of *Hamlet*.

Beside the fustian tradition, the tradition of cliché phrases, copies of Greek and Latin clause structure and phrase structure, two causes have removed the classics from us. On one hand we have ceased to read Greek with the aid of Latin cribs, and Latin is the only language into which any great amount of Greek can be in a lively fashion set over; secondly, there is no discrimination in classical studies. The student is told that all the classics are excellent and that it is a crime to think about what he reads. There is no use pretending that these literatures are read as literature. An apostolic succession of school teachers has become the medium of distribution.

The critical faculty is discouraged, the poets are made an exercise, a means of teaching the language. Even in this there is a great deal of buncombe. It is much better that a man should use a crib, and know the content of his authors than that he should be able to recite all the rules in Allen and Greenough's *Grammar*. Even the teaching by rules is largely a hoax. The Latin had certain *case feelings*. For the genitive he felt source, for the dative indirect action upon, for the accusative direct action upon, for the ablative all other peripheric sensation, i.e. it is less definitely or directly the source than the genitive, it is contributory circumstance; lump the locative with it, and one might call it the "circumstantial". Where it and the dative have the same form, we may conclude that there was simply a general indirect case.

The humanizing influence of the classics depends more on a wide knowledge, a reading knowledge, than on an ability to write exercises in Latin; it is ridiculous to pretend that a reading knowledge need imply more than a general intelligence of the minutiae of grammar. I am not assuming the position of those who objected to Erasmus's "tittle-tattles", but there is a sane order of importance.

When the classics were a new beauty and ecstasy people cared a damn sight more about the meaning of the authors, and a damn sight less about their grammar and philology.

We await, *vei jauzen lo jorn*, the time when the student will be encouraged to say which poems bore him to tears, and which he thinks rubbish, and whether there is any beauty in "Maecenas sprung from a line of kings". It is bad enough that so much of the finest poetry in the world should be distributed almost wholly through class-rooms, but if the first question to be asked were: "Gentlemen, are these verses worth reading?" instead of "What is the mood of 'manet'?" if, in short, the professor were put on his mettle to find poems worth reading instead of given the *facilem descensum*, the shoot, the supine shoot, of grammatical discussion, he might more dig out the vital spots in his authors, and meet from his class a less persistent undercurrent of conviction that all Latin authors are a trial.

The uncritical scholarly attitude has so spread, that hardly a living man can tell you at what points the Latin authors surpass the Greek, yet the comparison of their differences is full of all fascinations. Because Homer is better than Virgil, and Aeschylus, presumably, than Seneca, there has spread a superstition that the mere fact of a text being in Greek makes it of necessity better than a text written in Latin—which is buncombe.

Ovid indubitably added and invented much that is not in Greek, and the Greeks might be hard put to it to find a better poet among themselves than is their disciple Catullus. Is not Sappho, in comparison, a little, just a little Swinburnian?

I do not state this as dogma, but one should be open to such speculation.

I know that all classic authors have been authoritatively edited and printed by Teubner, and their wording ultimately

NOTES ON ELIZABETHAN CLASSICISTS

settled at Leipzig, but all questions concerning "the classics" are not definitely settled, cold-storaged, and shelved.

I may have been an ensanguined fool to spend so much time on mediaeval literature, or the time so "wasted" may help me to read Ovid with greater insight. I may have been right or wrong to read renaissance latinists, instead of following the professorial caution that "after all if one confined oneself to the accepted authors one was sure of reading good stuff, whereas there was a risk in hunting about among the unknown".

I am much more grateful for the five minutes during which a certain lecturer emphasized young Icarus begorming himself with Daedalus' wax than for all the dead hours he spent in trying to make me a scholar.

"... modo quas vaga moverat aura,
Captabat plumas: flavam modo pollice ceram
Mollibat; lusuque suo mirabile patris
Impediebat opus."

"Getting in both of their ways." My plagiarism was from the life and not from Ovid, the difference is perhaps unimportant.

Yet if after sixteen years a professor's words came back to one, it is perhaps important that the classics should be humanly, rather than philologically taught, even in classrooms. A barbaric age given over to *education* agitates for their exclusion and desuetude. Education is an onanism of the soul. Philology will be ascribed to De la Sade.

And there is perhaps more hope for the débutante who drawls in the last fashionable and outwearied die-away cadence "Ayh! Trois Contes? THAT's a good buk", than for the connoisseur stuffed full of catalogues; able to date any author and enumerate all the ranges of "influences".

NOTES ON ELIZABETHAN CLASSICISTS

IV

Meditation after further reading during which I found nothing of interest:

1

Beauty is a brief gasp between one cliché and another. In this case, between the "fourteeners" and the rhymed couplet of "pentameter".

2

"C. M." was a poet, likewise Golding, both facts already known to all "students of the period". Turbeyville or Turberuile is not a discovery.

. . . . .

Horace would seem to confer no boons upon his translators. With the exception of Chapman, the early translators of Homer seem less happy than the translators of Ovid. Horace's *Satires* are, we believe, the basis of much eighteenth-century satire. The earliest English version of any Horace that I have found is headed:

"A Medicinable Morall, that is 2 Bookes of Horace his Satyres, Englyshed according to the prescription of saint Hierome (Episto. ad Ruffin.) Quod malum est, muta, Quod bonum est, prode. The Wailyngs of the Prophet Hieremiah done into Englyshe verse also Epigrammes, by T. Drant. Perused and allowed according to the Queen Madiesties Iniunctions, London 1566".

The mutation of the satires is not inviting. The *Ars Poetica* opens as follows:

> "A Paynter if he shoulde adioyne
>   unto a womans heade
> A long maires necke and overspread
>   the corpse in everye steade

NOTES ON ELIZABETHAN CLASSICISTS

> With sondry feathers of straunge huie,
> the whole proportioned so
> Without all good congruitye
> the nether parts do goe
> Into a fishe, on hye a freshe
> welfavord womans face:
> My frinds let in to see this sighte
> could you not laugh a pace?"

By 1625 the Miltonic cliché is already formed. It is perhaps not particularly Milton's. Sir T. Hawkins is greeted by John Beaumont, but I do not find his translations very readable. I turn back, indeed, gratefully to Corinna (*Amores* I, 5) in a long loose gown

> "Her white neck hid with trellis hanging downe
> Resembling fair Semiramis going to bed
> Or Layis of a thousand lovers spread".

"C. M." gets quality even in the hackneyed topic:

> "What age of Varroes name shall not be told,
> And Iasons Argos, and the fleece of golde,
> Lofty Lucresius shall live that houre
> That Nature shall dissolve this earthly bowre.
> Eneas warre, and Titerius shall be read
> While Rome of all the conquering world is head.
> Till Cupid's bow and fierie shafts be broken,
> Thy verses, sweete Tibullus, shal be spoken".

As late as 1633 Saltonstall keeps some trace of good cadence, though it is manifestly departing.

> "Now Zephyrus warmes the ayre, the yeare is runne
> And the long seeming winter now is done,
> The Ramme which bore faire Hellen once away,
> Hath made the darke night equall to the day.

NOTES ON ELIZABETHAN CLASSICISTS

> Now boyes and girles do sweet Violets get,
> Which in the country often grow unset,
> Faire coloured flowers in the Meddowes spring,
> And now the Birds their untaught notes do sing."
> (*Tristia* XII.)

Turberuile in the 1567 edition of the *Heroides* does not confine himself to one measure, nor to rhyme. I think I have seen a mis-statement about the date of the earliest blank verse in English. These eight lines should prevent its being set too late. The movement is, to me at least, of interest, apart from any question of scholastic preciosity.

> "Aemonian Laodamia sendeth health,
> And greeting to Protesilaus hir spouse:
> And wisheth it, where he soiourns, to stay.
> Report hath spread in Aulide that you lie
> In rode, by meane of fierce and froward gale.
> Ah when thou me forsookste, where was the winde,
> Then broiling seas thine Oares should have withstood,
> That was a fitting time for wrathful waves."

His *Phaedra* has the "fourteener" measure.

> "My pleasure is to haughtie hills
> and bushie brakes to hie:
> To pitch my hay, or with my Houndes
> to rayse a lustie crie."

But there is an infinite monotony of fourteeners, and there is subsequently an infinite plethora of rhymed ten-syllable couplets. And they are all "exactly alike". Whether they translate Horace or Homer they are all exactly alike. Beauty is a gasp between clichés.

For every "great age" a few poets have written a few beautiful lines, or found a few exquisite melodies, and ten thousand people have copied them, until each strand of music is planed down to a dullness. The Sapphic stanza appears an exception, and yet,...Greece and Alexandria may have been embedded knee-deep in bad Sapphics, and it is easy to turn it to ridicule, comical, thumping.

V

There is a certain resonance in *Certain Bokes of Virgiles Aenaeis by Henry Earl of Surrey* (apud Ricardum Tottel 1557).

>"They whisted all, with fixed face attent
>When prince Aeneas from the royal seat
>Thus gan to speak, O Queene, it is thy will,
>I should renew a woe can not be told:
>How that the Grekes did spoile and overthrow
>The Phrygian wealth, and wailful realm of Troy,
>Those ruthful things that I myself beheld,
>And whereof no small part fel to my share,
>Which to expresse, who could refraine from teres,
>What Myrmidon, or yet what Dolopes?
>What stern Ulysses waged soldiar?
>
>And loe moist night now from the welkin falles
>And sterres declining counsel us to rest."

Still there is hardly enough here to persuade one to re-read or to read the *Aeneid*. Besides it is "so Miltonic". "Tho. Phaer, Docteur of Phisike" in 1562, published a version in older mould, whereof this tenebrous sample:

>"Even in ye porche, and first in Limbo iawes done wailings dwell
>And Cares on couches lyen, and Settled Mindes on vengeans fell
>Diseases leane and pale and combrous Age of dompishe yeres
>As Scillas and Centaurus, man before and beast behind

NOTES ON ELIZABETHAN CLASSICISTS

> In every doore they stampe, and Lyons sad with gnashing sound
> And Bugges with hundryd heades as Briary, and armid round
> Chimera fightes with flames and gastly Gorgon grim to see,
> Eneas sodenly for feare his glistering sword out toke".

He uses inner rhyme, and alliteration apparently without any design, merely because they happen. Such lines as "For as at sterne I stood, and steering strongly held my helme" do not compare favourably with the relatively free Saxon fragments. But when we come to

"The XIII BUKES of ENEADOS of the famose Poete Virgill, translatet out of Latyne verses into Scottish metir by the Reverend Father in God Mayster Gawin Douglas Bishop of Dunkel, unkil to the Erle of Angus, every book having hys particular prologe (printed in 1553)"*

we have to deal with a highly different matter.

> "The battellis and the man I will discrive
> Fra Troyis boundis, first that fugitive
> By fate to Italie, came and coist lauyne
> Ouer land and se, cachit with meikill pyne
> By force of goddis above, fra every stede
> Of cruel Juno, throw auld remembrit feid
> Grete payne in battelles, sufferit he also
> Or he his goddis, brocht in Latio
> And belt the ciete, fra quham of nobil fame
> The Latyne peopil, taken has thare name."

. . . . .

His commas are not punctuation, but indicate his caesurae.

* Written about 1512, i.e. early in the reign of Henry VIII, and by no means "Elizabethan".

Approaching the passage concerning the "hundryd headed Bugges" of Dr Phaer, Douglas translates as follows:

> "Fra thine strekis the way profound anone
> Depe unto hellis flude, of Acherone
> With holebisme, and hidduous swelth unrude
> Drumly of mude, and skaldand as it war wode.
>
> . . . . . .
>
> Thir riueris and thir watteris kepit war
> Be ane Charon, ane grisly ferrear
> Terribyl of schape, and sluggard of array
> Apoun his chin feill, chanos haris gray".

I am inclined to think that he gets more poetry out of Virgil than any other translator. At least he gives one a clue to Dante's respect for the Mantuan. In the first book Aeneas with the "traist Achates" is walking by the sea-board:

> "Amid the wod, his mother met them tuay
> Semand ane made, in vissage and array
> With wappinnis, like the Virgins of Spartha
> Or the stowt wensche, of Trace Harpalita
> Haistand the hors, her fadder to reskewe
> Spediar than Hebroun, the swift flude did persew.
> For Venus efter the gys, and maner thare
> Ane active bow, apoun her schulder bare
> As sche had bene, ane wilde huntreis
> With wind waffing, hir haris lowsit of trace".

This is not spoiled by one's memory of Chaucer's allusion.

> "Goyng in a queynt array
> As she hadde ben an hunteresse,
> With wynd blowynge upon hir tresse";

Douglas continues:

> "Hir skirt kiltit, till her bare knee
>   And first of uther, unto them, thus speike sche".

NOTES ON ELIZABETHAN CLASSICISTS

From Aeneas answer, these lines:

> "Quhidder thou be Diane, Phebus sister brycht
> Or than sum goddes, of thyr Nymphyis kynd
> Maistres of woddis beis to, us happy and kynd
> Relief our lang travell, quhat ever thow be".

And after her prophecy:

Vera incessu patuit dea.

> "Thus sayd sche, and turnand incontinent
> Hir nek schane, like unto the Rose in May
> Hir heuinly haris, glitterand bricht and gay
> Kest from her forehead, ane smell glorious and sueit
> Hir habit fell doune, couering to her feit
> And in hir passage, ane verray god did her kyith
> And fra that he knew, his moder alswith.
>
> . . . . . .
>
> Bot Venus with ane sop, of myst baith tway
> And with ane dirk cloud closit round about
> That na man sul tham se. . . .
>
> . . . . .
>
> Hir self uplyft, to Paphum past swyith
> To vesy her resting place, joly and blyith
> There is hir tempill, in Cipirland
> Quharin thare dois ane hundreth altaris stand
> Hait burning full of Saba, sence all houris
> Ane smelland swete, with fresch garland and flouris".
>
> . . . . .

Gawine Douglas was a great poet, and Golding has never had due praise since his own contemporaries bestowed it upon him. Caxton's *Virgil* (1490) is a prose redaction of a French version. The eclogue beginning

> "Tityrus, happilie thou lyste, tumbling under a beech tree"

is too familiar to quote here.

NOTES ON ELIZABETHAN CLASSICISTS

The celebrated distych:

"All trauellers doo gladlie report great praise of Vlysses
For that he knewe manie mens manners, and saw many citties"

is quoted by Wm. Webbe, in 1586, as a perfect example of English quantity, and ascribed to "Master Watson, fellow of S. John's", forty years earlier. If Master Watson continued his Odyssey there is alas no further trace of it.

. . . . . .

Conclusions after this reading:

1. The quality of translations declined in measure as the translators ceased to be absorbed in the subject matter of their original. They ended in the "Miltonian" cliché; in the stock and stilted phraseology of the usual English verse as it has come down to us.

2. This "Miltonian" cliché is much less Milton's invention than is usually supposed.

3. His visualization is probably better than I had thought. The credit due him for developing the resonance of the English blank verse paragraph is probably much less than most other people have until now supposed.

4. Gawine Douglas his works, should be made accessible by reprinting.

5. This will probably be done by some dull dog, who will thereby receive cash and great scholastic distinction. I, however, shall die in the gutter because I have not observed that commandment which says "Thou shalt respect the imbecilities of thine elders in order that thy belly shall be made fat from the jobs which lie in their charge".

6. That editors, publishers, and universities loathe the inquisitive spirit.

(1916 circa)

4

TRANSLATORS OF GREEK

EARLY TRANSLATORS OF HOMER

I. HUGHES SALEL

The dilection of Greek poets has waned during the last pestilent century, and this decline has, I think, kept pace with a decline in the use of Latin cribs to Greek authors. The classics have more and more become a baton exclusively for the cudgelling of schoolboys, and less and less a diversion for the mature.

I do not imagine I am the sole creature who has been well taught his Latin and very ill-taught his Greek (beginning at the age, say, of twelve, when one is unready to discriminate matters of style, and when the economy of the adjective cannot be wholly absorbing). A child may be bulldozed into learning almost anything, but man accustomed to some degree of freedom is loath to approach a masterpiece through five hundred pages of grammar. Even a scholar like Porson may confer with former translators.

We have drifted out of touch with the Latin authors as well, and we have mislaid the fine English versions: Golding's *Metamorphoses*; Gavine Douglas' *Æneids*; Marlowe's *Eclogues* from Ovid, in each of which books a great poet has compensated, by his own skill, any loss in transition; a new beauty has in each case been created. Greek in English remains almost wholly unsuccessful, or rather, there are glorious passages but no long or whole satisfaction. Chapman remains the best English "Homer", marred though he may be by excess of added ornament, and rather more marred by parentheses and inversions, to the point of being hard to read in many places.

And if one turn to Chapman for almost any favourite passage one is almost sure to be disappointed; on the other hand I think no one will excel him in the plainer passages of narrative, as of Priam's going to Achilles in the xxivth Iliad. Yet he breaks down in Priam's prayer at just the point where the language should be the simplest and austerest.

Pope is easier reading, and, out of fashion though he is, he has at least the merit of translating Homer into *something*. The nadir of Homeric translation is reached by the Leaf-Lang prose; Victorian faddism having persuaded these gentlemen to a belief in King James fustian; their alleged prose has neither the concision of verse nor the virtues of direct motion. In their preface they grumble about Chapman's "mannerisms", yet their version is full of "Now behold I" and "yea even as" and "even as when", tushery possible only to an affected age bent on propaganda. For, having, despite the exclusion of the *Dictionnaire Philosophique* from the island, finally found that the Bible couldn't be retained either as history or as private Reuter from J'hvh's Hebrew Press bureau, the Victorians tried to boom it, and even its wilfully bowdlerized translations, as literature.

"So spake he, and roused Athene that already was set thereon.... Even as the son of... even in such guise...."

perhaps no worse than

"With hollow shriek the steep of Delphos leaving"*

but bad enough anyway.

* Milton, of course, whom my detractors say I condemn without due circumspection.

TRANSLATORS OF GREEK

Of Homer two qualities remain untranslated: the magnificent onomatopœia, as of the rush of the waves on the sea-beach and their recession in:

παρὰ θῖνα πολυφλοίσβοιο θαλάσσης

untranslated and untranslatable; and, secondly, the authentic cadence of speech; the absolute conviction that the words used, let us say by Achilles to the "dog-faced" chicken-hearted Agamemnon, are in the actual swing of words spoken. This quality of actual speaking is *not* untranslatable. Note how Pope fails to translate it:

"There sat the seniors of the Trojan race
(Old Priam's chiefs, and most in Priam's grace):
The king, the first; Thymœtes at his side;
Lampus and Clytius, long in counsel try'd;
Panthus and Hicetaon, once the strong;
And next, the wisest of the reverend throng,
Antenor grave, and sage Ucalegon,
Lean'd on the walls, and bask'd before the sun.
Chiefs, who no more in bloody fights engage,
But wise through time, and narrative with age,
In summer days like grasshoppers rejoice,
A bloodless race, that send a feeble voice.
These, when the Spartan queen approach'd the tower,
In secret own'd resistless beauty's power:
They cried, No wonder, such celestial charms
For nine long years have set the world in arms!
What winning graces! What majestic mien!
She moves a goddess, and she looks a queen!
Yet hence, oh Heaven, convey that fatal face,
And from destruction save the Trojan race".

This is anything but the "surge and thunder", but it is, on the other hand, a definite idiom, within the limits of the rhymed pentameter couplet it is even musical in parts; there is imbecility in the antithesis, and bathos in "she looks a queen", but there is fine accomplishment in:

"Wise through time, and narrative with age",

Mr Pope's own invention, and excellent. What we definitely can *not* hear is the voice of the old men speaking. The simile of the grasshoppers is well rendered, but the old voices do not ring in the ear.

Homer (III, 156-60) reports their conversation:

Οὐ νέμεσις Τρῶας καὶ ἐϋκνήμιδας Ἀχαιοὺς
Τοιῇδ' ἀμφὶ γυναικὶ πολὺν χρόνον ἄλγεα πάσχειν·
Αἰνῶς ἀθανάτῃσι θεῇς εἰς ὦπα ἔοικεν·
Ἀλλὰ καὶ ὣς τοίη περ ἐοῦσ' ἐν νηυσὶ νεέσθω,
Μηδ' ἡμῖν τεκέεσσί τ' ὀπίσσω πῆμα λίποιτο.

Which is given in Sam. Clark's *ad verbum* translation:

"Non *est* indigne ferendum, Trojanos et bene-ocreatos
   Archivos
Tali de muliere longum tempus dolores pati:
Omnino immortalibus deabus ad vultum similis est.
Sed et sic, talis quamvis sit, in navibus redeat,
Neque nobis liberisque in posterum detrimentum
   relinquatur".

Mr Pope has given six short lines for five long ones, but he has added "fatal" to face (or perhaps only lifted it from νέμεσις), he has added "winning graces", "majestic", "looks a queen". As for owning beauty's resistless power secretly or in the open, the Greek is:

Τοῖοι ἄρα Τρώων ἡγήτορες ἦντ' ἐπὶ πύργῳ.
Οἳ δ' ὡς οὖν εἶδονθ' Ἑλένην ἐπὶ πύργον ἰοῦσαν,
Ἦκα πρὸς ἀλλήλους ἔπεα πτερόεντ' ἀγόρευον·

and Sam. Clark as follows:

"Tales utique Trojanorum proceres sedebant in turri. Hi autem ut viderunt Helenam ad turrim venientem, Submisse inter se verbis alatis dixerunt";

Ἦκα is an adjective of sound, it is purely objective, even *submisse** is an addition; though Ἦκα might, by a slight strain, be taken to mean that the speech of the old men came little by little, a phrase from each of the elders. Still it would be purely objective. It does not even say they spoke humbly or with resignation.

Chapman is no closer than his successor. He is so *galant* in fact, that I thought I had found his description in Rochefort. The passage is splendid, but splendidly unhomeric:

"All grave old men, and soldiers they had been, but for age
  Now left the wars; yet counsellors they were exceedingly sage.
And as in well-grown woods, on trees, cold spiny grasshoppers
Sit chirping, and send voices out, that scarce can pierce our ears
For softness, and their weak faint sounds; so, talking on the tow'r,
These seniors of the people sat; who when they saw the pow'r
Of beauty, in the queen, ascend, ev'n those cold-spirited peers,
Those wise and almost wither'd men, found this heat in their years,
That they were forc'd (though whispering) to say: 'What man can blame
The Greeks and Trojans to endure, for so admir'd a dame,

* I.e. Clark is "correct", but the words shade differently. Ἦκα means low, quiet, with a secondary meaning of "little by little". *Submisse* means low, quiet, with a secondary meaning of modesty, humbly.

So many mis'ries, and so long? In her sweet count'nance shine
Looks like the Goddesses. And yet (though never so divine)
Before we boast, unjustly still, of her enforced prise,
And justly suffer for her sake, with all our progenies,
Labour and ruin, let her go; the profit of our land
Must pass the beauty'. Thus, though these could bear so fit a hand
On their affections, yet, when all their gravest powers were us'd,
They could not choose but welcome her, and rather they accus'd
The Gods than beauty; for thus spake the most-fam'd king of Troy":

The last sentence representing mostly Ὥς ἄρ ἔφα in the line:

"Ὥς ἄρ' ἔφαν, Πρίαμος δ' Ἑλένην ἐκαλέσσατο φωνῇ·

"Sic dixerunt: Priamus ·utem Helenam vocavit voce".

Chapman is nearer Swinburne's ballad with:

"But those three following men", etc.

than to his alleged original.

Rochefort is as follows (*Iliade*, Livre III, M. de Rochefort, 1772):

"Hélène à ce discours sentit naître en son âme
Un doux ressouvenir de sa première flamme;
Le désir de revoir les lieux qu'elle a quittés
Jette un trouble inconnu dans ses sens agités.
Tremblante elle se lève et les yeux pleins de larmes,
D'un voile éblouissant elle couvre ses charmes;
De deux femmes suivie elle vole aux remparts.
Là s'étaient assemblés ces illustres vieillards
Qui courbés sous le faix des travaux et de l'âge
N'alloient plus au combat signaler leur courage,

Mais qui, près de leur Roi, par de sages avis,
Mieux qu'en leurs jeunes ans défendoient leur païs.
  Dans leurs doux entretiens, leur voix toujours égale
Ressembloit aux accents que forme la cigale,
Lorsqu'aux longs jours d'été cachée en un buisson,
Elle vient dans les champs annoncer la moisson.
Une tendre surprise enflamma leurs visages;
Frappés de ses appas, ils se disoient entre eux:
'Qui pourroit s'étonner que tant de Rois fameux,
Depuis neuf ans entiers aient combattu pour elle?
Sur le trône des cieux Vénus n'est pas plus belle.
Mais quelque soit l'amour qu'inspirent ses attraits,
Puisse Ilion enfin la perdre pour jamais,
Puisse-t-elle bientôt à son époux rendue,
Conjurer l'infortune en ces lieux attendue'".

Hugues Salel (1545), praised by Ronsard, is more pleasing:

"Le Roi Priam, et auec luy bon nombre
De grandz Seigneurs estoient à l'ombre
Sur les Crenaulx, Tymoetes et Panthus,
Lampus, Clytus, excellentz en vertus,
Hictaon renomme en bataille,
Ucalegon iadis de fort taille,
Et Antenor aux armes nompareil
Mais pour alors ne seruantz qu'en conseil.

Là, ces Vieillards assis de peur du Hasle
Causoyent ensemble ainsi que la Cigale
Ou deux ou trois, entre les vertes fueilles,
En temps d'Esté gazouillant à merveilles;
Lesquelz voyans la diuine Gregeoise,
Disoient entre eux que si la grande noise
De ces deux camps duroit longe saison,
Certainement ce n'estoit sans raison:
Veu la Beaulté, et plus que humain ouvrage,
Qui reluysoit en son diuin visaige.

Ce neantmoins il vauldrait mieulx la rendre,
(Ce disoyent ilz) sans guères plus attendre.
Pour éviter le mal qui peult venir,
Qui la voudra encores retenir".

Salel is a most delightful approach to the Iliads; he is still absorbed in the subject-matter, as Douglas and Golding were absorbed in their subject-matter. Note how exact he is in the rendering of the old men's mental attitude. Note also that he is right in his era. I mean simply that Homer *is* a little *rustre*, a little, or perhaps a good deal, mediaeval, he has not the dovetailing of Ovid. He has onomatopœia, as of poetry sung out; he has authenticity of conversation as would be demanded by an intelligent audience not yet laminated with aesthetics; capable of recognizing reality. He has the repetitions of the *chanson de geste*. Of all the French and English versions I think Salel alone gives any hint of some of these characteristics. Too obviously he is not onomatopœic, no. But he is charming, and readable, and "Briseis Fleur des Demoiselles" has her reality.

Nicolo Valla is, for him who runs, closer:

"Consili virtus, summis de rebus habebant
Sermones, et multa inter se et magna loquentes,
Arboribus quales gracili stridere cicadae
Saepe solent cantu, postquam sub moenibus altis
Tyndarida aspiciunt, procerum tum quisque fremebat,
Mutuasque exorsi, Decuit tot funera Teucros
Argolicasque pati, longique in tempore bellum
Tantus in ore decor cui non mortalis in artus
Est honor et vultu divina efflagrat imago.
Diva licet facies, Danaum cum classe recedat
Longius excido ne nos aut nostra fatiget
Pignora sic illi tantis de rebus agebant".

This hexameter is rather heavily accented. It shows, perhaps, the source of various "ornaments" in later English and

French translations. It has indubitable sonority even though monotonous.

It is the earliest Latin verse rendering I have yet come upon, and is bound in with Raphael of Volterra's first two Iliads, and some further renderings by Obsopeo.

Odyssea (Liber primus)

"Dic mihi musa uirum captae post tempora Troiae
Qui mores hominum multorum uidit et urbes
Multa quoque et ponto passus dum naufragus errat
Ut sibi tum sociis uitam seruaret in alto
Non tamen hos cupiens fato deprompsit acerbo
Ob scelus admissum extinctos ausumque malignum
Qui fame compulsu solis rapuere iuuencos
Stulti ex quo reditum ad patrias deus abstulit oras.
Horum itaque exitium memora mihi musa canenti".

Odyssea (Liber secundus)

"Cum primum effulsit roseis aurora quadrigis
Continuo e stratis proles consurgit Ulyxis
Induit et uestes humerosque adcomodat ensem
Molia denin pedibus formosis uincula nectit
Parque deo egrediens thalamo praeconibus omnis
Concilio cogunt extemplo mandat Achaeos
Ipse quoque ingentem properabat aedibus hastam
Corripiens: geminique canes comitantur euntem
Quumque illi mirum Pallas veneranda decorem
Preberet populus venientem suspicit omnis
Inque throno patrio ueteres cessere sedenti".

The charm of Salel is continued in the following excerpts. They do not cry out for comment. I leave Ogilby's English and the lines of Latin to serve as contrast or cross-light.

Iliade (Livre I), Hugues Salel (1545):*

* Abbé de St Chéron.

THE IRE

Ie te supply Déesse gracieuse,
Vouloir chanter l'Ire pernicieuse,
Dont Achilles fut tellement espris,
Que par icelle, ung grand nombre d'espritz
Des Princes Grecs, par dangereux encombres,
Feit lors descente aux infernales Umbres.
Et leurs beaulx Corps privéz de Sépulture
Furent aux chiens et aux oiseaulx pasture.

Iliade (Lib. III), John Ogilby (1660):

HELEN

Who in this chamber, sumpteously adornd
Sits on your ivory bed, nor could you say,
By his rich habit, he had fought to-day:
A reveller or masker so comes drest,
From splendid sports returning to his rest.
Thus did love's Queen warmer desires prepare.
But when she saw her neck so heavenly faire,
Her lovely bosome and celestial eyes,
Amazed, to the Goddess, she replies:
Why wilt thou happless me once more betray,
And to another wealthy town convey,
Where some new favourite must, as now at Troy
With utter loss of honour me enjoy.

Iliade (Livre VI), Salel:

GLAUCUS RESPOND À DIOMÈDE

Adonc Glaucus, auec grace et audace,
Luy respondit: "T'enquiers tu de ma race?
Le genre humain est fragile et muable
Comme la fueille et aussi peu durable.
Car tout ainsi qu'on uoit les branches uertes
Sur le printemps de fueilles bien couuertes

Qui par les uents d'automne et la froidure
Tombent de l'arbre et perdent leur uerdure
Puis de rechef la gelée passée,
Il en reuient à la place laissée :
Ne plus ne moins est du lignage humain :
Tel est huy uif qui sera mort demain.
S'il en meurt ung, ung autre reuint naistre.
Voylà comment se conserue leur estre".

Iliade (Lib. VI), as in Virgil, Dante, and others:

"Quasim gente rogas? Quibus et natalibus ortus?
Persimile est foliis hominum genus omne caducis
Quae nunc nata uides, pulchrisque, uirescere sylvis
Autumno ueniente cadunt, simul illa perurens
Incubuit Boreas: quaedam sub uerna renasci
Tempora, sic uice perpetua succrescere lapsis,
Semper item noua, sic aliis obeuntibus, ultro
Succedunt alii iuuenes aetate grauatis.
Quod si forte iuvat te qua sit quisque suorum
Stirpe satus, si natales cognoscere quaeris
Forte meos, referam, quae sunt notissima multis".

Iliade (Livre IX), Salel:

CALYDON

En Calydon règnoit
Oenéus, ung bon Roy qui donnoit
De ses beaulx Fruictz chascun an les Primices
Aux Immortelz, leur faisant Sacrifices.
Or il aduint (ou bien par son uouloir,
Ou par oubly) qu'il meit à nonchalloir
Diane chaste, et ne luy feit offrande,
Dont elle print Indignation grande
Encontre luy, et pour bien le punir
Feit ung Sanglier dedans ses Champs uenir

Horrible et fier qui luy feit grand dommage
Tuant les Gens et gastant le Fruictage.
Maintz beaulx Pomiers, maintz Arbres reuestuz
De Fleur et Fruict, en furent abattuz,
Et de la Dent aguisée et poinctue,
Le Bléd gasté et la Vigne tortue.
Méléager, le Filz de ce bon Roy,
Voyant ainsi le piteux Désarroy
De son Pays et de sa Gent troublée
Proposa lors de faire une Assemblée
De bons Veneurs et Leutiers pour chasser
L'horrible Beste et sa Mort pourchasser.
Ce qui fut faict. Maintes Gens l'y trouvèrent
Qui contre luy ses Forces éprouvèrent;
Mais à la fin le Sanglier inhumain
Receut la Mort de sa Royale Main.
Estant occis, deux grandes Nations
Pour la Dépouille eurent Contentions
Les Curetois disoient la mériter,
Ceulx d'Etolie en uouloient hériter.

Iliade (Livre x), Salel:

THE BATHERS

Quand Ulysses fut en la riche tente
Du compaignon, alors il diligente
De bien lier ses cheuaulx et les loge
Soigneusement dedans la même loge
Et au rang même où la belle monture
Du fort Gregeois mangeoit pain et pasture
Quand aux habitz de Dolon, il les pose
Dedans la nef, sur la poupe et propose
En faire ung jour à Pallas sacrifice,
Et luy offrir à jamais son seruice.
Bien tost après, ces deux Grecs de ualeur
Se cognoissant oppresséz de chaleur,

Et de sueur, dedans la mer entrèrent
Pour se lauer, et très bien so frotèrent
Le col, le dos, les jambes et les cuisses,
Ostant du corps toutes les immondices,
Estans ainsi refreichiz et bien netz,
Dedans des baingz souefs bien ordonnéz,
S'en sont entréz, et quand leurs corps
Ont esté oinctz d'huyle par le dehors
Puis sont allez manger, prians Minerue
Qu'en tous leurs faictz les dirige et conserue
En respandant du uin à pleine tasse,
(pour sacrifice) au milieu de la place.

II. ANDREAS DIVUS

In the year of grace 1906, 1908, or 1910 I picked from the Paris quais a Latin version of the *Odyssey* by Andreas Divus Justinopolitanus (Parisiis, In officina Christiani Wecheli, MDXXXVIII), the volume containing also the *Batrachomyomachia*, by Aldus Manutius, and the *Hymni Deorum* rendered by Georgius Dartona Cretensis. I lost a Latin *Iliads* for the economy of four francs, these coins being at that time scarcer with me than they ever should be with any man of my tastes and abilities.

In 1911 the Italian savant, Signore E. Teza, published his note, "Quale fosse la Casata di Andreas Divus Justinopolitanus?" This question I am unable to answer, nor do I greatly care by what name Andreas was known in the privacy of his life: Signore Dio, Signore Divino, or even Mijnheer van Gott may have served him as patronymic. Sannazaro, author of *De Partu Virginis*, and also of the epigram ending *hanc et sugere*, translated himself as Sanctus Nazarenus; I am myself known as Signore Sterlina to James Joyce's children, while the phonetic translation of my name into the Japanese tongue is so indecorous that I am seriously advised not to use it, lest it do me harm in Nippon. (Rendered back *ad verbum* into our maternal speech it gives for its meaning, "This picture of a phallus costs ten yen". There is no surety in shifting personal names from one idiom to another.)

Justinopolis is identified as Capodistria; what matters is Divus' text. We find for the "Nekuia" (*Odys.* XI):

"At postquam ad navem descendimus, et mare,
Nauem quidem primum deduximus in mare diuum,
Et malum posuimus et vela in navi nigra:
Intrò autem oues accipientes ire fecimus, intrò et ipsi
Iuimus dolentes, huberes lachrymas fundentes:
Nobis autem a tergo navis nigrae prorae
Prosperum ventum imisit pandentem velum bonum amicum
Circe benecomata gravis Dea altiloqua.
Nos autem arma singula expedientes in navi
Sedebamus: hanc autem ventusque gubernatorque dirigebat:
Huius āt per totum diem extensa sunt vela pontum transientis:
Occidit tunc Sol, obumbratae sunt omnes viae:
Haec autem in fines pervenit profundi Oceani:
Illic autem Cimmeriorum virorum populusque civitasque,
Caligine et nebula cooperti, neque unquam ipsos
Sol lucidus aspicit radiis,
Neque quando tendit ad coelum stellatum,
Neque quando retro in terram a coelo vertitur:
Sed nox pernitiosa extenditur miseris hominibus:
Navem quidem illuc venientes traximus, extra autem oves
Accepimus: ipsi autem rursus apud fluxum Oceani
Iuimus, ut in locum perveniremus quem dixit Circe:
Hic sacra quidem Perimedes Eurylochusque
Faciebant: ego autem ensem acutum trahens a foemore,
Foveam fodi quantum cubiti mensura hinc et inde:

Circum ipsam autem libamina fundimus omnibus mortuis;
Primum mulso, postea autem dulci vino:
Tertio rursus aqua, et farinas albas miscui:
Multum autem oravi mortuorum infirma capita:
Profectus in Ithacam, sterilem bovem, quae optima esset,
Sacrificare in domibus, pyramque implere bonis:
Tiresiae autem seorsum ovem sacrificare vovi
Totam nigram, quae ovibus antecellat nostris:
Has autem postquam votis precationibusque gentes mor-
    tuorum
Precatus sum, oves autem accipiens obtruncavi:
In fossam fluebat autem sanguis niger, congregataeque sunt
Animae ex Erebo cadaverum mortuorum,
Nymphaeque iuvenesque et multa passi senes,
Virginesque tenerae, nuper flebilem animum habentes,
Multi autem vulnerati aereis lanceis
Viri in bello necati, cruenta arma habentes,
Qui multi circum foveam veniebant aliunde alius
Magno clamore, me autem pallidus timor cepit.
Iam postea socios hortans iussi
Pecora, quae iam iacebant iugulata saevo aere,
Excoriantes comburere: supplicare autem Diis,
Fortique Plutoni, et laudatae Proserpinae.
At ego ensem acutum trahens a foemore,
Sedi, neque permisi mortuorum impotentia capita
Sanguinem prope ire, antequam Tiresiam audirem:
Prima autem anima Elpenoris venit socii:
Nondum enim sepultus erat sub terra lata,
Corpus enim in domo Circes reliquimus nos
Infletum et insepultum, quoniam labor alius urgebat:
Hunc quidem ego lachrymatus sum videns, misertusque
    sum animo,
Et ipsum clamando verba velocia allocutus sum:
   Elpenor, quomodo venisti sub caliginem obscuram:
Praevenisti pedes existens quam ego in navi nigra?

Sic dixi: hic autem mihi lugens respondit verbo:
Nobilis Laertiade, prudens Ulysse,
Nocuit mihi dei fatum malum, et multum vinum:
Circes autem in domo dormiens, non animadverti
Me retrogradum descendere eundo per scalam longam,
Sed contra murum cecidi: ast autem mihi cervix
Nervorum fracta est, anima autem in infernum descendit:
Nunc autem his qui venturi sunt postea precor non praesentibus
Per uxorem et patrem, qui educavit parvum existentem,
Telemachumque quem solum in domibus reliquisti.
Scio enim quod hinc iens domo ex inferni
Insulam in Aeaeam impellens benefabricatam navim:
Tunc te postea Rex iubeo recordari mei
Ne me infletum, insepultum, abiens retro, relinquas
Separatus, ne deorum ira fiam
Sed me combure cum armis quaecunque mihi sunt,
Sepulchrumque mihi accumula cani in litore maris,
Viri infelicis, et cuius apud posteros fama sit:
Haecque mihi perfice, figeque in sepulchro remum,
Quo et vivus remigabam existens cum meis sociis.
   Sic dixit: at ego ipsum, respondens, allocutus sum:
Haec tibi infelix perficiamque et faciam:
Nos quidem sic verbis respondentes molestis
Sedebamus: ego quidem separatim supra sanguinem ensem tenebam:
Idolum autem ex altera parte socii multa loquebatur:
Venit autem insuper anima matris mortuae
Autolyci filia magnanimi Anticlea,
Quam vivam dereliqui iens ad Ilium sacrum,
Hanc quidem ego lachrymatus sum videns miseratusque sum animo:
Sed neque sic sivi priorem licet valde dolens
Sanguinem prope ire, antequam Tiresiam audirem:
Venit autem insuper anima Thebani Tiresiae,

Aureum sceptrum tenens, me autem novit et allocuta est:
Cur iterum o infelix linquens lumen Solis
Venisti, ut videas mortuos, et iniucundam regionem?
Sed recede a fossa, remove autem ensem acutum,
Sanguinem ut bibam, et tibi vera dicam.
   Sic dixi: ego autem retrocedens, ensem argenteum
Vagina inclusi: hic autem postquam bibit sanguinem
   nigrum,
Et tunc iam me verbis allocutus est vates verus:
   Reditum quaeris dulcem illustris Ulysse:
Hunc autem tibi difficilem faciet Deus, non enim puto
Latere Neptunum, quam iram imposuit animo
Iratus, quod ei filium dilectum excaecasti:
   Sed tamen et sic mala licet passi pervenietis,
   Si volueris tuum animum continere et sociorum".

The meaning of the passage is, with a few abbreviations, as I have interpolated it in my Third Canto:

"And then went down to the ship, set keel to breakers,
Forth on the godly sea,
We set up mast and sail on the swart ship,
Sheep bore we aboard her, and our bodies also,
Heavy with weeping; and winds from sternward
Bore us out onward with bellying canvas,
Circe's this craft, the trim-coifed goddess.
Then sat we amidships—wind jamming the tiller—
Thus with stretched sail we went over sea till day's end.
Sun to his slumber, shadows o'er all the ocean,
Came we then to the bounds of deepest water,
To the Kimmerian lands and peopled cities
Covered with close-webbed mist, unpierced ever
With glitter of sun-rays,
Nor with stars stretched, nor looking back from heaven,
Swartest night stretched over wretched men there,
The ocean flowing backward, came we then to the place

Aforesaid by Circe.
Here did they rites, Perimedes and Eurylochus,
And drawing sword from my hip
I dug the ell-square pitkin,
Poured we libations unto each the dead,
First mead and then sweet wine, water mixed with white flour,
Then prayed I many a prayer to the sickly death's-heads,
As set in Ithaca, sterile bulls of the best
For sacrifice, heaping the pyre with goods.
Sheep, to Tiresias only; black and a bell sheep.
Dark blood flowed in the fosse,
Souls out of Erebus, cadaverous dead,
Of brides, of youths, and of much-bearing old;
Virgins tender, souls stained with recent tears,
Many men mauled with bronze lance-heads,
Battle spoil, bearing yet dreary arms,
These many crowded about me,
With shouting, pallor upon me, cried to my men for more beasts.
Slaughtered the herds, sheep slain of bronze,
Poured ointment, cried to the gods,
To Pluto the strong, and praised Proserpine,
Unsheathed the narrow sword,
I sat to keep off the impetuous, impotent dead
Till I should hear Tiresias.
But first Elpenor came, our friend Elpenor,
Unburied, cast on the wide earth,
Limbs that we left in the house of Circe,
Unwept, unwrapped in sepulchre, since toils urged other.
Pitiful spirit, and I cried in hurried speech:
'Elpenor, how art thou come to this dark coast?
Cam'st thou a-foot, outstripping seamen?'
      And he in heavy speech:
'Ill fate and abundant wine! I slept in Circe's ingle,

Going down the long ladder unguarded, I fell against the
    buttress,
Shattered the nape-nerve, the soul sought Avernus.
But thou, O King, I bid remember me, unwept, unburied,
Heap up mine arms, be tomb by sea-board, and inscribed:
"*A man of no fortune and with a name to come*".
And set my oar up, that I swung mid fellows'.
Came then another ghost, whom I beat off, Anticlea,
And then Tiresias, Theban,
Holding his golden wand, knew me and spoke first:
'Man of ill hour, why come a second time,
Leaving the sunlight, facing the sunless dead, and this
    joyless region?
Stand from the fosse, move back, leave me my bloody
    bever,
And I will speak you true speeches'.
        And I stepped back,
Sheathing the yellow sword. Dark blood he drank then,
And spoke: 'Lustrous Odysseus
Shalt return through spiteful Neptune, over dark seas,
Lose all companions'. Foretold me the ways and the
    signs.
Came then Anticlea, to whom I answered:
'Fate drives me on through these deeps. I sought Tiresias',
Told her the news of Troy. And thrice her shadow
Faded in my embrace".

It takes no more Latin than I have to know that Divus'
Latin is not the Latin of Catullus and Ovid; that it is *illepidus*
to chuck Latin nominative participles about in such profusion; that Romans did not use *habentes* as the Greeks used
ἔχοντες, etc. And *nos* in line 53 is unnecessary. Divus' Latin
has, despite these wems, its quality; it is even singable, there
are constant suggestions of the poetic motion; it is very
simple Latin, after all, and a crib of this sort may make just

the difference of permitting a man to read fast enough to get the swing and mood of the subject, instead of losing both in a dictionary.

Even *habentes* when one has made up one's mind to it, together with less obvious exoticisms, does not upset one as

"the steep of Delphos leaving".

One is, of necessity, more sensitive to botches in one's own tongue than to botches in another, however carefully learned.

For all the fuss about Divus' errors of elegance Samuelis Clarkius and Jo. Augustus Ernestus do not seem to have gone him much better—with two hundred years extra Hellenic scholarship at their disposal.

The first Aldine Greek Iliads appeared I think in 1504, Odyssey possibly later.* My edition of Divus is of 1538, and as it contains Aldus' own translation of the Frog-fight, it may indicate that Divus was in touch with Aldus in Italy, or quite possibly the French edition is pirated from an earlier Italian printing. A Latin Odyssey in some sort of verse was at that time infinitely worth doing.

Raphael of Volterra had done his prose Odyssey with the opening lines of several books and a few other brief passages in verse. This was printed with Laurenzo Valla's prose Iliads as early as 1502. He begins:

"Dic mihi musa virum captae post tempora Troiae
Qui mores hominum multorum vidit et urbes
Multa quoque et ponto passus dum naufragus errat
Ut sibi tum sotiis (sociis) vitam servaret in alto
Non tamen hos cupiens fato deprompsit acerbo".

* My impression is that I saw an *Iliad* by Andreas Divus on the Quais in Paris, at the time I found his version of the *Odyssey*, but an impression of this sort is, after eight years, untrustworthy, it may have been only a Latin *Iliad* in similar binding.

Probably the source of "Master Watson's" English quantitative couplet, but obviously not copied by Divus:

"Virum mihi dic musa multiscium qui valde multum
Erravit, ex quo Troiae sacram urbem depopulatus est:
Multorum autem virorum vidit urbes et mentem cognovit:
Multos autem hic in mare passus est dolores, suo in animo,
Liberans suamque animam et reditum sociorum".

On the other hand, it is nearly impossible to believe that Clark and Ernestus were unfamiliar with Divus. Clark calls his Latin crib a composite "non elegantem utique et venustam, sed ita Romanam, ut verbis verba". A good deal of Divus' *venustas* has departed. Clark's hyphenated compounds are, I think, no more Roman than are some of Divus' coinage; they may be a trifle more explanatory, but if we read a shade more of colour into ἀθέσφατος οἶνος than we can into *multum vinum*, it is not restored to us in Clark's *copiosum vinum*, nor does *terra spatiosa* improve upon *terra lata*, εὐρυοδείης being (if anything more than *lata*): "with wide ways or streets", the wide ways of the world, traversable, open to wanderers. The participles remain in Clark-Ernestus, many of the coined words remain unchanged. Georgius Dartona gives, in the opening of the second hymn to Aphrodite:

"Venerandam auream coronam habentem pulchram Venerem
Canam, quae totius Cypri munimenta sortita est
Maritimae ubi illam zephyri vis molliter spirantis
Suscitavit per undam multisoni maris,
Spuma in molli: hanc autem auricurae Horae
Susceperunt hilariter, immortales autem vestes induere:
Capite vero super immortali coronam bene constructam posuere
Pulchram, auream: tribus autem ansis
Donum orichalchi aurique honorabilis:

TRANSLATORS OF GREEK

Collum autem molle, ac pectora argentea
Monilibus aureis ornabant... ", etc.

Ernestus, adding by himself the appendices to the Epics, gives us:

"Venerandam auream coronam habentem pulchram Venerem
Canam, quae totius Cypri munimenta sortita est
Maritimae, ubi illam zephyri vis molliter spirantis
Tulit per undam multisoni maris
Spuma in molli: hanc autem auro comam religatae Horae
Susceperunt hilariter, immortales autem vestes induere:
Caput autem super immortale coronam bene constructam
    posuere
Pulchram, auream, perforatis autem auriculis
Donum orichalchi preciosi:
Collum autem molle ac pectora candida*
Monilibus aureis ornabant... ", etc.

"Which things since they are so" lead us to feel that we would have had no less respect for Messrs Clarkius and Ernestus if they had deigned to mention the names of their predecessors. They have not done this in their prefaces, and if any mention is made of the sixteenth-century scholars, it is very effectually buried somewhere in the voluminous Latin notes, which I have not gone through *in toto*. Their edition (Glasgow, 1814) is, however, most serviceable.

TRANSLATION OF AESCHYLUS

A search for Aeschylus in English is deadly, accursed, mind-rending. Browning has "done" the Agamemnon, or "done the Agamemnon in the eye" as the critic may choose to consider. He has written a modest and an apparently intelligent preface.

* Reading ἀργυφέοισιν, variant ἀργυρέοισιν, offered in footnote. In any case *argentea* is closer than *candida*.

"I should hardly look for an impossible transmission of the reputed magniloquence and sonority of the Greek; and this with the less regret, inasmuch as there is abundant musicality elsewhere, but nowhere else than in his poem the ideas of the poet".

He quotes Matthew Arnold on the Greeks: "their expression is so excellent, because it is so simple and so well subordinated, because it draws its force directly from the pregnancy of the matter which it conveys...not a word wasted, not a sentiment capriciously thrown in, stroke on stroke".

He is reasonable about the Greek spelling. He points out that γόνον ἰδὼν κάλλιστον ἀνδρῶν sounds very poorly as "Seeing her son the fairest of men" but is outshouted in "Remirando il figliuolo bellissimo degli uomini", and protests his fidelity to the meaning of Aeschylus.

His weakness in this work is where it essentially lay in all of his expression, it rests in the term "ideas".—"Thought" as Browning understood it—"ideas" as the term is current, are poor two-dimensional stuff, a scant, scratch covering. "Damn ideas, anyhow." An idea is only an imperfect induction from fact.

The solid, the "last atom of force verging off into the first atom of matter" is the force, the emotion, the objective sight of the poet. In the *Agamemnon* it is the whole rush of the action, the whole wildness of Kassandra's continual shrieking, the flash of the beacon fires burning unstinted wood, the outburst of

Τροίαν Ἀχαιῶν οὖσαν,

or the later

Τροίαν Ἀχαιοὶ τῇδ' ἔχουσ' ἐν ἡμέρᾳ.

"Troy is the Greeks'." Even Rossetti has it better than Browning: "Troy's down, tall Troy's on fire", anything, literally anything that can be shouted, that can be shouted uncontrolledly and hysterically. "Troy is the Greeks'" is an ambiguity for the ear. "Know that our men are in Ilion."

Anything but a stilted unsayable jargon. Yet with Browning we have

"Troia the Achaioi hold",

and later,

"Troia do the Achaioi hold",

followed by:

"this same day
I think a noise—no mixture—reigns i' the city
Sour wine and unguent pour thou in one vessel——"

And it does not end here. In fact it reaches the nadir of its bathos in a later speech of Klutaimnestra in the line

"The perfect man his home perambulating!"

We may add several exclamation points to the one which Mr Browning has provided. But then all translation is a thankless, or is at least most apt to be a thankless and desolate undertaking.

What Browning had not got into his sometimes excellent top-knot was the patent, or what should be the patent fact that inversions of sentence order in an uninflected language like English are not, simply and utterly *are not* any sort of equivalent for inversions and perturbations of order in a language inflected as Greek and Latin are inflected. That is the chief source of his error. In these inflected languages order has other currents than simple sequence of subject, predicate, object; and all sorts of departures from this Franco-English natural position are in Greek and Latin neither confusing nor delaying; they may be both simple and emphatic, they do not obstruct one's apperception of the verbal relations.

Obscurities *not inherent in* the matter, obscurities due not to the thing but to the wording, are a botch, and are *not* worth preserving in a translation. The work lives not by them but despite them.

Rossetti is in this matter sounder than Browning, when he says that the only thing worth bringing over is the beauty of the original; and despite Rossetti's purple plush and molasses trimmings he meant by "beauty" something fairly near what we mean by the "emotional intensity" of his original.

Obscurities inherent in the thing occur when the author is piercing, or trying to pierce into, uncharted regions; when he is trying to express things not yet current, not yet worn into phrase; when he is ahead of the emotional, or philosophic sense (as a painter might be ahead of the colour-sense) of his contemporaries.

As for the word-sense and phrase-sense, we still hear workmen and peasants and metropolitan bus-riders repeating the simplest sentences three and four times, back and forth between interlocutors: trying to get the sense "I sez to Bill, I'm goin' to 'Arrow" or some other such subtlety from one occiput into another.

"You sez to Bill, etc."

"Yus, I sez...etc."

"O!"

The first day's search at the Museum reveals "Aeschylus" printed by Aldus in 1518; by Stephanus in 1557; no English translation before 1777, a couple in the 1820's, more in the middle of the century, since 1880 past counting, and no promising names in the list. Sophocles falls to Jebb and does not appear satisfactory.

From which welter one returns thankfully to the Thomas Stanley Greek and Latin edition, with Saml. Butler's notes, Cambridge, "typis ac sumptibus academicis", 1811—once a guinea or half-a-guinea per volume, half leather, but now mercifully, since people no longer read Latin, picked up at

TRANSLATORS OF GREEK

2s. for the set (eight volumes in all), rather less than the price of their postage. Quartos in excellent type.

Browning shows himself poet in such phrases as "dust, mud's thirsty brother", which is easy, perhaps, but is English, even Browning's own particular English, as "dust, of mud brother thirsty", would not be English at all; and if I have been extremely harsh in dealing with the first passage quoted it is still undisputable that I have read Browning off and on for seventeen years with no small pleasure and admiration, and am one of the few people who know anything about his *Sordello*, and have never read his *Agamemnon*, have not even now when it falls into a special study been able to get through his *Agamemnon*.

Take another test passage:

> Οὗτός ἐστιν 'Αγαμέμνων, ἐμὸς   1413
> Πόσις, νεκρὸς δὲ τῆσδε δεξιᾶς χερός,
> Ἔργον δικαίας τέκτονος. Τάδ' ὧδ' ἔχει.

> "Hicce est Agamemnon, maritus
> Meus, hac dextra mortuus,
> Facinus justae artificis. Haec ita se habent".

We turn to Browning and find:

> "—this man is Agamemnon,
> My husband, dead, the work of this right hand here,
> Aye, of a just artificer: so things are".

To the infinite advantage of the Latin, and the complete explanation of why Browning's Aeschylus, to say nothing of forty other translations of Aeschylus, is unreadable.

Any bungling translation:

> "This is Agamemnon,
> My husband,
> Dead by this hand,
> And a good job. These, gentlemen, are the facts".

No, that is extreme, but the point is that any natural wording, anything which keeps the mind off theatricals and on Klutaimnestra actual, dealing with an actual situation, and not pestering the reader with frills and festoons of language, is worth all the convoluted tushery that the Victorians can heap together.*

I can conceive no improvement on the Latin, it saves by *dextra* for δεξιᾶς χερός, it loses a few letters in "se habent", but it has the same drive as the Greek.

The Latin can be a whole commentary on the Greek, or at least it can give one the whole parsing and order, and let one proceed at a comfortable rate with but the most rudimentary knowledge of the original language. And I do not think this a trifle; it would be an ill day if men again let the classics go by the board; we should fall into something worse than, or as bad as, the counter-reformation: a welter of gum-shoes, and cocoa, and Y.M.C.A. and Webbs, and social theorizing committees, and the general hell of a groggy doctrinaire obfuscation; and the very disagreeablizing of the classics, every pedagogy which puts the masterwork further from us, either by obstructing the schoolboy, or breeding affectation in dilettante readers, works toward such a detestable end. I do not know that strict logic will cover all of the matter, or that I can formulate anything beyond a belief that we test a translation by the feel, and particularly by the feel of being in contact with the force of a great original, and it does not seem to me that one can open this Latin text of the *Agamemnon* without getting such sense of contact:

> "Mox sciemus lampadum luciferarum   498
>   Signorumque per faces et ignis vices,
>   An vere sint, an, somniorum instar,

* In 1934, one would emend the last lines to:
    "I did it. That's how it is".

Gratum veniens illud lumen eluserit animum nostrum.
Praeconem hunc a littore video obumbratum
Ramis olivae: testatur autem haec mihi frater
Luti socius aridus pulvis,
Quod neque mutus, neque accendens facem
Materiae montanae signa dabit per fumum ignis".

Or

"Apollo, Apollo!   1095
Agyieu Apollo mi!
Ah! quo me tandem duxisti? ad qualem domum?

. . . . . .

"Heu, heu, ecce, ecce, cohibe a vacca   1134
Taurum: vestibus involvens
Nigricornem machina
Percutit; cadit vero in aquali vase.
Insidiosi lebetis casum ut intelligas velim.

. . . . . .

"Heu, heu, argutae lusciniae fatum *mihi tribuis*:

. . . . . .

"Heu nuptiae, nuptiae Paridis exitiales   1165
Amicis! eheu Scamandri patria unda!"

All this howling of Kassandra comes at one from the page, and the grimness also of the Iambics:

"Ohime! lethali intus percussus sum vulnere."   1352
"Tace: quis clamat vulnus lethaliter vulneratus?"
"Ohime! iterum secundo ictu sauciatus."
"Patrari facinus mihi videtur regis ex ejulatu."   1355
"At tuta communicemus consilia."
"Ego quidem vobis meam dico sententiam", etc.

Here or in the opening of the play, or where you like in this Latin, we are at once in contact with the action, something real is going on, we are keen and curious on the instant, but I cannot get any such impact from any part of the Browning.

"In bellum nuptam,
Autricemque contentionum, Helenam?   695
Quippe quae congruenter
Perditrix navium, perditrix virorum, perditrix urbium,
E delicatis
Thalami ornamentis navigavit
Zephyri terrigenae aura.

Et numerosi scutiferi,
Venatores secundum vestigia,
Remorum inapparentia
Appulerunt ad Simoentis ripas
Foliis abundantes
Ob jurgium cruentum."

"War-wed, author of strife,
Fitly Helen, destroyer of ships, of men,
Destroyer of cities,
From delicate-curtained room
Sped by land breezes.

Swift the shields on your track,
Oars on the unseen traces,
And leafy Simois
Gone red with blood."*

Contested Helen, 'Αμφινεικῆ.

"War-wed, contested,
(Fitly) Helen, destroyer of ships; of men;
Destroyer of cities,

From the delicate-curtained room
Sped by land breezes.

* For note on "H. D.'s" translations from Euripides, *vide* '*Instigations*'.

> Swift the shields on your track,
> Oars on the unseen traces.
> Red leaves in Simois!"

"Rank flower of love, for Troy."

"Quippe leonem educavit...   726
Mansuetum, pueris amabilem...
...divinitus sacerdos Ates (i.e. Paris)
In aedibus enutritus est."

"Statim igitur venit   746
Ad urbem Ilii,
Ut ita dicam, animus
Tranquillae serenitatis, placidum
Divitiarum ornamentum
Blandum oculorum telum,
Animum pungens flos amoris,
(*Helena*) accubitura. Perfecit autem
Nuptiarum acerbos exitus,
Mala vicina, malaque socia,
Irruens in Priamidas,
Ductu Jovis Hospitalis,
Erinnys luctuosa sponsis."

It seems to me that English translators have gone wide in two ways, first in trying to keep every adjective, when obviously many adjectives in the original have only melodic value, secondly they have been deaved with syntax; have wasted time, involved their English, trying first to evolve a definite logical structure for the Greek and secondly to preserve it, *and all its grammatical relations*, in English.

One might almost say that Aeschylus' Greek is agglutinative, that his general drive, especially in choruses, is merely to remind the audience of the events of the Trojan war; that syntax is subordinate, and duly subordinated, left out, that he is not austere, but often even verbose after a fashion (not Euripides' fashion).

A reading version might omit various things which would be of true service only if the English were actually to be sung on a stage, or chanted to the movements of the choric dance or procession.

Above suggestions should *not* be followed with intemperance. But certainly more sense and less syntax (good or bad) in translations of Aeschylus might be a relief.

Chor. Anapest:

"O iniquam Helenam, una quae multas,   1464
Multas admodum animas
Perdidisti ad Trojam!
Nunc vero nobilem memorabilem (*Agam. animam*),
Deflorasti per caedem inexpiabilem.
Talis erat tunc in aedibus
Eris viri domitrix aerumna".

Clytemnestra:

"Nequaquam mortis sortem exopta   1470
Hisce gravatus;
Neque in Helenam iram convertas,
Tanquam viriperdam, ac si una multorum
Virorum animas Graecorum perdens,
Intolerabilem dolorem effecerit".

. . . . . .

Clytemnestra:

"Mortem haud indignam arbitror   1530
Huic contigisse:
Neque enim ille insidiosam cladem
Aedibus intulit; sed meum ex ipso
Germen sublatum, multum defletam
Iphigeniam cum indigne affecerit,
Digna passus est, nihil in inferno
Glorietur, gladio inflicta
Morte luens quae prior perpetravit".

"Death not unearned, nor yet a novelty in this house;
  Let him make talk in hell concerning Iphigenia."

(If we allow the last as ironic equivalent of the literal "let him not boast in hell".)

"He gets but a thrust once given (by him)
  Back-pay, for Iphigenia."

One can further condense the English but at the cost of obscurity.

Morshead is bearable in Clytemnestra's description of the beacons:

"From Ida's top Hephaestos, Lord of fire,
Sent forth his sign, and on, and ever on,
Beacon to beacon sped the courier-flame
From Ida to the crag, that Hermes loves
On Lemnos; thence into the steep sublime
Of Athos, throne of Zeus, the broad blaze flared.
Thence, raised aloft to shoot across the sea
The moving light, rejoicing in its strength
Sped from the pyre of pine, and urged its way,
In golden glory, like some strange new sun,
Onward and reached Macistus' watching heights".

P.S. I leave these notes, rough as they are, to indicate a block of matter needing examination, the indication being necessary if the reader is to gauge the proportions and relations of other subjects here outlined.

5

FRENCH POETS*

The time when the intellectual affairs of America could be conducted on a monolingual basis is over. It has been irksome for long. The intellectual life of London is dependent on people who understand the French language about as well as their own. America's part in contemporary culture is based chiefly upon two men familiar with Paris: Whistler and Henry James. It is something in the nature of a national disgrace that a New Zealand paper, *The Triad*, should be more alert to, and have better regular criticism of, contemporary French publications than any American periodical has yet had.

I had wished to give but a brief anthology of French poems, interposing no comment of my own between author and reader; confining my criticism to selection. But that plan was not feasible. I was indebted to MM. Davray and Valette for cordial semi-permissions to quote the *Mercure* publications.

Certain delicate wines will not travel; they are not always the best wines. Foreign criticism may sometimes correct the criticism *du cru*. I cannot pretend to give the reader a summary of contemporary French opinion, but certain French poets have qualities strong enough to be perceptible to me, that is, to at least one alien reader; certain things are translatable from one language to another, a tale or an image will "translate"; music will, practically never, translate; and if a

* *The Little Review*, February, 1918.

work be taken abroad in the original tongue, certain properties seem to become less apparent, or less important. Fancy styles, questions of local "taste", lose importance. Even though I know the overwhelming importance of technique, technicalities in a foreign tongue cannot have for me the importance they have to a man writing in that tongue; almost the only technique perceptible to a foreigner is the presentation of content as free as possible from the clutteration of dead technicalities, fustian à la Louis XV; and from timidities of workmanship. This is perhaps the only technique that ever matters, the only *maestria*.

Mediocre poetry is, I think, the same everywhere; there is not the slightest need to import it; we search foreign tongues for *maestria* and for discoveries not yet revealed in the home product. The critic of a foreign literature must know a reasonable amount of the bad poetry of the nation he studies if he is to attain any sense of proportion.

He will never be as sensitive to fine shades of language as the native; he has, however, a chance of being less bound, less allied to some group of writers. It would be politic for me to praise as many living Frenchmen as possible, and thereby to increase the number of my chances for congenial acquaintance on my next trip to Paris, and to have a large number of current French books sent to me to review.

But these rather broad and general temptations can scarcely lead me to praise one man instead of another.

If I have thrown over current French opinion, I must urge that foreign opinion has at times been a corrective. England has never accepted the continental opinion of Byron; the right estimate lies perhaps between the two. Heine is, I have heard, better read outside Germany than within. The continent has never accepted the idiotic British adulation of Milton; on the other hand, the idiotic neglect of Landor has never been rectified by the continent.

Foreign criticism, if honest, can never be quite the same

as home criticism: it may be better or worse; it may have a value similar to that of a different decade or century and has at least some chance of escaping whims and stampedes of opinion.

I do not "aim at completeness". I believe that the American-English reader has heard in a general way of Baudelaire and Verlaine and Mallarmé; that Mallarmé, perhaps unread, is apt to be slightly overestimated; that Gautier's reputation, despite its greatness, is not yet as great as it should be.

After a man has lived a reasonable time with the two volumes of Gautier's poetry, he might pleasantly venture upon the authors whom I indicate in this essay; and he might have, I think, a fair chance of seeing them in proper perspective. I omit certain nebulous writers because I think their work bad; I omit the Parnassiens, Samain and Heredia, firstly because their work seems to me to show little that was not already implicit in Gautier; secondly, because America has had enough Parnassienism—perhaps second rate, but still enough. (The verses of La Comtesse de Noailles in the *Revue des Deux Mondes*, and those of John Vance Cheney in *The Atlantic* once gave me an almost identical pleasure.) I do not mean that all the poems here to be quoted are better than Samain's *Mon âme est une infante*... or his *Cléopâtre*.

We may take it that Gautier achieved hardness in *Emaux et Camées*; his earlier work did in France very much what remained for the men of the "nineties" to accomplish in England. Gautier's work done in the "thirties" shows a similar beauty, a similar sort of technique. If the Parnassiens were following Gautier they fell short of his merit. Heredia was perhaps the best of them. He tried to make his individual statements more "poetic"; but his whole, for all this, becomes frigid.

Samain followed him and began to go "soft"; there is

in him just a suggestion of muzziness. Heredia is "hard", but there or thereabouts he ends. Gautier is intent on being "hard"; is intent on conveying a certain verity of feeling, and he ends by being truly poetic. Heredia wants to be poetic *and* hard; the hardness appears to him as a virtue in the poetic. And one tends to conclude, from this, that all attempts to be poetic in some manner or other, defeat their own end; whereas an intentness on the quality of the emotion to be conveyed makes for poetry.

I intend here a qualitative analysis. The work of Gautier, Baudelaire, Verlaine, Mallarmé, Samain, Heredia, and of the authors I quote here should give an idea of the sort of poetry that has been written in France during the last half century, or at least during the last forty years. If I am successful in my choice, I will indicate most of the best and even some of the half-good. Van Bever and Léautaud's anthology contains samples of some forty or fifty more poets.*

After Gautier, France produced, as nearly as I can understand, three chief and admirable poets: Tristan Corbière, perhaps the most poignant writer since Villon; Rimbaud, a

---

* A testimony to the effect of anthologies, and to the prestige of Van Bever and Léautaud in forming French taste, and at the same time the most amazing response to my French number of *The Little Review*, was contained in a letter from one of the very poets I had chosen to praise:

"Je vous remercie de m'avoir révélé Laforgue que je connaissais seulement par les extraits publiés dans la première Anthologie en 1 volume par Van Bever et Léautaud".

This is also a reply to those who solemnly assured me that any foreigner attempting to criticize French poetry would meet nothing but ridicule from French authors.

I am free to say that Van B. and L.'s selections would have led me neither to Laforgue nor to Rimbaud. They were, however, my approach to many of the other poets, and their two-volume anthology is invaluable.

vivid and indubitable genius; and Laforgue—a slighter, but in some ways a finer "artist" than either of the others. I do not mean that he "writes better" than Rimbaud; and Eliot has pointed out the wrongness of Symons' phrase, "Laforgue the eternal adult, Rimbaud the eternal child". Rimbaud's effects seem often to come as the beauty of certain silver crystals produced by chemical means. Laforgue always knows what he is at; Rimbaud, the "genius" in the narrowest and deepest sense of the term, the "most modern", seems, almost without knowing it, to hit on the various ways in which the best writers were to follow him, slowly. Laforgue is the "last word": out of infinite knowledge of all the ways of saying a thing he finds the right way. Rimbaud, when right, is so because he cannot be bothered to exist in any other modality.

JULES LAFORGUE

(1860–1887)

Laforgue was the "end of a period"; that is to say, he summed up and summarized and dismissed nineteenth-century French literature, its foibles and fashions, as Flaubert in *Bouvard et Pécuchet* summed up nineteenth-century general civilization. He satirized Flaubert's heavy *Salammbô* manner inimitably, and he manages to be more than a critic, for in process of this ironic summary he conveys himself, *il raconte lui-même en racontant son âge et ses mœurs*, he delivers the moods and the passion of a rare and sophisticated personality: "point ce 'gaillard-là' ni le Superbe...mais au fond distinguée et franche comme une herbe"!

"Oh! laissez-moi seulement reprendre haleine,
Et vous aurez un livre enfin de bonne foi.

En attendant, ayez pitié de ma misère!
Que je vous sois à tous un être bienvenu!
Et que je sois absous pour mon âme sincère,
Comme le fut Phryné pour son sincère nu."

He is one of the poets whom it is practically impossible to "select". Almost any other six poems would be quite as "representative" as the six I am quoting.

PIERROTS

(On a des principes)

Elle disait, de son air vain fondamental:
"Je t'aime pour toi seul!" — Oh! là, là, grêle histoire;
Oui, comme l'art! Du calme, ô salaire illusoire
    Du capitaliste Idéal!

Elle faisait: "J'attends, me voici, je sais pas"...
Le regard pris de ces larges candeurs des lunes;
— Oh! là, là, ce n'est pas peut-être pour des prunes,
    Qu'on a fait ses classes ici-bas?

Mais voici qu'un beau soir, infortunée à point,
Elle meurt! — Oh! là, là; bon, changement de thème!
On sait que tu dois ressusciter le troisième
    Jour, sinon en personne, du moins

Dans l'odeur, les verdures, les eaux des beaux mois!
Et tu iras, levant encore bien plus de dupes
Vers le Zaïmph de la Joconde, vers la Jupe!
    Il se pourra même que j'en sois.

PIERROTS

III

Comme ils vont molester, la nuit,
Au profond des parcs, les statues,
Mais n'offrant qu'au moins dévêtues
Leur bras et tout ce qui s'ensuit,

En tête-à-tête avec la femme
Ils ont toujours l'air d'être un tiers,
Confondent demain avec hier,
Et demandent *Rien* avec âme!

Jurent "je t'aime" l'air là-bas,
D'une voix sans timbre, en extase,
Et concluent aux plus folles phrases
Par des: "Mon Dieu, n'insistons pas?"

Jusqu'à ce qu'ivre, Elle s'oublie,
Prise d'on ne sait quel besoin
De lune? dans leurs bras, fort loin
Des convenances établies.

COMPLAINTE DES CONSOLATIONS

Quia voluit consolari

Ses yeux ne me voient pas, son corps serait jaloux;
Elle m'a dit: "monsieur..." en m'enterrant d'un geste;
Elle est Tout, l'univers moderne et le céleste.
Soit, draguons donc Paris, et ravitaillons-nous,
    Tant bien que mal, du reste.

Les Landes sans espoir de ses regards brûlés,
Semblaient parfois des paons prêts à mettre à la voile...
Sans chercher à me consoler vers les étoiles,
Ah! Je trouverai bien deux yeux aussi sans clés,
    Au Louvre, en quelque toile!

Oh! qu'incultes, ses airs, rêvant dans la prison
D'un *cant* sur le qui-vive au travers de nos hontes!
Mais, en m'appliquant bien, moi dont la foi démonte
Les jours, les ciels, les nuits, dans les quatre saisons
    Je trouverai mon compte.

Sa bouche! à moi, ce pli pudiquement martyr
Où s'aigrissent des nostalgies de nostalgies!
Eh bien, j'irai parfois, très sincère vigie,
Du haut de Notre-Dame aider l'aube, au sortir,
      De passables orgies.

Mais, Tout va la reprendre! — Alors Tout m'en absout.
Mais, Elle est ton bonheur! — Non! je suis trop immense,
Trop chose. Comment donc! mais ma seule présence
Ici-bas, vraie à s'y mirer, est l'air de Tout:
      De la Femme au Silence.

LOCUTIONS DES PIERROTS

VI

Je te vas dire: moi, quand j'aime,
C'est d'un cœur, au fond sans apprêts,
Mais dignement élaboré
Dans nos plus singuliers problèmes.

Ainsi, pour mes mœurs et mon art,
C'est la période védique
Qui seule a bon droit revendique
Ce que j'en "attelle à ton char".

Comme c'est notre Bible hindoue
Qui, tiens, m'amène à caresser,
Avec ces yeux de cétacé,
Ainsi, bien sans but, ta joue.

   This sort of thing will drive many bull-moose readers to the perilous borders of apoplexy, but it may give pleasure to those who believe that man is incomplete without a certain amount of mentality. Laforgue is an angel with whom our modern poetic Jacob must struggle.

COMPLAINTE DES PRINTEMPS

    Permettez, ô sirène,
    Voici que votre haleine
    Embaume la verveine;
    C'est l'printemps qui s'amène!

— Ce système, en effet, ramène le printemps,
Avec son impudent cortège d'excitants.

    Otez donc ces mitaines;
    Et n'ayez, inhumaine,
    Que mes soupirs pour traîne:
    Ous'qu'il y a de la gêne...

— Ah! yeux bleus méditant sur l'ennui de leur art!
Et vous, jeunes divins, aux soirs crus de hasard!

    Du géant à la naine,
    Vois, tout bon sire entraîne
    Quelque contemporaine,
    Prendre l'air, par hygiène...

— Mais vous saignez ainsi pour l'amour de l'exil!
Pour l'amour de l'Amour! D'ailleurs, ainsi soit-il....

    T'ai-je fait de la peine?
    Oh! viens vers les fontaines
    Où tournent les phalènes
    Des Nuits Elyséennes!

— Pimbêche aux yeux vaincus, bellâtre aux beaux jarrets,
Donnez votre fumier à la fleur du Regret.

    Voilà que son haleine
    N'embaum' plus la verveine!
    Drôle de phénomène...
    Hein, à l'année prochaine?

— Vierges d'hier, ce soir traîneuses de fœtus,
A genoux! voici l'heure où se plaint l'Angélus.

Nous n'irons plus au bois,
Les pins sont éternels,
Les cors ont des appels!...
Neiges des pâles mois,
Vous serez mon missel!
— Jusqu'au jour de dégel.

COMPLAINTE DES PIANOS

Qu'on entend dans les Quartiers Aisés

Menez l'âme que les Lettres ont bien nourrie,
Les pianos, les pianos, dans les quartiers aisés!
Premiers soirs, sans pardessus, chaste flânerie,
Aux complaintes des nerfs incompris ou brisés.

    Ces enfants, à quoi rêvent-elles,
    Dans les ennuis des ritournelles?

    — "Préaux des soirs,
    Christs des dortoirs!

"Tu t'en vas et tu nous laisses,
Tu nous laiss's et tu t'en vas,
Défaire et refaire ses tresses,
Broder d'éternels canevas."

Jolie ou vague? triste ou sage? encore pure?
O jours, tout m'est égal? ou, monde, moi je veux?
Et si vierge, du moins, de la bonne blessure,
Sachant quels gras couchants ont les plus blancs aveux?

    Mon Dieu, à quoi donc rêvent-elles?
    A des Roland, à des dentelles?

    — "Cœurs en prison,
    Lentes saisons!

> "Tu t'en vas et tu nous quittes,
> Tu nous quitt's et tu t'en vas!
> Couvents gris, chœurs de Sulamites,
> Sur nos seins nuls croisons nos bras."

Fatales clés de l'être un beau jour apparues;
Psitt! aux hérédités en ponctuels ferments,
Dans le bal incessant de nos étranges rues;
Ah! pensionnats, théâtres, journaux, romans!

> Allez, stériles ritournelles,
> La vie est vraie et criminelle.
>
> — "Rideaux tirés,
> Peut-on entrer?
>
> "Tu t'en vas et tu nous laisses,
> Tu nous laiss's et tu t'en vas,
> La source des frais rosiers baisse,
> Vraiment! Et lui qui ne vient pas...."

Il viendra! Vous serez les pauvres cœurs en faute,
Fiancés au remords comme aux essais sans fond,
Et les suffisants cœurs cossus, n'ayant d'autre hôte
Qu'un train-train pavoisé d'estime et de chiffons.

> Mourir? peut-être brodent-elles,
> Pour un oncle à dot, des bretelles?
>
> — "Jamais! Jamais!
> Si tu savais!
>
> "Tu t'en vas et tu nous quittes,
> Tu nous quitt's et tu t'en vas,
> Mais tu nous reviendras bien vite
> Guérir mon beau mal, n'est-ce pas?"

Et c'est vrai! l'Idéal les fait divaguer toutes;
Vigne bohême, même en ces quartiers aisés.
La vie est là; le pur flacon des vives gouttes
Sera, *comme il convient*, d'eau propre baptisé.

> Aussi, bientôt, se joueront-elles
> De plus exactes ritournelles.
>
> — "Seul oreiller!
> Mur familier!
>
> "Tu t'en vas et tu nous laisses,
> Tu nous laiss's et tu t'en vas,
> Que ne suis-je morte à la messe!
> O mois, ô linges, ô repas!"

The journalist and his papers exist by reason of their "protective colouring". They must think as their readers think at a given moment.

It is impossible that Jules Laforgue should have written his poems in America in the "eighties". He was born in 1860, died in 1887 of *la misère*, of consumption and abject poverty in Paris. The vaunted sensitiveness of French perception, and the fact that he knew a reasonable number of wealthy and influential people, did nothing to prevent this. He had published two small volumes, one edition of each. The seventh edition of his collected poems is dated 1913, and doubtless they have been reprinted since then with increasing frequency.

> "Un couchant des Cosmogonies!
> Ah! que la Vie est quotidienne...
>
> Et, du plus vrai qu'on se souvienne,
> Comme on fut piètre et sans génie...."

What is the man in the street to make of this, or of the *Complainte des Bons Ménages*!

> "L'Art sans poitrine m'a trop longtemps bercé dupe.
> Si ses labours sont fiers, que ses blés décevants!
> Tiens, laisse-moi bêler tout aux plis de ta jupe
>   Qui fleure le couvent."

Delicate irony, the citadel of the intelligent, has a curious effect on these people. They wish always to be exhorted, at all times no matter how incongruous and unsuitable, to do things which almost any one will and does do whenever suitable opportunity is presented. As Henry James has said, "It was a period when writers besought the deep blue sea 'to roll'".

The ironist is one who suggests that the reader should think, and this process being unnatural to the majority of mankind, the way of the ironical is beset with snares and with furze-bushes.

Laforgue was a purge and a critic. He laughed out the errors of Flaubert, i.e. the clogging and cumbrous historical detail. He left *Cœur Simple, L'Education, Madame Bovary, Bouvard*. His *Salomé* makes game of the rest. The short story has become vapid because sixty thousand story writers have all set themselves to imitating De Maupassant, perhaps a thousand from the original.

Laforgue implies definitely that certain things in prose were at an end, and I think he marks the next phase after Gautier in French poetry. It seems to me that without a familiarity with Laforgue one cannot appreciate—i.e. determine the value of—certain positives and certain negatives in French poetry since 1890.

He deals for the most part with literary poses and clichés, yet he makes them a vehicle for the expression of his own very personal emotions, of his own unperturbed sincerity.

> "Je ne suis pas 'ce gaillard-là!' ni Le Superbe!
> Mais mon âme, qu'un cri un peu cru exacerbe,
> Est au fond distinguée et franche comme une herbe."

This is not the strident and satiric voice of Corbière, calling Hugo "*Garde Nationale épique*", and Lamartine "*Lacrymatoire d'abonnés*". It is not Tailhade drawing with rough strokes the people he sees daily in Paris, and bursting with guffaws over the Japanese in their mackintoshes, the West Indian mulatto behind the bar in the Quartier. It is not Georges Fourest burlesquing in a café; Fourest's guffaw is magnificent, he is hardly satirical. Tailhade draws from life and indulges in occasional squabbles.

Laforgue was a better artist than any of these men save Corbière. He was not in the least of their sort.

Beardsley's *Under the Hill* was until recently the only successful attempt to produce "anything like Laforgue" in our tongue. *Under the Hill* was issued in a limited edition. Laforgue's *Moralités Légendaires* was issued in England by the Ricketts and Hacon Press in a limited edition, and there the thing has remained. Laforgue can never become a popular cult because tyros cannot imitate him.

One may discriminate between Laforgue's tone and that of his contemporary French satirists. He is the finest wrought; he is most "verbalist". Bad verbalism is rhetoric, or the use of cliché unconsciously, or a mere playing with phrases. But there is good verbalism,* distinct from lyricism or imagism, and in this Laforgue is a master. He writes not the popular language of any country, but an international tongue common to the excessively cultivated, and to those more or less familiar with French literature of the first three-fourths of the nineteenth century.

He has dipped his wings in the dye of scientific terminology. Pierrot *imberbe* has

"Un air d'hydrocéphale asperge".

The tyro cannot play about with such things. Verbalism demands a set form used with irreproachable skill. Satire needs, usually, the form of cutting rhymes to drive it home.

Chautauquas, Mrs Eddy, Dr Dowies, Comstocks, Societies for the Prevention of All Human Activities, are impossible

* Gloze: later I applied the term *logopoeia*.

in the wake of Laforgue. And he is therefore an exquisite poet, a deliverer of the nations, a Numa Pompilius, a father of light. And to many people this mystery, the mystery why such force should reside in so fragile a book, why such power should coincide with so great a nonchalance of manner, will remain forever a mystery.

> "Que loin l'âme type
> Qui m'a dit adieu
> Parce que mes yeux
> Manquaient de principes!
>
> Elle, en ce moment.
> Elle, si pain tendre,
> Oh! peut-être engendre
> Quelque garnement.
>
> Car on l'a unie
> Avec un monsieur,
> Ce qu'il y a de mieux,
> Mais pauvre en génie."

Laforgue is incontrovertible. The "he man" of the kinema has not monopolized all the certitudes.

TRISTAN CORBIERE

(1845–1875)

Corbière seems to me the greatest poet of the period. *La Rapsodie Foraine et le Pardon de Sainte-Anne* is, to my mind, beyond all comment. He first published in 1873, remained practically unknown until Verlaine's essay in 1884, and was hardly known to "the public" until the Messein edition of his work in 1891.

LA RAPSODIE FORAINE ET LE PARDON DE SAINTE-ANNE

La Palud, 27 août, jour du Pardon

Bénite est l'infertile plage
Où, comme la mer, tout est nud.
Sainte est la chapelle sauvage
De Sainte-Anne-de-la-Palud...

De la Bonne Femme Sainte-Anne,
Grand'tante du petit Jésus,
En bois pourri dans sa soutane
Riche...plus riche que Crésus!

Contre elle la petite Vierge,
Fuseau frêle, attend l'*Angélus*;
Au coin, Joseph, tenant son cierge,
Niche, en saint qu'on ne fête plus....

C'est le Pardon. — Liesse et mystères —
Déjà l'herbe rase a des poux...
Sainte-Anne, Onguent des belles-mères!
Consolation des époux!...

Des paroisses environnantes:
De Plougastel et Loc-Tudy,
Ils viennent tous planter leurs tentes,
Trois nuits, trois jours, — jusqu'au lundi.

Trois jours, trois nuits, la palud grogne,
Selon l'antique rituel,
— Chœur séraphique et chant d'ivrogne —
LE CANTIQUE SPIRITUEL.

Mère taillée à coups de hache,
Tout cœur de chêne dur et bon;
Sous l'or de ta robe se cache
L'âme en pièce d'un franc Breton!

— Vieille verte à la face usée
Comme la pierre du torrent,
Par des larmes d'amour creusée,
Séchée avec des pleurs de sang...

— Toi, dont la mamelle tarie
S'est refait, pour avoir porté
La Virginité de Marie,
Une mâle virginité!

— Servante-maîtresse altière,
Très haute devant le Très-Haut;
Au pauvre monde, pas fière,
Dame pleine de comme-il-faut!

— Bâton des aveugles! Béquille
Des vieilles! Bras des nouveau-nés!
Mère de madame ta fille!
Parente des abandonnés!

— O Fleur de la pucelle neuve!
Fruit de l'épouse au sein grossi!
Reposoir de la femme veuve...
Et du veuf Dame-de-merci!

— Arche de Joachim! Aïeule!
Médaille de cuivre effacé!
Gui sacré! Trèfle quatre-feuille!
Mont d'Horeb! Souche de Jessé!

— O toi qui recouvrais la cendre,
Qui filais comme on fait chez nous,
Quand le soir venait à descendre,
Tenant l'Enfant sur tes genoux;

Toi qui fus là, seule, pour faire
Son maillot neuf à Bethléem,
Et là, pour coudre son suaire
Douloureux, à Jérusalem!...

Des croix profondes sont tes rides,
Tes cheveux sont blancs comme fils...
— Préserve des regards arides
Le berceau de nos petits-fils...

Fais venir et conserve en joie
Ceux à naître et ceux qui sont nés,
Et verse, sans que Dieu te voie,
L'eau de tes yeux sur les damnés!

Reprends dans leur chemise blanche
Les petits qui sont en langueur...
Rappelle à l'éternel Dimanche
Les vieux qui traînent en longueur.

— Dragon-gardien de la Vierge,
Garde la crèche sous ton œil.
Que, près de toi, Joseph-concierge
Garde la propreté du seuil!

Prends pitié de la fille-mère,
Du petit au bord du chemin...
Si quelqu'un leur jette la pierre,
Que la pierre se change en pain!

— Dame bonne en mer et sur terre,
Montre-nous le ciel et le port,
Dans la tempête ou dans la guerre...
O Fanal de la bonne mort!

Humble: à tes pieds n'as point d'étoile,
Humble...et brave pour protéger!
Dans la nue apparaît ton voile,
Pâle auréole du danger.

—Aux perdus dont la vie est grise,
(— Sauf respect — perdus de boisson)
Montre le clocher de l'église
Et le chemin de la maison.

Prête ta douce et chaste flamme
Aux chrétiens qui sont ici...
Ton remède de bonne femme
Pour tes bêtes-à-corne aussi!

Montre à nos femmes et servantes
L'ouvrage et la fécondité...
— Le bonjour aux âmes parentes
Qui sont bien dans l'éternité!

— Nous mettrons un cordon de cire,
De cire-vierge jaune autour
De ta chapelle et ferons dire
Ta messe basse au point du jour.

Préserve notre cheminée
Des sorts et du monde malin...
A Pâques te sera donnée
Une quenouille avec du lin.

Si nos corps sont puants sur terre,
Ta grâce est un bain de santé;
Répands sur nous, au cimetière,
Ta bonne odeur de sainteté.

— A l'an prochain! — Voici ton cierge:
(C'est deux livres qu'il a coûté)
...Respects à Madame la Vierge,
Sans oublier la Trinité.

...Et les fidèles, en chemise,
Sainte-Anne, ayez pitié de nous!
Font trois fois le tour de l'église
En se traînant sur leurs genoux,

Et boivent l'eau miraculeuse
Où les Job teigneux ont lavé
Leur nudité contagieuse...
Allez: la Foi vous a sauvé!

C'est là que tiennent leurs cénacles
Les pauvres, frères de Jésus.
— Ce n'est pas la cour des miracles,
Les trous sont vrais: *Vide latus!*

Sont-ils pas divins sur leurs claies
Qu'auréole un nimbe vermeil
Ces propriétaires de plaies,
Rubis vivants sous le soleil!...

En aboyant, un rachitique
Secoue un moignon désossé,
Coudoyant un épileptique
Qui travaille dans un fossé.

Là, ce tronc d'homme où croît l'ulcère,
Contre un tronc d'arbre où croît le gui,
Ici, c'est la fille et la mère
Dansant la danse de Saint-Guy.

Cet autre pare le cautère
De son petit enfant malsain:
— L'enfant se doit à son vieux père...
— Et le chancre est un gagne-pain!

Là, c'est l'idiot de naissance,
Un *visité par Gabriel*,
Dans l'extase de l'innocence...
— L'innocent est (tout) près du ciel! —

— Tiens, passant, regarde: tout passe.
L'œil de l'idiot est resté.
Car il est en état de grâce...
— Et la Grâce est l'Eternité! —

Parmi les autres, après vêpre,
Qui sont d'eau bénite arrosés,
Un cadavre, vivant de lèpre,
Fleurit, souvenir des croisés...

Puis tous ceux que les Rois de France
Guérissaient d'un toucher de doigts...
— Mais la France n'a plus de Rois,
Et leur dieu suspend sa clémence.

. . . . . .

Une forme humaine qui beugle
Contre le *calvaire* se tient;
C'est comme une moitié d'aveugle:
Elle est borgne et n'a pas de chien...
C'est une rapsodie foraine
Qui donne aux gens pour un liard
L'*Istoyre de la Magdalayne*,
Du *Juif Errant* ou d'*Abaylar*.
Elle hâle comme une plainte,
Comme une plainte de la faim,
Et, longue comme un jour sans pain,
Lamentablement, sa complainte...
— Ça chante comme ça respire,
Triste oiseau sans plume et sans nid
Vaguant où son instinct l'attire:
Autour du Bon-Dieu de granit...
Ça peut parler aussi, sans doute,
Ça peut penser comme ça voit:
Toujours devant soi la grand'route...
— Et, quand ç'a deux sous, ça les boit.
— Femme: on dirait, hélas! — sa nippe
Lui pend, ficelée en jupon;
Sa dent noire serre une pipe
Eteinte...Oh, la vie a du bon! —
Son nom...ça se nomme Misère.
Ça s'est trouvé né par hasard.
Ça sera trouvé mort par terre...
La même chose—quelque part.

Si tu la rencontres, Poète,
Avec son vieux sac de soldat:
C'est notre sœur...donne — c'est fête —
Pour sa pipe, un peu de tabac!...

Tu verras dans sa face creuse
Se creuser, comme dans du bois,
Un sourire; et sa main galeuse
Te faire un vrai signe de croix.

(*Les Amours Jaunes.*)

It is not long since a "strong, silent" American, who had been spending a year or so in Paris, complained to me that "all French poetry smelt of talcum powder". He did not specifically mention Corbière, who, with perhaps a few dozen other French poets, may have been outside the scope of his research. Corbière came also to "Paris".

I

Bâtard de Créole et Breton,
Il vint aussi là — fourmilière,
Bazar où rien n'est en pierre,
Où le soleil manque de ton.

— Courage! On fait queue...Un planton
Vous pousse à la chaîne — derrière! —
— Incendie éteint, sans lumière;
Des seaux passent, vides ou non. —

Là, sa pauvre Muse pucelle
Fit le trottoir en *demoiselle*.
Ils disaient: Qu'est-ce qu'elle vend?

— Rien. — Elle restait là, stupide,
N'entendant pas sonner le vide
Et regardant passer le vent...

II

Là: vivre à coups de fouet! — passer
En fiacre, en correctionnelle;
Repasser à la ritournelle,
Se dépasser, et trépasser! —

— Non, petit, il faut commencer
Par être grand — simple ficelle —
Pauvre: remuer l'or à la pelle;
Obscur: un nom à tout casser!...

Le coller chez les mastroquets,
Et l'apprendre à des perroquets
Qui le chantent ou qui le sifflent —

— Musique! — C'est le paradis
Des mahomets ou des houris,
Des vieux souteneurs qui se giflent!

People, at least some of them, think more highly of his Breton subjects than of the Parisian, but I cannot see that he loses force on leaving the sea-board; for example, his *Frère et Sœur Jumeaux* seems to me "by the same hand" and rather better than his *Roscoff*. His language does not need any particular subject matter, or prefer one to another. *Mannequin idéal, tête-de-turc du leurre, Fille de marbre, en rut!, Je voudrais être chien à une fille publique* are all, with a constant emission of equally vigorous phrases, to be found in the city poems. At his weakest he is touched with the style of his time, i.e. he falls into a phrase *à la Hugo*—but seldom. And he is conscious of the will to break from this manner, and is the first, I think, to satirize it, or at least the first to hurl anything as apt and violent as "garde nationale épique" or "inventeur de la larme écrite" at the romantico-rhetorico and the sentimento-romantico of Hugo and Lamartine. His nearest kinships in our period are to Gautier and Laforgue, though it is Villon whom most by life and temperament he must be said to resemble.

Laforgue was, for four or five years, "reader" to the ex-Kaiser's mama; he escaped to die of *la misère*. Corbière had, I believe, but one level of poverty:

> "Un beau jour — quel métier! — je faisais, comme ça
> Ma croisière. — Métier!... — Enfin. Elle passa.
> — Elle qui, — La Passante! Elle, avec son ombrelle!
> Vrai valet de bourreau, je la frôlai... — mais Elle
> Me regarda tout bas, souriant en dessous,
> Et — me tendit sa main, et...
>   m'a donné deux sous".

ARTHUR RIMBAUD
(1854-1891)

Rimbaud's first book appeared in 1873. His complete poems with a preface by Verlaine in 1895. Laforgue conveys his content by comment, Corbière by ejaculation, as if the words were wrenched and knocked out of him by fatality; by the violence of his feeling, Rimbaud presents a thick suave colour, firm, even.

AU CABARET VERT

Cinq heures du soir.

Depuis huit jours, j'avais déchiré mes bottines
Aux cailloux des chemins. J'entrais à Charleroi,
— *Au Cabaret Vert*: je demandai des tartines
De beurre et de jambon qui fût à moitié froid.

Bienheureux, j'allongeai les jambes sous la table
Verte: je contemplai les sujets très naïfs
De la tapisserie. — Et ce fut adorable,
Quand la fille aux tétons énormes, aux yeux vifs,

> — Celle-là, ce n'est pas un baiser qui l'épeure! —
> Rieuse, m'apporta des tartines de beurre,
> Du jambon tiède, dans un plat colorié,
>
> Du jambon rose et blanc parfumé d'une gousse
> D'ail, — et m'emplit la chope immense, avec sa mousse
> Que dorait un rayon de soleil arriéré.

The actual writing of poetry has advanced little or not at all since Rimbaud. Cézanne was the first to paint, as Rimbaud had written—in, for example, *Les Assis*:

> "Ils ont greffé dans des amours épileptiques
> Leur fantasque ossature aux grands squelettes noirs
> De leurs chaises; leurs pieds aux barreaux rachitiques
> S'entrelacent pour les matins et pour les soirs,
>
> Ces vieillards ont toujours fait tresse avec leurs sièges".

Or in the octave of

VENUS ANADYOMENE

> Comme d'un cercueil vert en fer-blanc, une tête
> De femme à cheveux bruns fortement pommadés
> D'une vieille baignoire émerge, lente et bête,
> Montrant des déficits assez mal ravaudés;
>
> Puis le col gras et gris, les larges omoplates
> Qui saillent; le dos court qui rentre et qui ressort,
> — La graisse sous la peau paraît en feuilles plates
> Et les rondeurs des reins semblent prendre l'essor.

Tailhade has painted his *Vieilles Actrices* at greater length, but smiling; Rimbaud does not endanger his intensity by a chuckle. He is serious as Cézanne is serious. Comparisons across an art are always vague and inexact, and there are no real parallels; still it is possible to think of Corbière a little as one thinks of Goya, without Goya's Spanish, with infinite differences, but with a macabre intensity, and a modernity that we have not yet surpassed. There are possible grounds for comparisons of like sort between Rimbaud and Cézanne.

Tailhade and Rimbaud were both born in 1854; I do not know who hit first on the form, but Rimbaud's *Chercheuses* is a very good example of a mould not unlike that into which Tailhade has cast his best poems.

LES CHERCHEUSES DE POUX

Quand le front de l'enfant plein de rouges tourmentes,
Implore l'essaim blanc des rêves indistincts,
Il vient près de son lit deux grandes sœurs charmantes
Avec de frêles doigts aux ongles argentins.

Elles asseoient l'enfant auprès d'une croisée
Grande ouverte où l'air bleu baigne un fouillis de fleurs,
Et, dans ses lourds cheveux où tombe la rosée,
Promènent leurs doigts fins, terribles et charmeurs.

Il écoute chanter leurs haleines craintives
Qui fleurent de longs miels végétaux et rosés
Et qu'interrompt parfois un sifflement, salives
Reprises sur la lèvre ou désirs de baisers.

Il entend leurs cils noirs battant sous les silences
Parfumés; et leurs doigts électriques et doux
Font crépiter, parmi ses grises indolences,
Sous leurs ongles royaux la mort des petits poux.

Voilà que monte en lui le vin de la Paresse,
Soupir d'harmonica qui pourrait délirer;
L'enfant se sent, selon la lenteur des caresses,
Sourdre et mourir sans cesse un désir de pleurer.

The poem is "not really" like Tailhade's, but the comparison is worth while. Many readers will be unable to "see over" the subject matter and consider the virtues of the style, but we are, let us hope, serious people; besides, Rimbaud's mastery is not confined to "the unpleasant"; "Roman" begins:

I

"On n'est pas sérieux, quand on a dix-sept ans.
— Un beau soir, foin des bocks et de la limonade,
Des cafés tapageurs aux lustres éclatants!
— On va sous les tilleuls verts de la promenade.

Les tilleuls sentent bon dans les bons soirs de juin!
L'air est parfois si doux, qu'on ferme la paupière;
Le vent chargé de bruits, — la ville n'est pas loin —
A des parfums de vigne et des parfums de bière...".

The sixth line is worthy of To-em-mei. But Rimbaud has not exhausted his idyllic moods or capacities in one poem. Witness:

COMEDIE EN TROIS BAISERS

Elle était fort déshabillée,
Et de grands arbres indiscrets
Aux vitres penchaient leur feuillée
Malinement, tout près, tout près.

Assise sur ma grande chaise,
Mi-nue elle joignait les mains.
Sur le plancher frissonnaient d'aise
Ses petits pieds si fins, si fins.

— Je regardai, couleur de cire
Un petit rayon buissonnier
Papillonner, comme un sourire
Sur son beau sein, mouche au rosier.

— Je baisai ses fines chevilles.
Elle eut un long rire très mal
Qui s'égrenait en claires trilles,
Une risure de cristal....

> Les petits pieds sous la chemise
> Se sauvèrent: "Veux-tu finir!"
> — La première audace permise,
> Le rire feignait de punir!
>
> — Pauvrets palpitant sous ma lèvre,
> Je baisai doucement ses yeux.
> — Elle jeta sa tête mièvre
> En arrière: "Oh! c'est encor mieux!..."
>
> "Monsieur, j'ai deux mots à te dire...."
> — Je lui jetai le reste au sein
> Dans un baiser, qui la fit rire
> D'un bon rire qui voulait bien...
>
> — Elle était fort déshabillée
> Et de grands arbres indiscrets,
> Aux vitres penchaient leur feuillée
> Malinement, tout près, tout près.

The subject matter is older than Ovid, and how many poets has it led to every silliness, every vulgarity! One has no instant of doubt here, nor, I think, in any line of any poem of Rimbaud's. How much I might have learned from the printed page that I have learned slowly from actualities. Or perhaps we never do learn from the page; but are only capable of recognizing the page after we have learned from actuality.

I do not know whether or no Rimbaud "started" the furniture poetry with *Le Buffet*; it probably comes, most of it, from the beginning of Gautier's *Albertus*. I cannot see that the *Bateau Ivre* rises above the general level of his work, though many people seem to know of this poem (and of the sonnet on the vowels) who do not know the rest of his writing. Both of these poems are in Van Bever and Léautaud. I wonder in what other poet will we find such firmness of colouring and such certitude.

TABLE

Laforgue 1860–1887; published 1885
Corbière 1845–1875; published 1872 and 1891
Rimbaud 1854–1891; published 1873
Remy de Gourmont 1858–1915
Merril 1868–1915
Tailhade 1854–1919
Verhaeren 1855–1916
Moréas 1856–1911

Living: (in 1919)
Vielé-Griffin 1864
Jammes 1868
De Régnier 1864
Spire 1868

Younger Men:
Klingsor, Romains, Vildrac

Other Dates:
Verlaine 1844–1896
Mallarmé 1842–1898
Samain 1858–1900
Elskamp, born 1862

REMY DE GOURMONT
(1858–1915)

As in prose, Remy de Gourmont found his own form, so also in poetry, influenced presumably by the mediaeval sequaires and particularly by Goddeschalk's quoted in *Le Latin Mystique*, he recreated the "litanies". It was one of the great gifts of "symbolisme", of the doctrine that one should "suggest" not "present"; it is, in his hand, an effective indirectness. The procession of all beautiful women moves before one in the *Litanies de la Rose*; and the rhythm is incomparable. It is not a poem to lie on the page, it must come to life in audition, or in the finer audition which one may have in imagining sound. One must "hear" it, in one way or another, and out of that intoxication comes beauty. One does no injustice to De Gourmont by giving this poem alone. The *Litany of the Trees* is of equal or almost equal beauty. The Sonnets in prose are different; they rise out of natural speech, out of conversation. Paul Fort perhaps began or re-began the use of conversational speech in rhyming prose paragraphs, at times charmingly.

LITANIES DE LA ROSE

A Henry de Groux.

Fleur hypocrite.
Fleur du silence.

Rose couleur de cuivre, plus frauduleuse que nos joies, rose couleur de cuivre, embaume-nous dans tes mensonges, fleur hypocrite, fleur du silence.

Rose au visage peint comme une fille d'amour, rose au cœur prostitué, rose au visage peint, fais semblant d'être pitoyable, fleur hypocrite, fleur du silence.

Rose à la joue puérile, ô vierges des futures trahisons, rose à la joue puérile, innocente et rouge, ouvre les rets de tes yeux clairs, fleur hypocrite, fleur du silence.

Rose aux yeux noirs, miroir de ton néant, rose aux yeux noirs, fais-nous croire au mystère, fleur hypocrite, fleur du silence.

Rose couleur d'or pur, ô coffre-fort de l'idéal, rose couleur d'or pur, donne-nous la clef de ton ventre, fleur hypocrite, fleur du silence.

Rose couleur d'argent, encensoir de nos rêves, rose couleur d'argent prends notre cœur et fais-en de la fumée, fleur hypocrite, fleur du silence.

Rose au regard saphique, plus pâle que les lys, rose au regard saphique, offre-nous le parfum de ton illusoire virginité, fleur hypocrite, fleur du silence.

Rose au front pourpre, colère des femmes dédaignées, rose au front pourpre, dis-nous le secret de ton orgueil, fleur hypocrite, fleur du silence.

Rose au front d'ivoire jaune, amante de toi-même, rose au front d'ivoire jaune, dis-nous le secret de tes nuits virginales, fleur hypocrite, fleur du silence.

Rose aux lèvres de sang, ô mangeuse de chair, rose aux lèvres de sang, si tu veux notre sang, qu'en ferions-nous? bois-le, fleur hypocrite, fleur du silence.

Rose couleur de soufre, enfer des désirs vains, rose couleur de soufre, allume le bûcher où tu planes, âme et flamme, fleur hypocrite, fleur du silence.

Rose couleur de pêche, fruit velouté de fard, rose sournoise, rose couleur de pêche, empoisonne nos dents, fleur hypocrite, fleur du silence.

Rose couleur de chair, déesse de la bonne volonté, rose couleur de chair, fais-nous baiser la tristesse de ta peau fraîche et fade, fleur hypocrite, fleur du silence.

Rose vineuse, fleur des tonnelles et des caves, rose vineuse, les alcools fous gambadent dans ton haleine: souffle-nous l'horreur de l'amour, fleur hypocrite, fleur du silence.

Rose violette, ô modestie des fillettes perverses, rose violette, tes yeux sont plus grands que le reste, fleur hypocrite, fleur du silence.

Rose rose, pucelle au cœur désordonné, rose rose, robe de mousseline, entr'ouvre tes ailes fausses, ange, fleur hypocrite, fleur du silence.

Rose en papier de soie, simulacre adorable des grâces incréées, rose en papier de soie, n'es-tu pas la vraie rose, fleur du silence.

Rose couleur d'aurore, couleur du temps, couleur de rien, ô sourire du Sphinx, rose couleur d'aurore, sourire ouvert sur le néant, nous t'aimerons, car tu mens, fleur hypocrite, fleur du silence.

Rose blonde, léger manteau de chrôme sur des épaules frêles, ô rose blonde, femelle plus forte que les mâles, fleur hypocrite, fleur du silence!

Rose en forme de coupe, vase rouge où mordent les dents quand la bouche y vient boire, rose en forme de coupe, nos morsures te font sourire et nos baisers te font pleurer, fleur hypocrite, fleur du silence.

Rose toute blanche, innocente et couleur de lait, rose toute blanche, tant de candeur nous épouvante, fleur hypocrite, fleur du silence.

Rose couleur de bronze, pâte cuite au soleil, rose couleur de bronze, les plus durs javelots s'émoussent sur ta peau, fleur hypocrite, fleur du silence.

Rose couleur de feu, creuset spécial pour les chairs réfractaires, rose couleur de feu, ô providence des ligueurs en enfance, fleur hypocrite, fleur du silence.

Rose incarnate, rose stupide et pleine de santé, rose incarnate, tu nous abreuves et tu nous leurres d'un vin très rouge et très bénin, fleur hypocrite, fleur du silence.

Rose en satin cerise, munificence exquise des lèvres triomphales, rose en satin cerise, ta bouche enluminée a posé sur nos chairs le sceau de pourpre de son mirage, fleur hypocrite, fleur du silence.

Rose au cœur virginal, ô louche et rose adolescence qui n'a pas encore parlé, rose au cœur virginal, tu n'as rien à nous dire, fleur hypocrite, fleur du silence.

Rose groseille, honte et rougeur des péchés ridicules, rose groseille, on a trop chiffonné ta robe, fleur hypocrite, fleur du silence.

Rose couleur du soir, demi-morte d'ennui, fumée crépusculaire, rose couleur du soir, tu meurs d'amour en baisant tes mains lasses, fleur hypocrite, fleur du silence.

Rose bleue, rose iridine, monstre couleur des yeux de

la Chimère, rose bleue, lève un peu tes paupières: as-tu peur qu-on te regarde, les yeux dans les yeux, Chimère, fleur hypocrite, fleur du silence!

Rose verte, rose couleur de mer, ô nombril des sirènes, rose verte, gemme ondoyante et fabuleuse, tu n'es plus que de l'eau dès qu'un doigt t'a touchée, fleur hypocrite, fleur du silence.

Rose escarboucle, rose fleurie au front noir du dragon, rose escarboucle, tu n'es plus qu'une boucle de ceinture, fleur hypocrite, fleur du silence.

Rose couleur de vermillon, bergère énamourée couchée dans les sillons, rose couleur de vermillon, le berger te respire et le bouc t'a broutée, fleur hypocrite, fleur du silence.

Rose des tombes, fraîcheur émanée des charognes, rose des tombes, toute mignonne et rose, adorable parfum des fines pourritures, tu fais semblant de vivre, fleur hypocrite, fleur du silence.

Rose brune, couleur des mornes acajous, rose brune, plaisirs permis, sagesse, prudence et prévoyance, tu nous regardes avec des yeux rogues, fleur hypocrite, fleur du silence.

Rose ponceau, ruban des fillettes modèles, rose ponceau, gloire des petites poupées, es-tu niaise ou sournoise, joujou des petits frères, fleur hypocrite, fleur du silence.

Rose rouge et noire, rose insolente et secrète, rose rouge et noire, ton insolence et ton rouge ont pâli parmi les compromis qu'invente la vertu, fleur hypocrite, fleur du silence.

Rose ardoise, grisaille des vertus vaporeuses, rose ardoise, tu grimpes et tu fleuris autour des vieux bancs solitaires, rose du soir, fleur hypocrite, fleur du silence.

Rose pivoine, modeste vanité des jardins plantureux, rose pivoine, le vent n'a retroussé tes feuilles que par hasard, et tu n'en fus pas mécontente, fleur hypocrite, fleur du silence.

Rose neigeuse, couleur de la neige et des plumes du cygne, rose neigeuse, tu sais que la neige est fragile et tu n'ouvres tes plumes de cygne qu'aux plus insignes, fleur hypocrite, fleur du silence.

Rose hyaline, couleur des sources claires jaillies d'entre les herbes, rose hyaline, Hylas est mort d'avoir aimé tes yeux, fleur hypocrite, fleur du silence.

Rose opale, ô sultane endormie dans l'odeur du harem, rose opale, langueur des constantes caresses, ton cœur connaît la paix profonde des vices satisfaits, fleur hypocrite, fleur du silence.

Rose améthyste, étoile matinale, tendresse épiscopale, rose améthyste, tu dors sur des poitrines dévotes et douillettes, gemme offerte à Marie, ô gemme sacristine, fleur hypocrite, fleur du silence.

Rose cardinale, rose couleur du sang de l'Eglise Romaine, rose cardinale, tu fais rêver les grands yeux des mignons et plus d'un t'épingla au nœud de sa jarretière, fleur hypocrite, fleur du silence.

Rose papale, rose arrosée des mains qui bénissent le monde, rose papale, ton cœur d'or est en cuivre, et les larmes qui perlent sur ta vaine corolle, ce sont les pleurs du Christ, fleur hypocrite, fleur du silence.

Fleur hypocrite,
Fleur du silence.

EMILE VERHAEREN

Verhaeren has been so well introduced to America by his obituary notices that I can scarcely hope to compete with them in this limited space. One can hardly represent him better than by the well known:

LES PAUVRES

Il est ainsi de pauvres cœurs
avec en eux, des lacs de pleurs,
qui sont pâles, comme les pierres
d'un cimetière.

Il est ainsi de pauvres dos
plus lourds de peine et de fardeaux
que les toits des cassines brunes,
parmi les dunes.

Il est ainsi de pauvres mains,
comme feuilles sur les chemins,
comme feuilles jaunes et mortes,
devant la porte.

Il est ainsi de pauvres yeux
humbles et bons et soucieux
et plus tristes que ceux des bêtes,
sous la tempête.

Il est ainsi de pauvres gens,
aux gestes las et indulgents
sur qui s'acharne la misère,
au long des plaines de la terre.

STUART MERRIL

I know that I have seen somewhere a beautiful and effective ballad of Merril's. His *Chambre D'Amour* would be more interesting if Samain had not written *L'Infante*, but Merril's painting is perhaps interesting as comparison. It begins:

"Dans la chambre qui fleure un peu la bergamote,
 Ce soir, lasse, la voix de l'ancien clavecin
 Chevrote des refrains enfantins de gavotte".

There is a great mass of this poetry full of highly cultured house furnishing; I think Catulle Mendès also wrote it. Merril's *Nocturne* illustrates a mode of symbolistic writing which has been since played out and parodied:

"La blême lune allume en la mare qui luit,
 Miroir des gloires d'or, un émoi d'incendie.
 Tout dort. Seul, à mi-mort, un rossignol de nuit
 Module en mal d'amour sa molle mélodie.

Plus ne vibrent les vents en le mystère vert
Des ramures. La lune a tu leurs voix nocturnes:
Mais à travers le deuil du feuillage entr'ouvert
Pleuvent les bleus baisers des astres taciturnes".

. . . . . .

There is no need to take this sort of tongue-twisting too seriously, though it undoubtedly was so taken in Paris during the late eighties and early nineties. He is better illustrated in *La Wallonie, vide infra.*

LAURENT TAILHADE
1854–1919

Tailhade's satires seem rough if one come upon them straight from reading Laforgue; and Laforgue will seem, and is presumably, the greatly finer artist; but one should not fail to note certain definite differences. Laforgue is criticizing, and conveying a mood. He is more or less literary, playing with words. Tailhade is painting contemporary Paris, with verve. His eye is on the thing itself. He has, *au fond*, not very much in common with Laforgue. He was born six years before Laforgue and in the same year as Rimbaud. Their temperaments are by no means identical. I do not know whether Tailhade wrote *Hydrothérapie* before Rimbaud had done *Les Chercheuses*. Rimbaud in that poem identifies himself more or less with the child and its feeling. Tailhade is detached. I do not say this as praise of either one or the other. I am only trying to keep things distinct.

HYDROTHERAPIE

Le vieux monsieur, pour prendre une douche ascendante,
A couronné son chef d'un casque d'hidalgo
Qui, malgré sa bedaine ample et son lumbago,
Lui donne un certain air de famille avec Dante.

Ainsi ses membres gourds et sa vertèbre à point
Traversent l'appareil des tuyaux et des lances,
Tandis que des masseurs, tout gonflés d'insolences,
Frottent au gant de crin son dos où l'acné pointe.

Oh! l'eau froide! la bonne et rare panacée
Qui, seule, raffermit la charpente lassée
Et le protoplasma des sénateurs pesants!

Voici que, dans la rue, au sortir de sa douche,
Le vieux monsieur qu'on sait un magistrat farouche
Tient des propos grivois aux filles de douze ans.

QUARTIER LATIN

Dans le bar où jamais le parfum des brévas
Ne dissipa l'odeur de vomi qui la navre
Triomphent les appas de la mère Cadavre
Dont le nom est fameux jusque chez les Howas.

Brune, elle fut jadis vantée entre les brunes,
Tant que son souvenir au Vaux-Hall est resté.
Et c'est toujours avec beaucoup de dignité
Qu'elle rince le zinc et détaille les prunes.

A ces causes, son cabaret s'emplit le soir,
De futurs avoués, trop heureux de surseoir
Quelque temps à l'étude inepte des *Digestes*,

Des Valaques, des riverains du fleuve Amoor
S'acoquinent avec des potards indigestes
Qui s'y viennent former aux choses de l'amour.

RUS

Ce qui fait que l'ancien bandagiste renie
Le comptoir dont le faste alléchait les passants,
C'est son jardin d'Auteuil où, veufs de tout encens,
Les zinnias ont l'air d'être en tôle vernie.

C'est là qu'il vient, le soir, goûter l'air aromal
Et, dans sa rocking-chair, en veston de flanelle,
Aspirer les senteurs qu'épanchent sur Grenelle
Les fabriques de suif et de noir animal.

Bien que libre-penseur et franc-maçon, il juge
Le dieu propice qui lui donna ce refuge
Où se meurt un cyprin emmy la pièce d'eau,
Où, dans la tour mauresque aux lanternes chinoises,
— Tout en lui préparant du sirop de framboises —
Sa "demoiselle" chante un couplet de Nadaud.

From this beneficent treatment of the amiable burgess; from this perfectly poetic inclusion of modernity, this un-rhetorical inclusion of the factories in the vicinity of Grenelle (inclusion quite different from the allegorical presentation of workmen's trousers in sculpture, and the grandiloquent theorizing about the socialistic up-lift or down-pull of smoke and machinery), Tailhade can move to personal satire, a personal satire impersonalized by its glaze and its finish.

RONDEL

Dans les cafés d'adolescents
Moréas cause avec Frémine:
L'un, d'un parfait cuistre a la mine,
L'autre beugle des contre-sens.

Rien ne sort moins de chez Classens
Que le linge de ces bramines.
Dans les cafés d'adolescents,
Moréas cause avec Frémine.

Désagrégeant son albumine,
La Tailhède offre quelque encens:
Maurras leur invente Commine
Et ça fait roter les passants,
Dans les cafés d'adolescents.

But perhaps the most characteristic phase of Tailhade is in his pictures of the bourgeoisie. Here is one depicted with all Tailhadian serenity. Note also the opulence of his vocables.

DINER CHAMPETRE

Entre les sièges où des garçons volontaires
Entassent leurs chalants parmi les boulingrins,
La famille Feyssard, avec des airs sereins,
Discute longuement les tables solitaires.

La demoiselle a mis un chapeau rouge vif
Dont s'honore le bon faiseur de sa commune,
Et madame Feyssard, un peu hommasse et brune,
Porte une robe loutre avec des reflets d'if.

Enfin ils sont assis! Or le père commande
Des écrevisses, du potage au lait d'amande,
Toutes choses dont il rêvait depuis longtemps.

Et, dans le ciel couleur de turquoises fanées,
Il voit les songes bleus qu'en ses esprits flottant
A fait naître l'ampleur des truites saumonées.

All through this introduction I am giving the sort of French poem least likely to have been worn smooth for us; I mean the kind of poem least represented in English. Landor and Swinburne have, I think, forestalled Tailhade's Hellenic poems in our affections. There are also his ballades to be considered.

FRANCIS JAMMES
(born 1868)

The bulk of Jammes' unsparable poetry is* perhaps larger than that of any man still living in France. The three first books of poems, and *Le Triomphe de la Vie* containing *Existences*, the more than *Spoon River* of France, must con-

---

* 1918.

tain about six hundred pages worth reading. *Existences* cannot be rendered in snippets. It is not a series of poems, but the canvas of a whole small town or half city, unique, inimitable and "to the life", full of verve. Only those who have read it and *L'Angélus de l'Aube*, can appreciate the full tragedy of Jammes' *débâcle*. Paul Fort had what his friends boasted as "tone", and he has diluted himself with topicalities; in Jammes' case it is more charitable to suppose some organic malady, some definite softening of the brain, for he seems perfectly simple and naïve in his collapse. It may be, in both cases, that the organisms have broken beneath the strain of modern existence. But the artist has no business to break.

Let us begin with Jammes earlier work:

> "J'aime l'âne si doux
> marchant le long des houx.
> Il prend garde aux abeilles
> et bouge ses oreilles;
> et il porte les pauvres
> et des sacs remplis d'orge.
> Il va, près des fossés
> d'un petit pas cassé.
> Mon amie le croit bête
> parce qu'il est poëte.
> Il réflechit toujours,
> ses yeux sont en velours.
> Jeune fille au doux cœur
> tu n'as pas sa douceur".

. . . . . .

The fault is the fault, or danger, which Dante has labelled "muliebria"; of its excess Jammes has since perished. But the poem to the donkey can, in certain moods, please one. In other moods the playful simplicity, at least in excess, is almost infuriating. He runs so close to sentimentalizing—

when he does not fall into that puddle—that there are numerous excuses for those who refuse him altogether. *J'allai à Lourdes* has pathos. Compare it with Corbière's *St-Anne* and the decadence is apparent; it is indeed a sort of half-way house between the barbaric Breton religion and the ultimate deliquescence of French Catholicism in Claudel, who (as I think it is James Stephens has said) "is merely lying on his back kicking his heels in it".

J'ALLAI A LOURDES

J'allai à Lourdes par le chemin de fer,
le long du gave qui est bleu comme l'air.

Au soleil les montagnes semblaient d'étain.
Et l'on chantait: sauvez! sauvez! dans le train,

Il y avait un monde fou, exalté,
plein de poussière et du soleil d'été.

Des malheureux avec le ventre en avant
étendaient leurs bras, priaient en les tordant.

Et dans une chaire où était du drap bleu,
un prêtre disait: "un chapelet à Dieu!"

Et un groupe de femmes, parfois, passait,
qui chantait: sauvez! sauvez! sauvez! sauvez!

Et la procession chantait. Les drapeaux
se penchaient avec leurs devises en or.

Le soleil était blanc sur les escaliers
dans l'air bleu, sur les cloches déchiquetées.

Mais sur un brancard, portée par ses parents,
son pauvre père tête nue et priant,

et ses frères qui disaient: "ainsi soit-il",
une jeune fille sur le point de mourir.

> Oh ! qu'elle était belle ! elle avait dix-huit ans,
> et elle souriait ; elle était en blanc.
>
> Et la procession chantait. Des drapeaux
> se penchaient avec leurs devises en or.
>
> Moi je serrais les dents pour ne pas pleurer,
> et cette fille, je me sentais l'aimer.
>
> Oh ! elle m'a regardé un grand moment,
> une rose blanche en main, souriant.
>
> Mais maintenant où es-tu ? dis, où es-tu,
> es-tu morte ? je t'aime, toi qui m'as vu.
>
> Si tu existes, Dieu, ne la tue pas,
> elle avait des mains blanches, de minces bras.
>
> Dieu, ne la tue pas ! — et ne serait-ce que
> pour son père nu-tête qui priait Dieu.

Jammes goes to pieces on such adjectives as "pauvre" and "petite", just as De Régnier slips on "cher", "aimée" and "tiède"; and in their train flock the herd whose adjectival centre appears to waver from "nue" to "frémissante". And there is, in many French poets, a fatal proclivity to fuss just a little too much over their subjects. Jammes has also the furniture tendency, and to it we owe several of his quite charming poems. However the strongest impression I get to-day, reading his work in inverse order (i.e. *Jean de Noarrieu* before these earlier poems), is of the very great stylistic advance made in that poem over his earlier work.

But he is very successful in saying all there was to be said in:

LA JEUNE FILLE

> La jeune fille est blanche,
> elle a des veines vertes
> au poignets, dans ses manches
> ouvertes.

On ne sait pas pourquoi
elle rit. Par moments
elle crie et cela
    est perçant.
Est-ce qu'elle se doute
qu'elle vous prend le cœur
en cueillant sur la route
    des fleurs.
On dirait quelquefois
qu'elle comprend des choses.
Pas toujours. Elle cause
    tout bas
"Oh! ma chère! oh! là, là...
...Figure-toi...mardi
je l'ai vu...j'ai ri" — Elle dit
    comme ça.
Quand un jeune homme souffre,
d'abord elle se tait:
elle ne rit plus, tout
    étonnée.
Dans les petits chemins
elle remplit ses mains
de piquants de bruyères
    de fougères.
Elle est grande, elle est blanche,
elle a des bras très doux,
elle est très droite et penche
    le cou.

The poem beginning:

"Tu seras nue dans le salon aux vieilles choses,
fine comme un fuseau de roseau de lumière
et, les jambes croisées, auprès du feu rose
    tu écouteras l'hiver"

loses, perhaps, or gains little by comparison with that of Heinrich von Morungen, beginning:

> "Oh weh, soll mir nun nimmermehr
> hell leuchten durch die Nacht
> noch weisser denn ein Schnee
> ihr Leib so wohl gemacht?
> Der trog die Augen mein,
> ich wähnt, es sollte sein
> des lichten Monden Schein,
> da tagte es".

Morungen had had no occasion to say "Je pense à Jean-Jacques", and it is foolish to expect exactly the same charm of a twentieth-century poet that we find in a thirteenth-century poet. Still it is not necessary to be Jammes-crazy to feel

IL VA NEIGER...

Il va neiger dans quelques jours. Je me souviens
de l'an dernier. Je me souviens de mes tristesses
au coin du feu. Si l'on m'avait demandé: qu'est-ce?
j'aurais dit: laissez-moi tranquille. Ce n'est rien.

J'ai bien réfléchi, l'année avant, dans ma chambre,
pendant que la neige lourde tombait dehors.
J'ai réfléchi pour rien. A présent comme alors
je fume une pipe en bois avec un bout d'ambre.

Ma vieille commode en chêne sent toujours bon.
Mais moi j'étais bête parce que ces choses
ne pouvaient pas changer et que c'est une pose
de vouloir chasser les choses que nous savons.

Pourquoi donc pensons-nous et parlons-nous? C'est drôle;
nos larmes et nos baisers, eux, ne parlent pas,
et cependant nous les comprenons, et les pas
d'un ami sont plus doux que de douces paroles.

If I at all rightly understand the words "vouloir chasser les choses que nous savons" they are an excellent warning against the pose of simplicity over-done that has been the end of Maeterlinck, and of how many other poets whose poetic machinery consists in so great part of pretending to know less than they do.

Jammes' poems are well represented in Miss Lowell's dilutation on *Six French Poets*, especially by the well-known *Amsterdam* and *Madame de Warens*, which are also in Van Bever and Léautaud. He reaches, as I have said, his greatest verve in *Existences* in the volume *Le Triomphe de la Vie*.

I do not wish to speak in superlatives, but *Existences*, if not Jammes' best work, and if not the most important single volume by any living French poet, either of which it well may be, is at any rate indispensable. It is one of the first half dozen books that a man wanting to know contemporary French work must indulge in. One can *not* represent it in snippets. Still I quote *Le Poète* (his remarks at a provincial soirée):

> "C'est drôle...Cette petite sera bête
> comme ces gens-là, comme son père et sa mère.
> Et cependant elle a une grâce infinie.
> Il y a en elle l'intelligence de la beauté.
> C'est délicieux, son corsage qui n'existe pas,
> son derrière et ses pieds. Mais elle sera bête
> comme une oie dans deux ans d'ici. Elle va jouer".
>
> (*Benette joue la Valse des Elfes.*)

In an earlier scene we have a good example of his rapidity in narrative.

La Servante
Il y a quelqu'un qui veut parler à monsieur.

Le Poète
Qui est-ce?

La Servante
Je ne sais pas.
Le Poète
Un homme ou une femme?

La Servante
Un homme.
Poète
Un commis-voyageur. Vous me le foutez belle!
La Servante
Je ne sais pas, monsieur.

Poète
Faites entrer au salon.
Laissez-moi achever d'achever ces cerises.

(*Next Scene*)
Le Poète (*dans son salon*)
A qui ai-je l'honneur de parler, monsieur?

Le Monsieur
Monsieur, je suis le cousin de votre ancienne maîtresse.

Le Poète
De quelle maîtresse? Je ne vous connais pas.
Et puis qu'est-ce que vous voulez?

Le Monsieur
Monsieur, écoutez-moi.
On m'a dit que vous êtes bon.

Poète
Ce n'est pas vrai.

La Pipe du Poète
Il me bourre avec une telle agitation
que je ne vais jamais pouvoir tirer de l'air.

Poète
D'abord, de quelle maîtresse me parlez-vous?
De qui, prétendez-vous? Non. Vous prétendez de qui j'ai été l'amant?

Le Monsieur
De Néomie.

Poète
De Néomie?

Le Monsieur
Oui, monsieur.

Poète
Où habitez-vous?

Le Monsieur
J'habite les environs de Mont-de-Marsan.

Poète
Enfin que voulez-vous?

Le Monsieur
Savoir si monsieur serait assez complaisant pour me donner quelque chose.

Poète
Et si je ne vous donne le pas, qu'est-ce que vous ferez?

Le Monsieur
Oh! Rien, monsieur. Je ne vous ferai rien. Non....

Le Poète
Tenez, voilà dix francs, et foutez-moi la paix.

(*Le monsieur s'en va, puis le poète sort.*)

The troubles of the Larribeau family, Larribeau and the *bonne*, the visit of the "Comtesse de Pentacosa", who is also staved off with ten francs, are all worth quoting. The whole small town is "Spoon-Rivered" with equal verve. *Existences* was written in 1900.

MOREAS

It must not be thought that these very "modern" poets owe their modernity merely to some magic chemical present in the Parisian *milieu*. Moréas was born in 1856, the year after Verhaeren, but his *Madeline-aux-serpents* might be William Morris on Rapunzel:

"Et votre chevelure comme des grappes d'ombres,
  Et ses bandelettes à vos tempes,
  Et la kabbale de vos yeux latents, —
  Madeline-aux-serpents, Madeline.
        Madeline, Madeline,
Pourquoi vos lèvres à mon cou, ah, pourquoi
Vos lèvres entre les coups du hache du roi!
Madeline, et les cordaces et les flûtes,
Les flûtes, les pas d'amour, les flûtes, vous les voulûtes,
Hélas! Madeline, la fête, Madeline,
Ne berce plus les flots au bord de l'Ile,
Et mes bouffons ne crèvent plus des cerceaux
Au bord de l'Ile, pauvres bouffons.
Pauvres bouffons que couronne la sauge!
Et mes litières s'effeuillent aux ornières, toutes mes litières
    à grand pans
De nonchaloir, Madeline-aux-serpents".…

A difference with Morris might have arisen, of course, over the now long-discussed question of *vers libre*, but who are we to dig up that Babylon? The schoolboys' papers of Toulouse had learnt all about it before the old gentlemen of *The Century* and *Harper's* had discovered that such things exist.

One will not have understood the French poetry of the last half-century unless one makes allowance for what they call the Gothic as well as the Roman or classic influence. We should probably call it (their "Gothic") "mediaevalism", its tone is that of their thirteenth-century poets, Crestien de Troyes, Marie de France, or perhaps even D'Orléans. Tailhade in his *Hymne Antique* displays what we would call Swinburnism (Greekish). Tristan Klingsor (a *nom de plume* showing definite tendencies) exhibits these things a generation nearer to us:

> "Dans son rêve le vieux Prince de Touraine
> voit passer en robe verte à longue traîne
> Yeldis aux yeux charmeurs de douce reine".
>
> . . . . . .
>
> Or
>
> "Au verger où sifflent les sylphes d'automne
> mignonne Isabelle est venue de Venise
> et veut cueillir des cerises et des pommes".
>
> . . . . . .

He was writing rhymed *vers libre* in 1903, possibly stimulated by translations in a volume called *Poésie Arabe*. This book has an extremely interesting preface. I have forgotten the name of the translator, but in excusing the simplicity of Arab songs he says: "The young girl in Germany, educated in philosophy in Kant and Hegel, when love comes to her, at once exclaims 'Infinite!', and allies her vocabulary with the transcendental. The little girl in the tents 'ne savait comparer fors que sa gourmandise'". In Klingsor for 1903, I find:

> "Croise tes jambes fines et nues
> Dans ton lit,
> Frotte de tes mignonnes mains menues
> Le bout de ton nez;
> Frotte de tes doigts potelés et jolis,
> Les deux violettes de tes yeux cernés,
> Et rêve.
> Du haut du minaret arabe s'échappe
> La mélopée triste et brève

> De l'indiscret muezzin
> Qui nasillonne et qui éternue,
> Et toi tu bâilles comme une petite chatte,
> Tu bâilles d'amour brisée,
> Et tu songes au passant d'Ormuz ou d'Endor
> Qui t'a quittée ce matin
> En te laissant sa légère bourse d'or
> Et les marques bleues de ses baisers".

Later he turns to Max Elskamp, addressing him as if he, Klingsor, at last had "found Jesus":

> "Je viens vers vous, mon cher Elskamp
> Comme un pauvre varlet de cœur et de joie
> Vient vers le beau seigneur qui campe
> Sous sa tente d'azur et de soie".

. . . . . .

However I believe Moréas was a real poet, and, being stubborn, I have still an idea which got imbedded in my head some years ago: I mean that Klingsor is a poet. As for the Elskamp phase and cult, I do not make much of it. Jean de Bosschère has written a book upon Elskamp, and he assures me that Elskamp is a great and important poet, and some day, perhaps, I may understand it. De Bosschère seems to me to see or to feel perhaps more keenly than any one else certain phases of modern mechanical civilization: the ant-like madness of men bailing out little boats they never will sail in, shoeing horses they never will ride, making chairs they never will sit on, and all with a frenzied intentness. I may get my conviction as much from his drawings as from his poems. I am not yet clear in my mind about it. His opinion of Max Elskamp cannot be lightly passed over. (*Vide infra*, "De Bosschère on Elskamp".)

FRENCH POETS OF OUR DECADE

Early in 1912 *L'Effort*, since called *L'Effort Libre*, published an excellent selection of poems mostly by men born since 1880: Arcos, Chennevière, Duhamel, Spire, Vildrac, and Jules Romains, with some of Léon Bazalgette's translations from Whitman.

SPIRE
(Born 1868)

André Spire, writing in the style of the generation which has succeeded him, is well represented in this collection by his *Dames Anciennes*. The contents of his volumes are of very uneven value: Zionist propaganda, addresses, and a certain number of well-written poems.

DAMES ANCIENNES

En hiver, dans la chambre claire,
Tout en haut de la maison,
Le poêle de faïence blanche,
Cerclé de cuivre, provincial, doux,
Chauffait mes doigts et mes livres.
Et le peuplier mandarine,
Dans le soir d'argent dédoré,
Dressait, en silence, ses branches,
Devant ma fenêtre close.

— Mère, le printemps aux doigts tièdes
A soulevé l'espagnolette
De mes fenêtres sans rideaux.
Faites taire toutes ces voix qui montent
Jusqu'à ma table de travail.

— Ce sont les amies de ma mère
Et de la mère de ton père,
Qui causent de leurs maris morts,
Et de leurs fils partis.

— Avec, au coin de leurs lèvres,
Ces moustaches de café au lait?
Et dans leurs mains ces tartines?
Dans leurs bouches ces Kouguelofs?

— Ce sont des cavales anciennes
Qui mâchonnent le peu d'herbe douce
Que Dieu veut bien leur laisser.

— Mère, les maîtres sensibles
Lâchent les juments inutiles
Dans les prés, non dans mon jardin!

— Sois tranquille, mon fils, sois tranquille,
Elles ne brouteront pas tes fleurs.

— Mère, que n'y occupent-elles leurs lèvres,
Et leurs trop courtes dents trop blanches
De porcelaine trop fragile!

— Mon fils, fermez votre fenêtre.
Mon fils, vous n'êtes pas chrétien!

JULES ROMAINS

The reader who has gone through Spire, Romains, and Vildrac, will have a fair idea of the poetry written by this group of men. Romains has always seemed to me, and is, I think, generally recognized as, the nerve-centre, the dynamic centre of the group.

"Les marchands sont assis aux portes des boutiques;
Ils regardent. Les toits joignent la rue au ciel
Et les pavés semblent féconds sous le soleil
    Comme un champ de maïs.
Les marchands ont laissé dormir près du comptoir
Le désir de gagner qui travaille dès l'aube.
On dirait que, malgré leur âme habituelle,

Une autre âme s'avance et vient au seuil d'eux-mêmes
Comme ils viennent au seuil de leurs boutiques noires."

We are regaining for cities a little of what savage man has for the forest. We live by instinct; receive news by instinct; have conquered machinery as primitive man conquered the jungle. Romains feels this, though his phrases may not be ours. Wyndham Lewis on giants is nearer Romains than anything else in English, but vorticism is, in the realm of biology, the hypothesis of the dominant cell. Lewis on giants comes perhaps nearer Romains than did the original talks about the Vortex. There is in inferior minds a passion for unity, that is, for a confusion and melting together of things which a good mind will want kept distinct. Uninformed English criticism has treated Unanimism as if it were a vague general propaganda, and this criticism has cited some of our worst and stupidest versifiers as a corresponding manifestation in England. One can only account for such error by the very plausible hypothesis that the erring critics have not read *Puissances de Paris*.

Romains is not to be understood by extracts and fragments. He has felt this general replunge of mind into instinct, or this development of instinct to cope with a metropolis and with metropolitan conditions; in so far as he has expressed the emotions of this consciousness he is poet; he has, aside from that, tried to formulate this new consciousness, and in so far as such formulation is dogmatic, debatable, intellectual, hypothetical, he is open to argument and dispute; that is to say he is philosopher, and his philosophy is definite and defined. Vildrac's statement "Il a changé la pathétique" is perfectly true. Many people will prefer the traditional and familiar and recognizable poetry of writers like Klingsor. I am not dictating people's likes and dislikes. Romains has made a new kind of poetry. Since the scrapping of the Aquinian, Dantescan system, he is perhaps the first person who had dared put up so definite a philosophical framework for his emotions.*

I do not mean, by this, that I agree with Jules Romains; I am prepared to go no further than my opening sentence of this section, concerning our growing, or returning, or perhaps only newly-noticed, sensitization to crowd feeling; to the metropolis and its peculiar sensations. Turn to Romains:

> "Je croyais les murs de ma chambre imperméables.
> Or ils laissent passer une tiède bruine
> Qui s'épaissit et qui m'empêche de me voir,
> Le papier à fleurs bleues lui cède. Il fait le bruit
> Du sable et du cresson qu'une source traverse.
> L'air qui touche mes nerfs est extrêmement lourd.
> Ce n'est pas comme avant le pur milieu de vie
> Où montait de la solitude sublimée.
>
> Voilà que par osmose
> Toute l'immensité d'alentour le sature.
>
> . . . . . .
>
> Il charge mes poumons, il empoisse les choses,
> Il sépare mon corps des meubles familiers,
>
> . . . . . .
>
> Les forces du dehors s'enroulent à mes mains".

In *Puissances de Paris* he states that there are beings more "real than the individual". Here, I can but touch upon salients.

> "Rien ne cesse d'être intérieur.
> La rue est plus intime à cause de la brume."

Lines like Romains', so well packed with thought, and in which he is so careful that you will get the idea, cannot

---

* Gloze 1929. C. W. Wood took to writing quite ably on similar topics, about 1927.

be poured out by the bushel like those of contemporary rhetoricians, like those of Claudel and Fort. The best poetry has always a content, it may not be an intellectual content; in Romains the intellectual statement is necessary to keep the new emotional content coherent.

The opposite of Lewis' giant appears in:

"Je suis l'esclave heureux des hommes dont l'haleine
　Flotte ici. Leur vouloir s'écoule dans mes nerfs;
　Ce qui est moi commence à fondre".

This statement has the perfectly simple order of words. It is the simple statement of a man saying things for the first time, whose chief concern is that he shall speak clearly. His work is perhaps the fullest statement of the poetic consciousness of our time, or the scope of that consciousness. I am not saying he is the most poignant poet; simply that in him we have the fullest poetic *exposition*.

You can get the feel of Laforgue or even of Corbière from a few poems; Romains is a subject for study. I do not say this as praise, I am simply trying to define him. His *Un Etre en Marche* is the narrative of a girls' school, of the "crocodile" or procession going out for its orderly walk, its collective sensations and adventures.

Troupes and herds appear in his earlier work:

"Le troupeau marche, avec ses chiens et son berger,
　Il a peur. Çà et là des réverbères brûlent,
　Il tremble d'être poursuivi par les étoiles.

　　　·　·　·　·　·

　La foule traîne une écume d'ombrelles blanches

　　　·　·　·　·　·

　La grande ville s'évapore,
　Et pleut à verse sur la plaine
　　　　Qu'elle sature".

His style is not a "model", it has the freshness of grass, not of new furniture polish. In his work many nouns meet their verbs for the first time, as, perhaps, in the last lines above quoted. He needs, as a rule, about a hundred pages to turn round in. One cannot give these poems in quotation; one wants about five volumes of Romains. In so far as I am writing "criticism", I must say that his prose is just as interesting as his verse. But then his verse is just as interesting as his prose. Part of his method is to show his subject in a series of successive phases, thus in *L'Individu*:

V

Je suis un habitant de ma ville, un de ceux
Qui s'assoient au théâtre et qui vont par les rues.

. . . . . .

VI

Je cesse lentement d'être moi. Ma personne
Semble s'anéantir chaque jour un peu plus,
C'est à peine si je le sens et m'en étonne.

His poetry is not of single and startling emotions, but—for better or worse—of progressive states of consciousness. It is as useless for the disciple to try and imitate Romains, without having as much thought of his own, as it is for the tyro in words to try imitations of Jules Laforgue. The limitation of Romains' work, as of a deal of Browning's, is that, having once understood it, one may not need or care to re-read it. This restriction applies also in a wholly different way to *Endymion*; having once filled the mind with Keats' colour, or the beauty of things described, one gets no new thrill from the re-reading of them in not very well-written verse. This limitation applies to all poetry that is not implicit in its own medium, that is, which is not indissolubly bound in with the actual words, word music, the fineness and firmness of the actual writing, as in Villon, or in *Collis O Heliconii*.

FRENCH POETS

But one cannot leave Romains unread. His interest is more than a prose interest, he has verse technique, rhyme, terminal syzygy, but that is not what I mean. He is poetry in:

"On ne m'a pas donné de lettres, ces jours-ci;
Personne n'a songé, dans la ville, à m'écrire,
Oh! je n'espérais rien; je sais vivre et penser
Tout seul, et mon esprit, pour faire une flambée,
N'attend pas qu'on lui jette une feuille noircie.
Mais je sens qu'il me manque un plaisir familier,
J'ai du bonheur aux mains quand j'ouvre une enveloppe";

. . . . . .

But such statements as:

TENTATION

Je me plais beaucoup trop à rester dans les gares;
Accoudé sur le bois anguleux des barrières,
Je regarde les trains s'emplir de voyageurs.

. . . . . .

and:

"Mon esprit solitaire est une goutte d'huile
Sur la pensée et sur le songe de la ville
Qui me laissent flotter et ne m'absorbent pas".

. . . . . .

would not be important unless they were followed by exposition. The point is that they *are* followed by exposition, to which they form a necessary introduction, defining Romains' angle of attack; and, as a result, the force of Romains is cumulative. His early books gather meaning as one reads through the later ones.

And I think if one opens him almost anywhere one can discern the authentic accent of a man saying something, not the desultory impagination of rehash.

Charles Vildrac is an interesting companion figure to his brilliant friend Romains. He conserves himself, he is never carried away by Romains' theories. He admires, differs, and occasionally formulates a corrective or corollary as in *Gloire*.

Compare this poem with Romains' *Ode to the Crowd Here Present* and you get the two angles of vision.

Henry Spiess, a Genevan lawyer, has written an interesting series of sketches of the court-room. He is a more or less isolated figure. I have seen amusing and indecorous poems by George Fourest, but it is quite probable that they amuse because one is unfamiliar with their genre; still *La Blonde Négresse* (the heroine of his title), his satire of the symbolo-rhapsodicoes in the series of poems about her: "La négresse blonde, la blonde négresse", gathering into its sound all the swish and woggle of the sound-over-sensists; the poem on the beautiful blue-behinded baboon; that on the gentleman "qui ne craignait ni la vérole ni dieu"; "Les pianos du Casino au bord de la mer" (Laforgue plus the four-hour touch), are an egregious and diverting guffaw. (I do not think the book is available to the public. J. G. Fletcher once lent me a copy, but the edition was limited and the work seems rather unknown.*)

Romains is my chief concern. I cannot give a full exposition of Unanimism on a page or two. Among all the younger writers and groups in Paris, the group centring in Romains is the only one which seems to me to have an energy comparable to that of the *Blast* group in London,† and is the only group in which the writers for *Blast* can be expected to take very much interest.

Romains in the flesh does not seem so energetic as Lewis in the flesh, but then I have seen Romains only once and I am well acquainted with Lewis. Romains is, in his writing,

* Reprinted about 1920.
† Gloze: statement dated Feb. 1918.

more placid, the thought seems more passive, less impetuous. As for those who will not have Lewis "at any price", there remains to them no other course than the acceptance of Romains, for these two men hold the two tenable positions: the Mountain and the Multitude. It might be fairer to Romains to say simply he has chosen, or specialized in, the collected multitude as a subject matter, and that he is quite well on a mountain of his own.

My general conclusions, re-doing and reviewing this period of French poetry, are (after re-reading most of what I had read before):

1. As stated in my opening, that mediocre poetry is about the same in all countries; that France has as much drivel, gas, mush, etc., poured into verse, as has any other nation.

2. That it is impossible "to make a silk purse out of a sow's ear", or poetry out of nothing; that all attempts to "expand" a subject into poetry are futile, fundamentally; that the subject matter must be coterminous with the expression. Tasso, Spenser, Ariosto, prose poems, diffuse forms of all sorts are a preciosity, a parlour-game, and dilutations go to the scrap heap.

3. That Corbière, Rimbaud, Laforgue are permanent; that probably some of De Gourmont's and Tailhade's poems are permanent, or at least reasonably durable; that Romains is indispensable, for the present at any rate; that people who say they "don't like French poetry" are possibly matoids, and certainly ignorant of the scope and variety of French work. In the same way people are ignorant of the qualities of French people; ignorant that if they do not feel at home in Amiens (as I do not), there are other places in France. In the Charente if you walk across country you meet people exactly like the nicest people you can meet in the American country and *they are not "foreign"*.

All France is not to be found in Paris. The adjective "French" is current in America with a dozen erroneous or stupid connotations. If it means, as it did in the mouth of my contemporary, "talcum powder" and surface neatness, the selection of poems I have given here would almost show the need of, or at least a reason for, French Parnassienism; for it shows the French poets violent, whether with the violent words of Corbière, or the quiet violence of the irony of Laforgue, the sudden annihilations of his "turn-back" on the subject. People forget that the incision of Voltaire is no more all of French Literature than is the *robustezza* of Brantôme. (Burton of the *Anatomy* is our only writer who can match him.) They forget the two distinct finenesses of the Latin French and of the French "Gothic", that is of the eighteenth century, of Bernard (if one take a writer of no great importance to illustrate a definite quality), or of D'Orléans and of Froissart in verse. From this delicacy, if they cannot be doing with it, they may turn easily to Villon or Basselin. Only a general distaste for literature can be operative against all of these writers.

UNANIMISME

The English translation of Romains' *Mort de Quelqu'un* has provoked various English and American essays and reviews. His published works are *L'Ame des Hommes*, 1904; *Le Bourg Régénéré*, 1906; *La Vie Unanime*, 1908; *Premier Livre de Prières*, 1909; *La Foule qui est Ici*, 1909; in 1910 and 1911 *Un Etre en Marche, Deux Poèmes, Manuel de Deification, L'armée dans la Ville, Puissances de Paris*, and *Mort de Quelqu'un*, employing the three excellent publishing houses of the Mercure, Figuière and Sansot.

His "Reflexions" at the end of *Puissances de Paris* are so good a formulation of the Unanimiste Aesthetic, or *Pathétique*, that quotation of them will do more to disabuse readers misled by stupid English criticism than would any amount of talk about Romains. I let him speak for himself:

FRENCH POETS

REFLEXIONS

"Many people are now ready to recognize that there are in the world beings more real than man. We admit the life of entities greater than our own bodies. Society is not merely an arithmetical total, or a collective designation. We even credit the existence of groups intermediate between the individual and the state. But these opinions are put forth by abstract deduction or by experimentation of reason.

"People employ them to complete a system of things and with the complacencies of analogy. If they do not follow a serious study of social data, they are at least the most meritorious results of observations; they justify the method, and uphold the laws of a science which struggles manfully to be scientific.

"These fashions of knowing would seem both costly and tenuous. Man did not wait for physiology to give him a notion of his body, in which lack of patience he was intelligent, for physiology has given him but analytic and exterior information concerning things he had long known from within. He had been conscious of his organs long before he had specified their modes of activity. As spirals of smoke from village chimneys, the profound senses of each organ had mounted toward him; joy, sorrow, all the emotions are deeds more fully of consciousness than are the thoughts of man's reason. Reason makes a concept of man, but the heart perceives the flesh of his body.

"In like manner we must know the groups that englobe us, not by observation from without, but by an organic consciousness. And it is by no means sure that the rhythms will make their nodes in us, if we be not the centres of groups. We have but to become such. Dig deep enough in our being, emptying it of individual reveries, dig enough little canals so that the souls of the groups will flow of necessity into us.

"I have attempted nothing else in this book. Various groups have come here into consciousness. They are still rudimentary, and their spirit is but a perfume in the air. Beings with as little consistence as la Rue du Havre, and la Place de la Bastille, ephemeral as the company of people in an omnibus, or the audience at L'Opéra Comique, cannot have complex organism or thoughts greatly elaborate. People will think it superfluous that I should unravel such shreds in place of re-carding once more the enormous heap of the individual soul.

"Yet I think the groups are in the most agitated stage of their evolution. Future groups will perhaps deserve less affection, and we shall conceal the basis of things more effectively. Now the incomplete and unstable contours have not yet learned to stifle any tendency (any inclination). Every impact sets them floating. They do not coat the infantile matter with a hard or impacting envelope. A superior plant has realized but few of the possibilities swarming in fructificatory mould. A mushroom leads one more directly to the essential life quality than do the complexities of the oak tree.

"Thus the groups prepare more future than is strictly required. Thus we have the considerable happiness of watching the commencement of reign, the beginning of an organic series which will last as did others, for a thousand ages, before the cooling of the earth. This is not a progression, it is a creation, the first leap-out of a different series. Groups will not continue the activities of animals, nor of men; they will start things afresh according to their own need, and as the consciousness of their substance increases they will refashion the image of the world.

"The men who henceforth can draw the souls of groups to converge within themselves, will give forth the coming dream, and will gather, to boot, certain intuitions of human habit. Our ideas of the being will undergo a correction; will hesitate rather more in finding a distinction between the existent and non-existent. In passing successively from the Place de l'Europe to the Place des Vosges, and then to a gang of navvies, one perceives that there are numerous shades of difference between nothing and something. Before resorting to groups one is sure of discerning a being of a simple idea. One knows that a dog exists, that he has an interior and independent unity; one knows that a table or a mountain does not exist; nothing but our manner of speech cuts it off from the universal non-existing. But streets demand all shades of verbal expression (from the non-existing up to the autonomous creature).

"One ceases to believe that a definite limit is the indispensable means of existence. Where does la Place de la Trinité begin? The streets mingle their bodies. The squares isolate themselves with great difficulty. The crowd at the theatre takes on no contour until it has lived for some time, and with vigour. A being (*être*) has a centre, or centres in harmony, but a being is not compelled to have limits. He exists a great deal in one place, rather less in others, and, further on, a second being commences before the first has left off. Every being has, somewhere in space, its maximum. Only ancestored individuals possess affirmative contours, a skin which cuts them off from the infinite.

"Space is no one's possession. No being has succeeded in appropriating one scrap of space and saturating it with his own unique existence. Everything over-crosses, coincides, and cohabits. Every point is a perch for a thousand birds. Paris, the Rue Montmartre, a crowd, a man, a protoplasm are on the same spot of pavement. A thousand existences are concentric. We see a little of some of them.

"How can we go on thinking that an individual is a solitary thing which is born, grows, reproduces itself and dies? This is a superior and inveterate manner of being an individual. But groups are not truly born. Their life makes and unmakes itself like an unstable state of matter, a condensation which does not endure. They show us that life, at its origin, is a provisory attitude, a moment of exception, an intensity between two relaxations, not continuity, nothing decisive. The first entireties take life by a sort of slow success, and extinguish themselves without catastrophe, the single elements do not perish because the whole is disrupted.

"The crowd before the Baraque Foraine starts to live little by little, as water in a kettle begins to sing and evaporate. The passages of the Odéon do not live by night, each day they are real, a few hours. At the start life seems the affair of a moment, then it becomes intermittent. To be durable; to become a development and a destiny; to be defined and finished off at each end by birth and death, it needs a deal of accustomedness.

"The primitive forms are not coequal. There is a natural hierarchy among groups. Streets have no set middle, no veritable limitations; they hold a long vacillating sort of life which night flattens out almost to nothingness. Cross-roads and squares take on contour, and gather up the nodes of their rhythms. Other groups have a fashioned body, they endure but a little space, but they have learned, almost, to die; they even resurrect themselves as by a jerk or dry spasm, they begin the habit of being, they strive toward it, and this puts them out of breath.

"I have not yet met a group fully divine. None has had a real consciousness, none has addressed me, saying: I exist. The day when the first group shall take its soul in its hands, as one lifts up a child in order to look in its face, that day there will be a new god upon earth. This is the god I await, with my labour of annunciation."

This excerpt from Romains gives the tone of his thought. In so far as he writes in the present tense he carries conviction. He broaches truly a "new", or at least contemporary "*pathétique*". He utters, in original vein, phases of consciousness whereinto we are more or less drifting, in measure of our proper sensibility.

I retain, however, my full suspicion of agglomerates.

I also reprint for the first time my earlier note on Vildrac.

VILDRAC

Vildrac's *Gloire* is in a way commentary on Romains' *Ode to the Crowd*; a critique of part, at least, of unanimism.

> "Il avait su gagner à lui
> Beaucoup d'hommes ensemble,
>
> . . . . . .
>
> Et son bonheur était de croire,
> Quand il avait quitté la foule,
> Que chacun des hommes l'aimait
> Et que sa présence durait
> Innombrable et puissante en eux,
>
> . . . . . .
>
> Or un jour il en suivit un
> Qui retournait chez soi, tout seul,
> Et il vit son regard s'éteindre
> Dès qu'il fût un peu loin des autres."
>
> . . . . . .

(The full text of this appeared in *Poetry*, August, 1913.)

Vildrac's two best known poems are *Une Auberge* and *Visite*; the first a forlorn scene, not too unlike a Van Gogh, though not done with Van Gogh's vigour.

> "C'est seulement parce qu'on a soif qu'on entre y boire;
> C'est parce qu'on se sent tomber qu'on va s'y asseoir.
> On n'y est jamais à la fois qu'un ou deux
> Et l'on n'est pas forcé d'y raconter son histoire.
>
> . . . . . .
>
> Celui qui entre...
>
> . . . . . .

> Mange lentement son pain
> Parce que ses dents sont usées;
> Et il boit avec beaucoup de mal
> Parce qu'il a de peine plein sa gorge.
>
> Quand il a fini,
> Il hésite, puis timide
> Va s'asseoir un peu
> A côté du feu.
>
> Ses mains crevassées épousent
> Les bosselures dures de ses genoux."

Then of the other man in the story:

> "qui n'était pas des nôtres....
> Mais comme il avait l'air cependant d'être des nôtres!"

The story or incident in *Visite* is that of a man stirring himself out of his evening comfort to visit some pathetic dull friends.

. . . . . .

> "Ces gens hélas, ne croyaient pas
> Qu'il fût venu à l'improviste
> Si tard, de si loin, par la neige...
> Et ils attendaient l'un et l'autre
> Que brusquement et d'un haleine il exposât
> La grave raison de sa venue."

Only when he gets up to go, "ils osèrent comprendre".

. . . . . .

> "Il leur promit de revenir.
>
> . . . . . .
>
> Mais avant de gagner la porte
> Il fixa bien dans sa mémoire
> Le lieu où s'abritait leur vie.
> Il regarda bien chaque objet

FRENCH POETS

Et puis aussi l'homme et la femme,
Tant il craignait au fond de lui
De ne plus jamais revenir."

DE BOSSCHERE'S STUDY OF ELSKAMP*

I

I confessed in my February essay my inability to make anything of Max Elskamp's poetry, and I have tacitly confessed my inability to find any formula for hawking De Bosschère's own verse to any public of my acquaintance; De Bosschère's study of Elskamp, however, requires no advocacy; I do not think it even requires to be a study of Max Elskamp; it drifts as quiet canal water; the protagonist may or not be a real man.

"Ici, la solitude est plus accentuée: souvent, pendant de longues minutes, les rues sont désertes.... Les portes ne semblent pas, ainsi que dans les grandes villes, s'ouvrir sur un poumon de vie, et être une cellule vivante de la rue. Au contraire, toutes sont fermées. Aussi bien, les façades de ce quartier sont pareilles aux murs borgnes. Un mince ruban de ciel roux et gris, à peine bleu au printemps, découpe les pignons, se tend sur le marché désert et sur le puits profond des cours."

From this Antwerp, De Bosschère derives his subject, as Gautier his "Albertus" from

"Un vieux bourg flamand tel que peint Téniers";

trees bathing in water.

"Son univers était limité par: 'le grand peuplier'; une

---

* "*Max Elskamp*"; essai par Jean De Bosschère. Bibliothèque de l'Occident, 17 rue Eblé, Paris. fr. 3.50.

statue de Pomone, 'le grand rocher', et 'la grande grenouille'; ceci était un coin touffu où il y avait de l'eau et où il ne vit jamais qu'une seule grenouille, qu'il croyait immortelle." De Bosschère's next vision of Elskamp is when his subject is pointed out as "le poète décadent", for no apparent reason save that he read Mallarmé at a time when Antwerp did not. The study breaks into a cheerful grin when Elskamp tells of Mallarmé's one appearance in the sea-port:

"Le bruit et les cris qui furent poussés pendant la conférence de Mallarmé, l'arrêtèrent plusieurs fois. L'opinion du public sur sa causerie est contenue en ces quelques mots, dits par un général retraité, grand joueur de billard, et qui du reste ne fit qu'une courte absence de la salle de jeu, pour écouter quelques phrases du poète. 'Cet homme est ivre ou fou', dit il fort haut, en quittant la salle, où son jugement fit loi. Anvers, malgré un léger masque de snobisme, qui pourrait tromper, n'a pas changé depuis. Mallarmé, même pour les *avertis*, est toujours l'homme ivre ou fou".

The billiard player is the one modern touch in the book; for the rest Elskamp sails with sea-captains, apparently in sailing ships to Constantinople, or perhaps one should call it Byzantium. He reads Juan de la Cruz and Young's *Night Thoughts*, and volumes of demonology, in the properly dim library of his maternal grandfather, "Sa passion en rhétorique fut pour Longfellow, il traduisait 'Song of (*sic*) Hiawatots'".

The further one penetrates into De Bosschère's delightful narrative the less real is the hero; the less he needs to be real. A phantom has been called out of De Foe's period, delightful phantom, taking on the reality of the fictitious; in the end the author has created a charming figure, but I am as far as ever from making head or tail of the verses attributed to this creation. I have had a few hours' delightful reading, I have loitered along slow canals, behind a small window sits Elskamp doing something I do not in the least understand.

II

So was I at the end of the first division "Sur la Vie" de Max Elskamp. The second division, concerned with "Œuvre et Vie", but raised again the questions that had faced me in reading Elskamp's printed work. He has an undercurrent, an element everywhere present, differentiating his poems from other men's poems. De Bosschère scarcely helps me to name it. The third division of the book, at first reading, nearly quenched the curiosity and the interest aroused by the first two-thirds. On second reading I thought better of it. Elskamp, plunged in the Middle Ages, in what seems almost an atrophy, as much as an atavism, becomes a little more plausible. (For what it is worth, I read the chapter upon a day of almost complete exhaustion.)

"Or, quand la vision lâche comme une proie vidée le saint, il demeure avec les hommes."

"Entre le voyant et ceux qui le sanctifient il y a un précipice insondable. Seul l'individu est béatifié par sa croyance; mais il ne peut *l'utiliser* au temporel ni la partager avec les hommes, et c'est peut-être la forme unique de la justice sur terre."

The two sentences give us perhaps the tone of De Bosschère's critique *Sur le Mysticisme* of Elskamp.

It is, however, not in De Bosschère, but in *La Wallonie* that I found the clue to this author:

CONSOLATRICE DES AFFLIGÉS

Et l'hiver m'a donné la main.
J'ai la main d'Hiver dans les mains,

et dans ma tête, au loin, il brûle
les vieux étés de canicule;

et dans mes yeux, en candeurs lentes,
très blanchement il fait des tentes,

dans mes yeux il fait des Sicile,
puis des îles, encore des îles.

Et c'est tout un voyage en rond
trop vite pour la guérison

à tous les pays où l'on meurt
au long cours des mers et des heures;

et c'est tout un voyage au vent
sur les vaisseaux de mes lits blancs

qui houlent avec des étoiles
à l'entour de toutes les voiles.

Or j'ai le goût de mer aux lèvres
comme une rancœur de genièvre

bu pour la très mauvaise orgie
des départs dans les tabagies;

puis ce pays encore me vient:
un pays de neiges sans fin....

Marie des bonnes couvertures,
faites-y la neige moins dure

et courir moins comme des lièvres
mes mains sur mes draps blancs de fièvre.

Max Elskamp in "La Wallonie", 1892.

 The poem appears in Van Bever and Léautaud's anthology and there may be no reason for my not having thence received it; but there is, for all that, a certain value in finding a man among his native surroundings, and in finding Elskamp at home, among his contemporaries, I gained first the advantage of comprehension.

FRENCH POETS

ALBERT MOCKEL AND *LA WALLONIE**

I recently received a letter from Albert Mockel, written with a graciousness not often employed by English and American writers in communication to their juniors. Indeed, the present elder generation of American "respectable" authors having all their lives approached so nearly to death, have always been rather annoyed that American letters did not die utterly in *their* personal desiccations. Signs of vitality; signs of interest in, or cognizance of other sections of this troubled planet have been steadily and papier-mâchéedly deprecated. The rubbish bins *Harper's* and the *Century* have opened their receptive lids not to new movements but only to the diluted imitations of new movers, etc.

La Wallonie, beginning as *L'Elan Littéraire* in 1885, endured seven years. It announced for a full year on its cover that its seventh year was its last. Albert Mockel has been gracious enough to call it "Notre *Little Review* à nous", and to commend the motto on our cover, in the letter here following:

109, *Avenue de Paris*　　　　　　　　　　　　　　8 *mai*, 1918
La Malmaison Rueil

Monsieur et cher confrère,
　Merci de votre aimable envoi. La *Little Review* m'est sympathique à l'extrême. En la feuilletant j'ai cru voir renaître ce temps doré de ferveur et de belle confiance où, adolescent encore, et tâtonnant un peu dans les neuves régions de l'Art, je fondai à Liége notre *Little Review* à nous, *La Wallonie*. Je retrouve justement quelques livraisons de cette revue et je vous les envoie; elles ont tout au moins le mérite de la rareté.
　Vous mon cher confrère, déjà ne marchez plus à tâtons mais je vous soupçonne de n'être pas aussi terriblement, aussi

* *Little Review*, Oct. 1918.

criminellement jeune que je l'étais à cette époque-là. Et puis trente ans ont passé sur la littérature, et c'est de la folie d'hier qu'est faite la sagesse d'aujourd'hui. Alors le Symbolisme naissait; grâce à la collaboration de mes amis, grâce à Henri de Régnier et Pierre M. Olin qui dirigèrent la revue avec moi, *La Wallonie* en fut l'un des premiers foyers. Tout était remis en question. On aspirait à plus de liberté, à une forme plus intense et plus complète, plus musicale et plus souple, à une expression nouvelle de l'éternelle beauté. On s'ingéniait, on cherchait.... Tâtonnements? Certes et ils étaient inévitables. Mais vif et ardent effort, désintéressement absolu, foi juvénile et surtout "No compromise with the public taste".... N'y a-t-il point là quelques traits de ressemblance avec l'œuvre que vous tentez aujourd'hui en Amérique, et, à trente années d'intervalle, une sorte de cousinage? C'est pourquoi mon cher confrère, j'ai lu avec tant de plaisir la *Little Review* dont vous avez eu la gentillesse de m'adresser la collection.

Croyez-moi sympathiquement vôtre,
ALBERT MOCKEL.

With a native mistrust of *la belle phrase*; of "*temps doré*", "*ferveur*", "*belle confiance*", etc., and with an equally native superiority to any publication not printed LARGE, I opened *La Wallonie*. The gropings, "tâtonnements", to which M. Mockel so modestly refers, appear to have included some of the best work of Mallarmé, of Stuart Merrill, of Max Elskamp and Emile Verhaeren. Verlaine contributed to *La Wallonie*, De Régnier was one of its editors.... Men of since popular fame—Bourget, Pierre Louys, Maeterlinck—appeared with the rarer spirits.

If ever the "amateur magazine" in the sense of magazine by lovers of art and letters, for lovers of art and letters, in contempt of the commerce of letters, has vindicated itself, that vindication was *La Wallonie*. Verhaeren's *Les Pauvres*

FRENCH POETS

first appeared there as the second part of the series: *Chansons des Carrefours* (January, 1892).... The Elskamp I have just quoted appeared there with other poems of Max Elskamp. Mallarmé is represented by the exquisite:

SONNET

Ses purs ongles très haut dédiant leur onyx,
L'Angoisse, ce minuit, soutient, lampadophore,
Maint rêve vespéral brûlé par le Phénix
Que ne recueille pas de cinéraire amphore

Sur les crédences, au salon vide: nul ptyx,
Aboli bibelot d'inanité sonore.
(Car le Maître est allé puiser des pleurs au Styx
Avec ce seul objet dont le Néant s'honore.)

Mais proche la croisée au nord vacante, un or
Agonise selon peut-être le décor
Des licornes ruant du feu contre une nixe,

Elle, défunte nue en le miroir; encor
Que, dans l'oubli fermé par le cadre, se fixe
De scintillations sitôt le septuor.

Mallarmé in "La Wallonie", January, 1889.

An era of Franco-American intercourse is marked by:

BILLET A WHISTLER

Pas les rafales à propos
De rien comme occuper la rue
Sujette au noir vol de chapeaux;
Mais une danseuse apparue

Tourbillon de mousseline ou
Fureur éparses en écumes
Que soulève par son genou
Celle même dont nous vécûmes

> Pour tout, hormis lui, rebattu
> Spirituelle, ivre, immobile
> Foudroyer avec le tutu,
> Sans se faire autrement de bile
>
> Sinon rieur que puisse l'air
> De sa jupe éventer Whistler.
>
> *Mallarmé in "Wallonie", November, 1890.*

If I owe Albert Mockel a great debt in having illuminated my eye for Elskamp I owe him no less the pleasure of one of Merrill's most delicate triumphs in the opening of

BALLET
Pour Gustave Moreau

> En casque de cristal rose les baladines,
> Dont les pas mesurés aux cordes des kinnors
> Tintent sous les tissus de tulle roidis d'ors,
> Exultent de leurs yeux pâles de xaladines.
>
> Toisons fauves sur leurs lèvres incarnadines,
> Bras lourds de bracelets barbares, en essors
> Moelleux vers la lueur lunaire des décors,
> Elles murmurent en malveillantes sourdines:
>
> "Nous sommes, ô mortels, danseuses du Désir,
> Salomés dont les corps tordus par le plaisir
> Leurrent vos heurs d'amour vers nos pervers arcanes.
>
> Prosternez-vous avec des hosannas, ces soirs!
> Car, surgissant dans des aurores d'encensoirs,
> Sur nos cymbales nous ferons tonner vos crânes".
>
> *Stuart Merrill in "La Wallonie", July, 1888.*

The period was "glauque" and "nacre", it had its pet and too-petted adjectives, the handles for parody; but it had also a fine care for sound, for sound fine-wrought, not mere swish and resonant rumble, not

> "Dolores, O hobble and kobble Dolores.
> O perfect obstruction on track".

The particular sort of fine workmanship shown in this sonnet of Merrill's has of late been too much let go by the board. One may do worse than compare it with the Syrian syncopation of Διώνα and Ἄδωνιν in Bion's *Adonis*.

Hanton is gently didactic:

LE BON GRAIN

"Déjà peinent maints moissonneurs dont la mémoire est destinée à vivre."   *Celestin Demblon.*

Amants des rythmes en des strophes cadencées,
Des rimes rares aux splendeurs évocatoires,
Laissant en eux comme un écho de leurs pensées,
Comme un parfum de leurs symboles en histoires :

Tels les poètes vont cherchant en vrais glaneurs
Les blonds épis qui formeront leur riche écrin.
Ils choisiront, comme feraient les bons vanneurs,
Parmi les blés passés au crible, le beau grain.

Et germera cette semence bien choisie,
Entre les roses et les lys, pour devenir
Riche moisson de la fertile fantaisie.

L'ardent soleil de Messidor fera jaunir
Les tiges souples d'une forte poésie
Qui dresseront leurs fiers épis vers l'avenir !

              Edmond Hanton in "La Wallonie", July, 1888.

Delaroche is, at least in parts, utterly incomprehensible, but there is an interesting experiment in sound-sequence which begins:

SONNETS SYMPHONIQUES

En la langueur
accidentelle
de ta dentelle
où meurt mon cœur

Un profil pleure
et se voit tel
en le pastel
du divin leurre

Qu'or végétal
de lys s'enlise
au froid santal

Si n'agonise
occidental
qui s'adonise.

Achille Delaroche in "La Wallonie", February, 1889.

I do not know that we will now be carried away by Albert Saint-Paul's chinoiserie, or that she-devils are so much in fashion as when Jules Bois expended, certainly, some undeniable emotion in addressing them:

PETALES DE NACRE

En sa robe où s'immobilisent les oiseaux,
Une émerge des fleurs comme une fleur plus grande.
Comme une fleur penchée au sourire de l'eau,

Ses mains viennent tresser la traînante guirlande
Pour enchaîner le Dragon vert—et de légende!
Qui de ses griffes d'or déchire les roseaux,

Les faisceaux de roseaux: banderolles et lances.

Et quand le soir empourprera le fier silence
De la forêt enjôleuse de la Douleur,
Ses doigts, fuseaux filant au rouet des murmures
Les beaux anneaux fleuris liant les fleurs aux fleurs,

Ses doigts n'auront saigné qu'aux épines peu dures.
Albert Saint-Paul in "La Wallonie", January, 1891.

POUR LA DEMONE

Un soir de joie, un soir d'ivresse, un soir de fête,
— Et quelle fête, et quelle ivresse, et quelle joie! —
Tu vins. L'impérial ennui sacrait ta tête;
Et tu marchais dans un bruit d'armure et de soie.

Tu dédaignas tous les bijoux et l'oripeau
De ruban, de dentelle et d'éphémère fleur....
Hermétique, ta robe emprisonnait ta peau.
Oui, la fourrure seule autour de ta pâleur.

Tu parus. Sous tes yeux que le kh'ol abomine,
Le bal fut la lugubre et dérisoire histoire.
Les hommes des pantins qu'un vice mène et mine.
Les femmes, cœurs et corps fanés, —— et quel déboire!

POUR LA DEMONE

V

Elle est folle, c'est sûr, elle est folle la chère;
Elle m'aime à n'en pas douter, mais elle est folle,
Elle m'aime et, compatissez à ma misère,
Avec tous, avec toutes, elle batifole.

Un passe.... Elle s'élance à lui, cœur présumé....
Elle s'offre et le provoque, puis elle fuit
Vers ailleurs...si fidèle encore au seul-aimé,
Mais elle est folle et je m'éplore dans la nuit.

Pour quelque amie aux délicatesses félines,
Elle glisse vers les caresses trop profondes.
..."Tu vas, folle, oublier mes rancœurs orphelines".
Mais sa lèvre pensive hésite aux toisons blondes.
>> *Jules Bois in "La Wallonie", September,* 1890.

In part we must take our reading of *La Wallonie* as a study of the state of symbolism from 1885 to 1892.

Rodenbach displays the other leaf of the diptych: the genre, the homely Wallon landscape, more familiar to the outer world in Verhaeren, but not, I think, better painted.

PAYSAGES SOUFFRANTS

II

A Emile Verhaeren.

Là-bas, tant de petits hameaux sous l'avalanche
De la neige qui tombe adoucissante et blanche,
Tant de villages, tant de chaumines qui sont
Pour le reste d'un soir doucement assoupies,
Car la neige s'étend en de molles charpies
Sur les blessures des vieilles briques qui n'ont
Rien senti d'une Sœur sur leur rougeur qui saigne!
Mais, ô neige, c'est toi la Sœur au halo blanc
Qui consoles les murs malades qu'on dédaigne
Et mets un peu d'ouate aux pierres s'éraflant.

Las! rien ne guérira les chaumines—aïeules
Qui meurent de l'hiver et meurent d'être seules....
Et leurs âmes bientôt, au gré des vents du nord.
Dans la fumée aux lents départs, seront parties
Cependant que la neige, à l'heure de leur mort,
Leur apporte ses refraîchissantes hosties!
>> *Georges Rodenbach in "La Wallonie", January,* 1888.

Rodenbach is authentic.

Vielé-Griffin, who, as Stuart Merrill, has always been

known in France as "an American", contributed largely to *La Wallonie*. His *Au Tombeau d'Hélène* ends:

HELENE

Me voici:
J'étais là dès hier, et dès sa veille,
Ailleurs, ici;
Toute chair, a paré, un soir, mon âme vieille
Comme l'éternité du désir que tu vêts.
La nuit est claire au firmament...
Regarde avec tes yeux levés:
Voici — comme un tissu de pâle feu fatal
Qui fait épanouir la fleur pour la flétrir —
Mon voile où transparaît tout assouvissement
Qui t'appelle à la vie et qui t'en fait mourir.
La nuit est claire au firmament vital....
Mes mythes, tu les sais:
Je suis fille du Cygne,
Je suis la lune dont s'exubèrent les mers
Qui montent, tombent, se soulèvent;
Et c'est le flot de vie exultante et prostrée,
le flot des rêves,
le flot des chairs,
le flux et le reflux de la vaste marée.

Mon doute — on dit l'Espoir — fait l'action insigne:
Je suis reine de Sparte et celle-là de Troie,
Par moi, la douloureuse existence guerroie,
Je meus toute inertie aux leurres de ma joie,
Hélène, Séléné, flottant de phase en phase,
Je suis l'Inaccédée et la tierce Hypostase
Et si je rejetais, désir qui m'y convies,
Mon voile qui promet et refuse l'extase,
Ma nudité de feu résorberait les Vies....

Vielé-Griffin in "La Wallonie", December, 1891.
(*Complete number devoted to his poems.*)

Mockel is represented by several poems rather too long to quote—*Chantefable un peu naïve*, *L'Antithèse*, suggestive of the Gourmont litany; by prose comment, by work over various pseudonyms. *A Clair Matin* is a suitable length to quote, and it is better perhaps to represent him here by it than by fragments which I had first intended to cut from his longer poems.

A CLAIR MATIN

La nuit au loin s'est effacée
comme les lignes tremblantes d'un rêve;
la nuit s'est fondue au courant du Passé
et le jour attendu se lève.

Regardez! en les courbes molles des rideaux
une heure attendue se révèle
et ma fenêtre enfin s'éclaire,
cristalline du givre où se rit la lumière.

Une parure enfantine de neiges
habille là-bas d'immobiles eaux
et c'est les cortèges des fées nouvelles
à tire d'ailes, à tire d'ailes
du grand lointain qui toutes reviennent
aux flocons de ce jour en neiges qui s'épèle.

Des courbes de mes rideaux clairs
— voici! c'est un parfum de ciel! —
blanc des guirlandes de l'hiver
le jeune matin m'est apparu
avec un visage de fiancée.

Des fées
(ah je ne sais quelles mortelles fées)
jadis elles vinrent toucher la paupière
d'un être enfantin qui mourut.
Son âme, où se jouait en songes la lumière,

diaphane corolle épanouie au jour
son âme était vive de toute lumière!
Lui, comme un frère il suivait ma course
et nous allions en confiants de la montagne à la vallée
par les forêts des chênes, des hêtres
— car eux, les ancêtres, ils ont le front grave,
ils virent maints rêves des autres âges
et nous parlent, très doucement, comme nos Pères.

Mais voyez! à mes rideaux pâles
le matin glisse des sourires;
car la Fiancée est venue
car la Fiancée est venue
avec un simple et très doux visage,
avec des mots qu'on n'entend pas,
en silence la Fiancée est apparue
comme une grande sœur de l'enfant qui mourut;
et les hêtres, les chênes royaux des forêts
par douce vocalise égrenant leur parure,
les voix ressuscitées en la plaine sonore
et toute la forêt d'aurore
quand elle secoue du crépuscule sa chevelure,
tout chante, bruit, pétille et rayonne
car la céleste Joie que la clarté délivre
d'un hymne répercute aux miroirs du futur
le front pâle où scintille en étoiles le givre.
 Albert Mockel in "La Wallonie", Dernier fascicule, 1892.

 I have left Gide and Van Lerberghe unquoted, unmentioned, but I have, I dare say, given poems enough to indicate the quality and the scope of the poetry in *La Wallonie*.

 In prose their cousinage is perhaps more quickly apparent. Almost the first sentence I come upon (I suspect it is Mockel's) runs as follows:

"*La Revue des deux Mondes* publie un roman de Georges Ohnet ce qui ne surprendra personne".

This is the proper tone to use when dealing with elderly muttonheads; with the *Harpers* of yester year. *La Wallonie* found it out in the eighties. The symboliste movement flourished on it. American letters did not flourish, partly perhaps for the lack of it, and for the lack of unbridled uncompromising magazines run by young men who did not care for *réputations surfaites*, for elderly stodge and stupidity.

If we turn to Mockel's death notice for Jules Laforgue we will find *La Wallonie* in 1887 awake to the value of <u>contemporary</u> achievement:

JULES LAFORGUE

Nous apprenons avec une vive tristesse, la mort de Jules Laforgue, l'un des plus curieux poètes de la littérature aux visées nouvelles. Nous l'avons désigné, ja deux mois: un Tristan Corbière plus argentin, moins âpre.... Et telle est bien sa caractéristique. Sans le moindre soupçon d'imitation ou de réminiscences, Jules Laforgue a sauvegardé une originalité vivace. Seulement, cette originalité, par bien des saillies, touche à celle de Tristan Corbière. C'est une même raillerie de la Vie et du Monde; mais plus de sombre et virile amertume émouvait en l'auteur des *Amours Jaunes*, dont cette pièce donnera quelque idée:

LE CRAPAUD

Un chant dans une nuit sans air...
— La lune plaque en métal clair
Les découpures du vert sombre.
...Un chant; comme un écho, tout vif
Enterré, là, sous le massif...
— Ça se tait; viens, c'est là, dans l'ombre...
Un crapaud!
       — Pourquoi cette peur,
Près de moi, ton soldat fidèle!

Vois-le, poète tondu, sans aile,
Rossignol de la boue...
   — Horreur! —
...Il chante. — Horreur!! — Horreur pourquoi?
Vois-tu pas son œil de lumière...
Non, il s'en va, froid, sous sa pierre.

   . . . . .

Bonsoir — ce crapaud-là c'est moi.

Chez Laforgue, il y a plus de gai sans-souci, de coups de batte de pierrot donnés à toutes choses, plus de "vaille-que-vaille la vie", dit d'un air de moqueuse résignation. Sa rancœur n'est pas à qui encombrante. Il était un peu l'enfant indiscipliné qui rit à travers les gronderies, et fait la moue à sa fantaisie; mais son haussement d'épaules gamin, et ses "Après tout?" qu'il jette comme une chiquenaude au visage du Temps, cachent toujours au fond de son cœur un lac mélancolique, un lac de tristesse et d'amours flétris, où vient se refléter sa claire imagination. Témoins ces fragments pris aux *Complaintes*:

Mon cœur est une urne où j'ai mis certains défunts,
Oh! chut, refrains de leurs berceaux! et vous, parfums.

   . . . . .

Mon cœur est un Néron, enfant gâté d'Asie,
Qui d'empires de rêve en vain se rassasie.
Mon cœur est un noyé vidé d'âme et d'essors,
Qu'étreint la pieuvre Spleen en ses ventouses d'or.
C'est un feu d'artifice, hélas! qu'avant la fête,
A noyé sans retour l'averse qui s'embête.
Mon cœur est le terrestre Histoire-Corbillard
Que traînent au néant l'instinct et le hazard
Mon cœur est une horloge oubliée à demeure
Qui, me sachant défunt, s'obstine à marquer l'heure.

Et toujours mon cœur ayant ainsi déclamé,
En revient à sa complainte: Aimer, être aimé!

Et cette pièce, d'une ironie concentrée:

COMPLAINTE DES BONS MENAGES

L'Art sans poitrine m'a trop longtemps bercé dupe.
Si ses labours sont fiers, que ses blés décevants!
Tiens, laisse-moi bêler tout aux plis de ta jupe
      Qui fleure le couvent.
La Génie avec moi, serf, a fait des manières;
Toi, jupe, fais frou-frou, sans t'inquiéter pourquoi....

. . . .

Mais l'Art, c'est l'Inconnu! qu'on y dorme et s'y vautre,
On ne peut pas l'avoir constamment sur les bras!
Et bien, ménage au vent! Soyons Lui, Elle et l'Autre.
      Et puis n'insistons pas.

Et puis? et puis encore un pied de nez mélancolique à la destinée:

      Qui m'aima jamais? Je m'entête
      Sur ce refrain bien impuissant
      Sans songer que je suis bien bête
      De me faire du mauvais sang.

Jules Laforgue a publié outre les *Complaintes*, un livret de vers dégingandés, d'une raillerie splénétique, à froid, comme celle qui sied aux hommes du Nord. Mais il a su y ajouter ce sans-façon de choses dites à l'aventure, et tout un parfum de lumière argentine, comme les rayons de *Notre-Dame la Lune* qu'il célèbre. Le manque de place nous prive d'en citer quelques pages. Nous avons lu aussi cette étrange Nuit d'Etoiles: le *Conseil Féerique*, un assez court poème édité par la "Vogue"; divers articles de revue, entre lesquels cette page ensoleillée, parue dans la *Revue Indépendante*: *Pan et la Syrinx*. Enfin un nouveau livre était annoncé: **de la Pitié**, *de la Pitié!*, déjà préparé par l'une des Invocations du volume précédent, et dont nous croyons voir l'idée en ces vers des *Complaintes*:

> Vendange chez les Arts enfantins; sois en fête
> D'une fugue, d'un mot, d'un ton, d'un air de tête.
>
> . . . . . .
>
> Vivre et peser selon le Beau, le Bien, le Vrai?
> O parfums, ô regards, ô fois! soit, j'essaierai.
>
> . . . . . .
>
> ...Va, que ta seule étude
> Soit de vivre sans but, fou de mansuétude —
>
> *Albert Mockel in "La Wallonie"*, 1887.

I have quoted but sparingly, and I have thought quotation better than comment, but despite the double meagreness I think I have given evidence that *La Wallonie* was worth editing.

It began as *L'Elan Littéraire* with sixteen pages, and an edition of 200 copies; it should convince any but the most stupid that size is not the criterion of permanent value, and that a small magazine may outlast much bulkier printings.

After turning the pages of *La Wallonie*, perhaps after reading even this so brief excerpt, one is ready to see some sense in even so lyric a phrase as "temps doré, de ferveur et de belle confiance".

In their seven years' run these editors, one at least beginning in his "teens", had published a good deal of the best of Verhaeren, had published work by Elskamp, Merrill, Griffin, Louys, Maeterlinck, Verlaine, Van Lerberghe, Gustave Kahn, Moréas, Quillard, André Gide; had been joined in their editing board by De Régnier (remember that they edited in Liége, not in Paris; they were not at the hub of the universe, but in the heart of French Belgium); they had not made any compromise. Permanent literature, and the seeds of permanent literature, had gone through proof-sheets in their office.

There is perhaps no greater pleasure in life, and there certainly can have been no greater enthusiasm than to have been young and to have been part of such a group of writers working in fellowship at the beginning of such a course, of such a series of courses as were implicated in *La Wallonie*.

If the date is insufficiently indicated by Mallarmé's allusion to Whistler, we may turn to the art notes:

"eaux-fortes de Mlle Mary Cassatt...Lucien Pissaro, Sisley...lithographies de Fantin-Latour...Odillon Redon".

"J'ai été un peu à Paris, voir Burne Jones, Moreau, Delacroix...la danse du ventre, et les adorables Javanaises. C'est mon meilleur souvenir, ces filles 'très parées' dans l'étrange demi-jour de leur case et qui tournent lentement dans la stridente musique avec de si énigmatiques inflexions de mains et de si souriantes poursuites les yeux dans les yeux."

Prose poetry, that doubtful connection, appears at times even to advantage:

"Séléné, toi l'essence et le regard des infinis, ton mal nous serait la félicité suprême. O viens à nous, Tanit, Vierge Tanit, fleur métallique épanouie aux plaines célestes!"— *Mockel*.

POSTSCRIPT (anno XII)

Attempts to eliminate a small amount of unnecessary matter from the foregoing notes have not been very successful. There are a couple of pages of quotation no longer necessary to anyone's general knowledge, save in so far as they emphasize the discrepancy between the two zones of writing, and for that I am ready to leave them.

The reader in 1934 will be puzzled by the amount of attention given to Jammes. That belongs to an almost forgotten transition. Perhaps no one who wasn't in London about 1912 will understand one's interest in "that sort of thing". That sort of thing being an attempt to get rid of wooden and rhetorical phraseology. It had begun or had had a new impulse with Madox Ford's *English Review* (1908 to 1910 I think). The young reader will now wonder how Tagore had anything to do with it. This sort of thing belongs to memoirs rather than to analytical criticism. I happen to remember Yeats being very emphatic: "Those ducks are the ducks of real life and not out of literature!" Tagore's word for shawl-tip worn in a particular manner was the precise word in Bengali whatever it ultimately became in later translations. I remember Yeats (at what you would consider the antipodes of Madox Ford's critical disposition): "I have spent the whole of my life trying to get rid of rhetoric". (This must have been along between 1912-18.)

"I have got rid of one kind of rhetoric and have merely set up another." Being a serious character, at least along certain lines, he set about getting rid of THAT.

Chronicles or reports on current publication in Paris implied a very different sort of activity. From 1911 to 1917 or 1918, my sifting out of French verse implied a search for what we didn't know. Writing from Paris after 1920, I was merely reporting on current publication that was good enough to merit interest or respect outside of France. I cannot honestly say that I now recall much more than a few poems of Guy Charles Cros, a half dozen or less by Vlaminck, and Cocteau's general work. The former can be judged from quotation. The discussion of Cocteau would require a very long essay. My meeting with Abbé Rousselot belongs to memoirs. He invented a machine for measuring the length of spoken sounds, that is a machine very useful for getting the facts of quantitative verse disentangled from theory.

GUY CHARLES CROS
(About 1921)

"Je suis seul au milieu de tout comme une pierre au milieu du courant
Qui ne bouge ni à droite ni à gauche et qui reste là cent ans:
Une pierre au milieu de l'eau, de l'eau qui tremble et qui frisonne.
Je n'ai rien qui soit à moi et je ne suis à personne.

Etre tout seul, seul à jamais, le reconnaître et le savoir,
Est-il un rêve qui vaille cette certitude sans espoir?

L'eau qui coule sans remous est lente et profonde —
Ai-je cru un seul instant à la réalité du monde?"

MAURICE VLAMINCK
(About 1921)

Quand Jean Pierre Marie
Fils de Marie Jean Jules Pierre
Vint au monde
Il comprit qu'en somme
C'était une mauvaise affaire
On l'avait invité
Sans lui mettre son couvert
Sa mère était pauvre,
Son père était décédé
Sans rien lui laisser....

Or of Jean-Jules-Marie Pierre:

...Il dit: j'ai de quoi payer!
Entra dans un bistro
Où mangeaient des cochers
Et dégusta du gigot.

En appelant le patron
Il cria: L'addition!
Fier
Sur le zinc,
Il posa sa croix de guerre,
En pensant: ça vaut beaucoup!
Le patron le regarda de travers
— Cette monnaie là, dit-il,
Ne vaut plus rien du tout,
La guerre est finie!
Ça passe pour cette fois-ci
Mais ne reviens pas ici!
Et il ajouta d'un air bonasse:
— Qu'est-ce que tu veux que j'en fasse!

Or Marie:

MARIE

Elle était coquette et pas belle
Elle s'appelait Marie
Comme la Vierge et les bonnes.
Des bonnes s'appellent Marie
La Vierge aussi.
Elle était coquette et pas belle.
Son père était tourneur
Il était mort à la peine
Avant la journée de huit heures.
Sa mère faisait des ménages
Marie ne pensait qu'à l'amour
Toujours.
Ça devait finir très mal pour elle
Elle était coquette et pas belle.
Un matin je l'ai rencontrée
Elle avait beaucoup de chagrin,
Elle était enceinte d'un Américain
Qui reprenait le train.

6

HENRY JAMES AND REMY DE GOURMONT

HENRY JAMES

HENRY JAMES AND REMY DE GOURMONT

I

HENRY JAMES*

This essay on James is a dull grind of an affair, a Baedecker to a continent.

I set out to explain, not why Henry James is less read than formerly—I do not know that he is. I tried to set down a few reasons why he ought to be, or at least might be, more read.

Some may say that his work was over, well over, finely completed; there is mass of that work, heavy for one man's shoulders to have borne up, labour enough for two lifetimes; still we would have had a few more years of his writing. Perhaps the grasp was relaxing, perhaps we should have had no strongly-planned book; but we should have had paragraphs here and there, and we should have had, at least, conversation, wonderful conversation; even if we did not hear it ourselves, we should have known that it was going on somewhere. The massive head, the slow uplift of the hand, *gli occhi onesti e tardi*, the long sentences piling themselves up in elaborate phrase after phrase, the lightning incision, the pauses, the slightly shaking admonitory gesture

* *Little Review*, Aug. 1918.

with its "wu-a-wait a little, wait a little, something will come"; blague and benignity and the weight of so many years' careful, incessant labour of minute observation always there to enrich the talk. I had heard it but seldom, yet it is all unforgettable.

The man had this curious power of founding affection in those who had scarcely seen him and even in many who had not, who but knew him at second hand.

No man who has not lived on both sides of the Atlantic can well appraise Henry James; his death marks the end of a period. *The Times* says: "The Americans will understand his changing his nationality", or something of that sort. The "Americans" will understand nothing whatsoever about it. They have understood nothing about it. They do not even know what they lost. They have not stopped for eight minutes to consider the meaning of his last public act. After a year of ceaseless labour, of letter writing, of argument, of striving in every way to bring in America on the side of civilization, he died of apoplexy. On the side of civilization—civilization* against barbarism, civilization, not Utopia, not a country or countries where the right always prevails in six weeks! After a life-time spent in trying to make two continents understand each other, in trying, and only his thoughtful readers can have any conception of how he had tried, to make three nations intelligible one to another. I am tired of hearing pettiness talked about Henry James' style. The subject has been discussed enough in all conscience, along

---

* 1929. I should probably be incapable of writing this paragraph now. But that is how things looked in 1918 and I see no reason to pretend that I saw them otherwise. I still believe that a Hohenzollern victory would have meant an intolerable post-war world. I think I write this without animus, and that I am quite aware of the German component indispensable to a complete civilization.

with the minor James. Yet I have heard no word of the major James, of the hater of tyranny; book after early book against oppression, against all the sordid petty personal crushing oppression, the domination of modern life; not worked out in the diagrams of Greek tragedy, not labelled "epos" or "Aeschylus". The outbursts in *The Tragic Muse*, the whole of *The Turn of the Screw*, human liberty, personal liberty, the rights of the individual against all sorts of intangible bondage!* The passion of it, the continual passion of it in this man who, fools said, didn't "feel". I have never yet found a man of emotion against whom idiots didn't raise this cry.

And the great labour, this labour of translation, of making America intelligible, of making it possible for individuals to meet across national borders. I think half the American idiom is recorded in Henry James' writing, and whole decades of American life that otherwise would have been utterly lost, wasted, rotting in the unhermetic jars of bad writing, of inaccurate writing. No English reader will ever know how good are his New York and his New England; no one who does not see his grandmother's friends in the pages of the American books. The whole great assaying and weighing, the research for the significance of nationality, French, English, American.

"An extraordinary old woman, one of the few people who are really doing anything good." There were the cobwebs

* This holds, despite anything that may be said of his fuss about social order, social tone. I naturally do not drag in political connotations, from which H. J. was, we believe, wholly exempt. What he fights is "influence", the impinging of family pressure, the impinging of one personality on another; all of them in highest degree damn'd, loathsome and detestable. Respect for the peripheries of the individual may be, however, a discovery of our generation; I doubt it, but it seems to have been at low ebb in some districts (not rural) for some time.

about connoisseurship, etc., but what do they matter? Some yokel writes in the village paper, as Henley had written before, "James' stuff was not worth doing". Henley has gone pretty completely. America has not yet realized that never in history had one of her great men abandoned his citizenship out of shame. It was the last act—the last thing left. He had worked all his life for the nation and for a year he had laboured for the national honour. No other American was of sufficient importance for his change of allegiance to have constituted an international act; no other American would have been welcome in the same public manner. America passes over these things, but the thoughtful cannot pass over them.

Armageddon, the conflict? I turn to James' *A Bundle of Letters*; a letter from "Dr Rudolph Staub" in Paris, ending:

"You will, I think, hold me warranted in believing that between precipitate decay and internecine enmities, the English-speaking family is destined to consume itself and that with its decline the prospect of general pervasiveness to which I allude above, will brighten for the deep-lunged children of the fatherland!"

We have heard a great deal of this sort of thing since; it sounds very natural. My edition of the volume containing these letters was printed in 1883, and the imaginary letters were written somewhat before that. I do not know that this calls for comment. Henry James' perception came thirty years before Armageddon. That is all I wish to point out. Flaubert said of the War of 1870: "If they had read my *Education Sentimentale*, this sort of thing wouldn't have happened". Artists are the antennae of the race, but the bullet-headed many will never learn to trust their great artists. If it is the business of the artist to make humanity aware of itself; here the thing was done, the pages of diagnosis. The multitude of wearisome fools will not learn their right hand from their left or seek out a meaning.

HENRY JAMES AND REMY DE GOURMONT

It is always easy for people to object to what they have not tried to understand.

I am not here to write a full volume of detailed criticism, but two things I do claim which I have not seen in reviewers' essays. First, that there was emotional greatness in Henry James' hatred of tyranny; secondly, that there was titanic volume, weight, in the masses he sets in opposition within his work. He uses forces no whit less specifically powerful than the proverbial "doom of the house"—Destiny, *Deus ex machina*,—of great traditional art. His art was great art as opposed to over-elaborate or over-refined art by virtue of the major conflicts which he portrays. In his books he showed race against race, immutable; the essential Americanness, or Englishness or Frenchness—in *The American*, the difference between one nation and another; not flag-waving and treaties, not the machinery of government, but "why" there is always misunderstanding, why men of different race are not the same.

We have ceased to believe that we conquer anything by having Alexander the Great make a gigantic "joy-ride" through India. We know that conquests are made in the laboratory, that Curie with his minute fragments of things seen clearly in test tubes, in curious apparatus, makes conquests. So, too, in these novels, the essential qualities which make up the national qualities, are found and set working, the fundamental oppositions made clear. This is no contemptible labour. No other writer had so assayed three great nations or even thought of attempting it.

Peace comes of communication. No man of our time has so laboured to create means of communication as did the late Henry James. The whole of great art is a struggle for communication. All things that oppose this are evil, whether they be silly scoffing or obstructive tariffs.

And this communication is not a levelling, it is not an elimination of differences. It is a recognition of differences, of the right of differences to exist, of interest in finding things different. Kultur is an abomination; philology is an abomination, all repressive uniforming education is an evil.

A SHAKE DOWN

I have forgotten the moment of lunar imbecility in which I conceived the idea of a "Henry James" number.* The pile of typescript on my floor can but annoyingly and too palpably testify that the madness has raged for some weeks.

Henry James was aware of the spherical form of the planet, and susceptible to a given situation, and to the tone and tonality of persons as perhaps no other author in all literature. The victim and the votary of the "scene", he had no very great narrative sense, or at the least, he attained the narrative faculty but *per aspera*, through very great striving.

It is impossible to speak accurately of "his style", for he passed through several styles which differ greatly one from another; but in his last, his most complicated and elaborate, he is capable of great concision; and if, in it, the single sentence is apt to turn and perform evolutions for almost pages at a time, he nevertheless manages to say on one page more than many a more "direct" author would convey only in the course of a chapter.

His plots and incidents are often but adumbrations or symbols of the quality of his "people", illustrations invented, contrived, often factitiously and almost transparently, to show what acts, what situations, what contingencies would befit or display certain characters. We are hardly asked to accept them as happening.†

He did not begin his career with any theory of art for art's sake, and a lack of this theory may have damaged his earlier work.

* *Little Review*, Aug. 1918.
† Cf. Stendhal's rather unconvincing apology for the ultimate female in *Le Rouge et le Noir*.

HENRY JAMES AND REMY DE GOURMONT

If we take *French Poets and Novelists* as indication of his then (1878) opinions, and novels of the nineties showing a later bias, we might contend that our subject began his career with a desire to square all things to the ethical standards of a Salem mid-week Unitarian prayer meeting, and that to almost the end of his course he greatly desired to fit the world into the social exigencies of Mrs Humphry Ward's characters.

Out of these unfortunate cobwebs he emerged into his greatness, I think, by two causes: first by reason of his hatred of personal intimate tyrannies working at close range; and secondly, in later life, because the actual mechanism of his scriptorial processes became so bulky, became so huge a contrivance for record and depiction, that the old man simply couldn't remember or keep his mind on or animadvert on anything but the authenticity of his impression.

I take it as the supreme reward for an artist; the supreme return that his artistic conscience can make him after years spent in its service, that the momentum of his art, the sheer bulk of his processes, the (*si licet*) size of his fly-wheel, should heave him out of himself, out of his personal limitations, out of the tangles of heredity and of environment, out of the bias of early training, of early predilections, whether of Florence, A.D. 1300, or of Back Bay of 1872, and leave him simply the great true recorder.

This reward came to Henry James in the ripeness of his talents; even further perhaps it entered his life and his conversation. The stages of his emergence are marked quite clearly in his work. He displays himself in *French Poets and Novelists*, constantly balancing over the question of whether or no the characters presented in their works are, or are not, fit persons to be received in the James family back-parlour.

In *The Tragic Muse* he is still didactic quite openly. The things he believes still leap out nakedly among the people and things he is portraying; the parable is not yet wholly incarnate in the narrative.

HENRY JAMES AND REMY DE GOURMONT

To lay all his faults on the table, we may begin with his self-confessed limitation, that "he never went down town". He displayed in fact a passion for high life comparable only to that supposed to inhere in the readers of a magazine called *Forget-me-not*.

Hardy, with his eye on the Greek tragedians, has produced an epic tonality, and *The Mayor of Casterbridge* is perhaps more easily comparable to the Grettir Saga than to the novels of Mr Hardy's contemporaries. Hardy is, on his other side, a contemporary of Sir Walter Scott.

Balzac gains what force his crude writing permits him by representing his people under the ἀνάγκη of modernity, cash necessity; James, by leaving cash necessity nearly always out of the story, sacrifices, or rather fails to attain, certain intensities.

He never manages the classic, I mean as Flaubert gives us in each main character: *Everyman*. One may conceivably be bored by certain pages in Flaubert, but one takes from him a solid and concrete memory, a property. Emma Bovary and Frederic and M. Arnoux are respectively every woman and every man of their period. Maupassant's *Bel Ami* is not. Neither are Henry James' people. They are always, or nearly always, the bibelots.

But he does, nevertheless, treat of major forces, even of epic forces, and in a way all his own. If Balzac tried to give a whole civilization, a whole humanity, James was not content with a rough sketch of one country.

As Armageddon has only too clearly shown, national qualities are the great gods of the present and Henry James spent himself from the beginning in an analysis of these potent chemicals; trying to determine from the given microscopic slide the nature of the Frenchness, Englishness, Germanness, Americanness, which chemicals too little regarded, have in our time exploded for want of watching. They are the permanent and fundamental hostilities and incompatibles.

HENRY JAMES AND REMY DE GOURMONT

We may rest our claim for his greatness in the magnitude of his protagonists, in the magnitude of the forces he analysed and portrayed. This is not the bare matter of a number of titled people, a few duchesses and a few butlers. Whatever Flaubert may have said about his *Education Sentimentale* as a potential preventive of the débâcle of 1870, *if people had* read it, and whatever Gautier's friend may have said about *Emaux et Camées* as the last resistance to the Prussians, from Dr Rudolph Staub's paragraph in *The Bundle of Letters* to the last and almost only public act of his life, James displayed a steady perception and a steady consideration of the qualities of different Western races, whose consequences none of us can escape.

And these forces, in precisely that they are not political and executive and therefore transient, factitious, but in precisely that they are the forces of race temperaments, are major forces and are indeed as great protagonists as any author could have chosen. They are firmer ground than Flaubert's when he chooses public events as in the opening of the third part of *Education Sentimentale*

The portrayal of these forces, to seize a term from philology, may be said to constitute "original research"—to be Henry James' own addendum; not that this greatly matters. He saw, analysed, and presented them. He had most assuredly a greater awareness than was granted to Balzac or to Mr Charles Dickens or to M. Victor Hugo who composed the *Légende des Siècles*.

His statement that he never went down town has been urged greatly against him. A butler is a servant, tempered with upper-class contacts. Mr Newman, the American, has emerged from the making of wash-tubs; the family in *The Pupil* can scarcely be termed upper-class, however, and the factor of money, Balzac's ἀνάγκη, scarcely enters his stories.

We may leave Hardy writing Sagas. We may admit that there is a greater *robustezza* in Balzac's messiness, simply

HENRY JAMES AND REMY DE GOURMONT

because he is perpetually concerned, inaccurately, with the factor of money, of earning one's exiguous living.

We may admit the shadowy nature of some of James' writing, and agree whimsically with "R. H. C."* (in the *New Age*) that James will be quite comfortable after death, as he had been dealing with ghosts all his life.

James' third donation is perhaps a less sweeping affair and of more concern to his compatriots than to any one who might conceivably translate him into an alien tongue, or even to those who publish his writings in England.

He has written history of a personal sort, social history well documented and incomplete, and he has put America on the map both in memoir and fiction, giving to her a reality such as is attained only by scenes recorded in the arts and in the writing of masters. Mr Eliot has written, and I daresay most other American admirers have written or will write, that, whatever any one else thinks of Henry James, no one but an American can ever know, really know, how good he is at the bottom, how good his "America" is.

No Englishman can, and in less degree can any continental, or in fact any one whose family was not living on, say, West 23rd Street in the old set-back, two-story-porched red brick vine-covered houses, etc., when Henry James was being a small boy on East 23rd Street; no one whose ancestors had not been presidents or professors or founders of Ha'avwd College or something of that sort, or had not heard of a time when people lived on 14th Street, or had known of some one living in Lexington or Newton "Old Place" or somewhere of that sort in New England, or had heard of the New York that produced "Fanny", New York the jocular and uncritical, or of people who danced with General Grant or something of that sort, would quite know *Washington Square* or *The Europeans* to be so autochthonous, so authentic

* Pseudonym used by A. R. Orage.

to the conditions. They might believe the things to be "real", but they would not know how closely they corresponded to an external reality.

Perhaps only an exile from these things will get the range of the other half of James' presentations! Europe to the Transpontine, New York of brown stone that he detested, the old and the new New York in *Crapey Cornelia* and in *The American Scene*, which more than any other volumes give us our peculiar heritage, an America with an interest, with a tone of time not overstrained, not jejunely over-sentimentalized, which is not a re-doing of school histories or the laying out of a fabulous period; and which is in relief, if you like, from Dickens or from Mark Twain's *Mississippi*. He was not without sympathy for his compatriots as is amply attested by Mr and Mrs B. D. Hayes of New York (*vide The Birthplace*) with whom he succeeds, I think, rather better than with most of his princely continentals. They are, at any rate, his bow to the Happy Genius of his country—as distinct from the gentleman who displayed the "back of a banker and a patriot", or the person whose aggregate features could be designated only as a "mug".

In his presentation of America he is greatly attentive, and, save for the people in *Cœur Simple*, I doubt if any writer has done more of "this sort of thing" for his country, this portrayal of the typical thing in timbre and quality—balanced, of course, by the array of spittoons in the Capitol (*The Point of View*).

Still if one is seeking a Spiritual Fatherland, if one feels the exposure of what he would not have scrupled to call, two clauses later, such a wind-shield, *The American Scene* greatly provides it. It has a mermaid note, almost to outvie the warning, the sort of nickel-plate warning which is hurled at one in the saloon of any great transatlantic boat; the awfulness that engulfs one when one comes, for the first time unexpectedly on a pile of all the *Murkhn* magazines laid, shingle-wise on a brass-studded, screwed-into-place, baize-covered steamer table. The first glitter of the national weapons for driving off quiet and all closer signs of intelligence.*

Attempting to view the jungle of the work as a whole, one notes that, despite whatever cosmopolitan upbringing Henry James may have had, as witness *A Small Boy's Memoirs* and *Notes of a Son and Brother*, he nevertheless began in *French Poets and Novelists* with a provincial attitude from which it took him a long time to work free. Secondly, we see various phases of the "style" of his presentation or circumambience.

There is a small amount of prentice work. Let us say *Roderick Hudson, Casamassima*. There are lucky first steps in *The American* and *The Europeans*, a precocity of result, for certainly some of his early work is as permanent as some of the ripest, and more so than a deal of the intervening. We find (for in the case before us criticism must be in large part a weeding-out) that his first subject matter provides him with a number of good books and stories: *The American, The Europeans, Eugene Pickering, Daisy Miller, The Pupil, Brooksmith, A Bundle of Letters, Washington Square, The Portrait of a Lady*, before 1882 and, rather later, *Pandora, The Four Meetings*, perhaps *Louisa Pallant*. He ran out of his first material.

We next note a contact with the *Yellow Book*, a dip into "cleverness", into the epigrammatic genre, the bare epi-

* I differ, beyond that point, with our author. I enjoy ascent as much as I loathe descent in an elevator. I do not mind the click of brass doors. I had indeed for my earliest toy, if I was not brought up in it, the rather slow and well-behaved elevator in a quiet and quietly bright huge sanatorium. The height of high buildings, the chasms of New York are delectable; but this is beside the point; one is not asked to share the views and tastes of a writer.

grammatic style. It was no better than other writers, not so successful as Wilde. We observe him to be not so hard and fine a satirist as is George S. Street.

We come then to the period of allegories (*The Real Thing, Dominick Ferrand, The Liar*). There ensues a growing discontent with the short sentence, epigram, etc., in which he does not at this time attain distinction; the clarity is not satisfactory, was not satisfactory to the author, his *donnée* being radically different from that of his contemporaries. The "story" not being really what he is after, he starts to build up his medium; a thickening, a chiaroscuro is needed, the long sentence; he wanders, seeks to add a needed opacity, he overdoes it, produces the cobwebby novel, emerges or justifies himself in *Maisie* and manages his long-sought form in *The Awkward Age*. He comes out the triumphant stylist in the *American Scene* and in all the items of *The Finer Grain** collection and in the posthumous *Middle Years*.

This is not to damn incontinent all that intervenes, but I think the chief question addressed to me by people of goodwill who do not, but are yet ready and willing to, read James, is: Where the deuce shall I begin? One cannot take even the twenty-four volumes, more or less selected volumes of the Macmillan edition all at once, and it is, alas, but too easy to get so started and entoiled as never to finish this author or even come to the best of him.

The laziness of an uncritical period can be nowhere more blatant than in the inherited habit of talking about authors as a whole. It is perhaps the sediment from an age daft over great figures, or a way of displaying social gush, the desire for a celebrity at all costs, rather than a care of letters.

To talk in any other way demands an acquaintance with

---

* Volume now labelled *Maud Evelyn* in the Macmillan collected edition. The titles in my essay are those of their "New York" edition.

the work of an author, a price few conversationalists care to pay, *ma chè*! It is the man with inherited opinions who talks about "Shelley", making no distinction between the author of the Fifth Act of *The Cenci* and of the *Sensitive Plant*. Not but what there may be a personal *virtù* in an author—appraised, however, from the best of his work when, that is, it is correctly appraised. People ask me what James to read. He is a very uneven author; not all of his collected edition has marks of permanence.

One can but make one's own suggestion:

The American, French Poets and Novelists, The Europeans, Daisy Miller, Eugene Pickering, Washington Square, A Bundle of Letters, Portrait of a Lady, Pandora, The Pupil, Brooksmith, What Maisie Knew, and *The Awkward Age* (if one is "doing it all"), *Europe, Four Meetings, The Ambassadors, The American Scene, The Finer Grain* (all the volume, i.e. "The Velvet Glove", "Mona Montravers", "Round of Visits", "Crapey Cornelia", "Bench of Desolation"), *The Middle Years* (posthumous), *The Ivory Tower* (notes first), and *The Sacred Fount*.

I "go easy" on the more cobwebby volumes; the most Jamesian are indubitably *The Wings of a Dove* and *The Golden Bowl*; upon them devotees will fasten, but the potential devotee may as well find his aptitude in the stories of *The Finer Grain* volume where certain exquisite titillations will come to him as readily as anywhere else. If he is to bask in Jamesian tickle, nothing will restrain him and no other author will to any such extent afford him equal gratifications.

If, however, the reader does not find delectation in the list given above, I think it fairly useless for him to embark on the rest.

Part of James is a caviare, part I must reject according to my lights as bad writing; another part is a *spécialité*, a pleasure for certain temperaments only; the part I have set together above seems to me maintainable as literature. One can definitely say: "this is good"; hold the argumentative field, suffer comparison with other writers; with, say, the Goncourt, or Maupassant. I am not impertinently throwing books on the scrap-heap; there are certain valid objections to James; there are certain standards which one may believe in, and having stated them, one is free to state that any author does not comply with them; granting always that there may be other standards with which he complies, or over which he charmingly or brilliantly triumphs.

James does not "feel" as solid as Flaubert; he does not give us *Everyman*, but, on the other hand, he was aware of things whereof Flaubert was not aware and in certain things supersedes the author of *Madame Bovary*.

He appears at times to write around and around a thing and not always to emerge from the "amorous plan" of what he wanted to present, into definite presentation.

He does not seem to me at all times evenly skilful in catching the intonations of speech. He recalls the New England "a" in the "Lady's" small brothers "Ha-ard" (Hnaah-d) but only if one is familiar with the phonetics described; but (*vide* the beginning of *The Birthplace*) one is not convinced that he really knows (by any sure instinct) how people's voices would sound. Some remarks are in key, some obviously factitious.

He gives us more of his characters by description than he can by any attribution of conversation, save perhaps by the isolated and discreet remarks of Brooksmith.

His emotional centre is in being sensitive to the feel of the place or to the tonality of the person.

It is with his own so beautiful talk, his ability to hear his own voice in the rounded paragraph, that he is aptest to charm one. I find it often, though not universally, difficult to "hear" his characters speaking. I have observed various places where the character notably stops speaking and the author interpolates words of his own; sentences that no one but Henry James could in any circumstances have used.

Beyond which statements I see no great concision or any clarity to be gained by rearranging my perhaps too elliptical comments on individual books.

Honest criticism, as I conceive it, cannot get much further than saying to one's reader exactly what one would say to the friend who approaches one's bookshelf asking: "What the deuce shall I read?" Beyond this there is the "parlour game", the polite essay, and there is the official pronouncement, with neither of which we are concerned.

Of all exquisite writers James is the most colloquial, yet in the first edition of his *French Poets and Novelists*, his style, save for a few scattered phrases, is so little unusual that most of the book seems, superficially, as if it might have been written by almost anyone. It contains some surprising lapses...as bad as any in Mr Hueffer or even in Mr Mencken. It is interesting largely in that it shows us what our subject had to escape from.

Let us grant at once that his novels show him, all through his life, possessed of the worst possible taste in pictures,* of almost as great a lack of taste as that which he attributes to the hackwork and newspaper critiques of Théophile Gautier. Let us admit that "painting" to Henry James probably meant, to the end of his life, the worst possible late Renaissance conglomerations.

Let us admit that in 1876, or whenever it was, his taste in poetry inclined to the swish of De Musset; that it very likely never got any further. By "poetry" he very possibly meant the "high-falutin" and he eschewed it in certain forms; himself taking still higher falutes in a to-be-developed mode of his own.

I doubt if he ever wholly outgrew that conception of the (by him so often invoked) Daughters of Memory. He arrived

---

* 1929. There are, however, signs of personal observation and appreciation of paintings in his sketches of Italy.

truly at a point from which he could look back upon people who "besought the deep blue sea to roll". Poetry to him began, perhaps, fullfledged, springing Minerva-like from the forehead of George Gordon, Lord Byron, and went pretty much to the bad in Charles Baudelaire; it did not require much divination by 1914 (*The Middle Years*) to note that he had found Tennyson rather vacuous and that there "was something in" Browning.

James was so thoroughly a recorder of people, of their atmospheres, society, personality, setting; so wholly the artist of this particular genre, that it was, perhaps, impossible for him ever to hold a critical opinion of art out of key with the opinion about him—except in so far as he might have ambitions for the novel, for his own particular métier. His critical opinions were simply an extension of his being in key with the nice people who "impressed" themselves on his gelatine "plate". (This is a theoretical generalization and must be taken *cum grano*.)

We may, perhaps, take his adjectives on De Musset as a desperate attempt to do "justice" to a man with whom he knew it impossible for him to sympathize. There is, however, nothing to hinder our supposing that he saw in De Musset's "gush" something for him impossible and that he wished to acknowledge it. Side by side with this are the shreds of Back Bay or Buffalo, the mid-week-prayer-meeting point of view.

His most egregious slip is in the essay on Baudelaire, the sentence quoted by Hueffer.* Notwithstanding this, he does effectively put his nippers on Baudelaire's weakness:

"A good way to embrace Baudelaire at a glance is to say that he was, in his treatment of evil, exactly what Hawthorne

---

* "For a poet to be realist is of course nonsense", and, as Hueffer says, such a sentence from such a source is enough to make one despair of human nature.

was not—Hawthorne, who felt the thing at its source, deep in the human consciousness. Baudelaire's infinitely slighter volume of genius apart, he was a sort of Hawthorne reversed. It is the absence of this metaphysical quality in his treatment of his favourite subjects (Poe was his metaphysician, and his devotion sustained him through a translation of 'Eureka!') that exposes him to that class of accusations of which M. Edmond Scherer's accusation of feeding upon *pourriture* is an example; and, in fact, in his pages we never know with what we are dealing. We encounter an inextricable confusion of sad emotions and vile things, and we are at a loss to know whether the subject pretends to appeal to our conscience or—we were going to say—to our olfactories. 'Le Mal?' we exclaim; 'you do yourself too much honour. This is not Evil; it is not the wrong; it is simply the nasty!' Our impatience is of the same order as that which we should feel if a poet, pretending to pluck 'the flowers of good', should come and present us, as specimens, a rhapsody on plum-cake and *eau de Cologne*".

Here as elsewhere his perception, apart from the readability of the work, is worthy of notice.

Hueffer says* that James belauds Balzac. I cannot see it. I can but perceive Henry James wiping the floor with the author of *Eugénie Grandet*, pointing out all his qualities, but almightily wiping the floor with him. He complains that Gautier is lacking in a concern about supernatural hocus-pocus and that Flaubert is lacking. If Balzac takes him to any great extent in, James with his inherited Swedenborgianism is perhaps thereby laid open to Balzac.

It was natural that James should write more about the bulky author of *La Comédie Humaine* than about the others; here was his richest quarry, here was there most to note and to emend and to apply so emended to processes of his own.

* Ford Madox Hueffer's volume on Henry James.

HENRY JAMES AND REMY DE GOURMONT

From Maupassant, the Goncourt or Baudelaire there was nothing for him to acquire.

His dam'd fuss about furniture is foreshadowed in Balzac, and all the paragraphs on Balzac's house-furnishing propensities are of interest in proportion to our interest in, or our boredom with, this part of Henry James' work.

What, indeed, could he have written of the Goncourt save that they were a little dull but tremendously right in their aim? Indeed, but for these almost autobiographical details pointing to his growth out of Balzac, all James would seem but a corollary to one passage in a Goncourt preface:

"Le jour où l'analyse cruelle que mon ami, M. Zola, et peut-être moi-même avons apportée dans la peinture du bas de la société sera reprise par un écrivain de talent, et employée à la reproduction des hommes et des femmes du monde, dans les milieux d'éducation et de distinction—ce jour-là seulement le classicisme et sa queue seront tués....

"Le Réalisme n'a pas en effet l'unique mission de décrire ce qui est bas, ce qui est répugnant....

"Nous avons commencé, nous, par la canaille, parce que la femme et l'homme du peuple, plus rapprochés de la nature et de la sauvagerie, sont des créatures simples et peu compliquées, tandis que le Parisien et la Parisienne de la société, ces civilisés excessifs, dont l'originalité tranchée est faite toute de nuances, toute de demi-teintes, toute de ces riens insaisissables, pareils aux riens coquets et neutres avec lesquels se façonne le caractère d'une toilette distinguée de femme, demandent des années pour qu'on les perce, pour qu'on les sache, pour qu'on les *attrape*—et le romancier du plus grand génie, croyez-le bien, ne les devinera jamais ces gens de salon, avec les *racontars* d'amis qui vont pour lui à la découverte dans le monde....

"Ce projet de roman qui devait se passer dans le grand monde, dans le monde le plus quintessencié, et dont nous rassemblions lentement et minutieusement les éléments

HENRY JAMES AND REMY DE GOURMONT

délicats et fugaces, je l'abandonnais après la mort de mon frère, convaincu de l'impossibilité de le réussir tout seul".

But this particular paragraph could have had little to do with the matter. *French Poets and Novelists* was published in 1878 and Edmond de Goncourt signed the preface to *Les Frères Zemganno* in 1879. The paragraphs quoted are interesting, however, as showing Goncourt's state of mind in that year. He had probably been preaching in this vein long before setting the words on paper, before getting them printed.

If ever one man's career was foreshadowed in a few sentences of another, Henry James' is to be found in this paragraph.

It is very much as if he said: I will not be a megatherium botcher like Balzac; there is nothing to be said about these Goncourt, but one must try to be rather more interesting than they are in, let us say, *Madame Gervaisais*.*

Proceeding with the volume of criticism, we find that "Le Jeune H." simply didn't "get" Flaubert; that he was much alive to the solid parts of Turgenev. He shows himself very apt, as we said above, to judge the merits of a novelist on the ground that the people portrayed by the said novelist are or are not suited to reception into the household of Henry James senior; whether, in short, Emma Bovary or Frederic or M. Arnoux would have spoiled the so delicate atmosphere, have juggled the so fine susceptibilities of a refined 23rd Street family at the time of the Philadelphia "Centennial".

* It is my personal feeling at the moment that *La Fille Elisa* is worth so much more than all Balzac that the things are as out of scale as a sapphire and a plum pudding, and that *Elisa*, despite the dull section, is worth most of James' writing. This is, however, aside from the question we are discussing. 1929. Not having re-read *Elisa* in the interim, this earlier opinion of mine now appears to me gross exaggeration. E. P.

HENRY JAMES AND REMY DE GOURMONT

I find the book not so much a sign that Henry James was "disappointed", as Hueffer puts it, as that he was simply and horribly shocked by the literature of his continental forbears and contemporaries.

It is only when he gets to the Théâtre Français that he finds something which really suits him. Here there is order, tradition, perhaps a slight fustiness (but a quite pardonable fustiness, an arranged and suitable fustiness having its recompense in a sort of spiritual quiet); here, at any rate, was something decorous, something not to be found in Concord or in Albany. And it is easy to imagine the young James, not illuminated by Goncourt's possible conversation or writing, not even following the hint given in his essay on Balzac and Balzacian furniture, but sitting before Madame Nathalie in *Le Village* and resolving to be the Théâtre Français of the novel.

A resolution which he may be said to have carried out to the great enrichment of letters.

Strictures on the work of this period are no great detraction. *French Poets and Novelists* gives us a point from which to measure Henry James' advance. Genius showed itself partly in the escape from some of his original limitations, partly in acquirements. His art at length became "second nature", became perhaps half unconscious; or in part wholly unconscious; in other parts perhaps too highly conscious. At any rate in sunnier circumstances he talked exactly as he wrote, the same elaborate paragraph beautifully attaining its climax; the same sudden incision when a brief statement could dispose of a matter.

Be it said for his style: he is seldom or never involved when a direct bald statement will accurately convey his own meaning, *all of it*. He is not usually, for all his wide leisure, verbose. He may be highly and bewilderingly figurative in his language (*vide* Mr Hueffer's remarks on this question).

HENRY JAMES AND REMY DE GOURMONT

Style apart, I take it that the hatred of tyrannies was as great a motive as any we can ascribe to Galileo or Leonardo or to any other great figure, to any other mythic Prometheus; for this driving force we may well overlook personal foibles, the early Bostonese bias, the heritage from his father's concern in commenting Swedenborg, the later fusses about social caution and conservation of furniture. Hueffer rather boasts about Henry James' innocence of the classics. It is nothing to brag of, even if a man struggling against natural mediaevalism have entrenched himself in impressionist theory. If James *had* read his classics, the better Latins especially, he would not have so excessively cobwebbed, fussed, blathered, worried about minor mundanities. We may *conspuer* with all our vigour Henry James' concern with furniture, the Spoils of Poynton, connoisseurship, Mrs Ward's tea-party atmosphere, the young Bostonian of the immature works. We may relegate these things mentally to the same realm as the author's pyjamas and collar buttons, to his intellectual instead of his physical valeting. There remains the capacious intelligence, the searching analysis of things that cannot be so relegated to the scrap-heap and to the wash-basket.

Let us say that English freedom legally and traditionally has its basis in property. Let us say, à la Balzac, that most modern existence is governed by, or at least interfered with by, the necessity to earn money; let us also say that a Frenchman is not an Englishman or a German or an American, and that despite the remark that the aristocracies of all people, the upper classes, are the same everywhere, racial differences are *au fond* differences; they are likewise major subjects.

Writing, as I am, for the reader of good-will, for the bewildered person who wants to know where to begin, I need not apologize for the following elliptical notes. James, in his prefaces, has written explanation to death (with sometimes a very pleasant necrography). Leaving the *French*

Poets and Novelists, I take the novels and stories as nearly as possible in their order of publication (as distinct from their order as rearranged and partially weeded out in the collected edition*).

1875. (U.S.A.) *A Passionate Pilgrim and other Tales.* Eugene Pickering is the best of this lot and most indicative of the future James. Contains also the title story and *Madame de Mauves*. Other stories inferior.

1876. (U.S.A.) *Roderick Hudson*, prentice work. First novel not up to the level of *Pickering*.

1877. *The American*; essential James, part of the permanent work. *Watch and Ward*, discarded by the author.

1878. *French Poets and Novelists*, already discussed.

1878. *Daisy Miller.* (The big hit and one of his best.) *An International Episode, Four Meetings*, good work.

1880. Short stories first printed in England with additions, but no important ones.

1880. *Confidence*, not important.

1881. *Washington Square*, one of his best, "putting America on the map", giving us a real past, a real background. *Pension Beaurepas* and *Bundle of Letters*, especially the girls' letters, excellent, already mentioned.

1881. *The Portrait of a Lady*, one of his best. Charming Venetian preface in the collected edition.

1884. *Tales of Three Cities*, stories dropped from the collected edition, save *Lady Barbarina*.

1884. *Lady Barbarina*, a study in English blankness comparable to that exposed in the letters of the English young lady in *A Bundle of Letters*. There is also New York of the period.

"But if there was one thing Lady Barb disliked more than another it was describing Pasterns. She had always lived with people who knew of themselves what such a place

---

* Either the New York or present "collected".

would be, without demanding these pictorial effects, proper only, as she vaguely felt, to persons belonging to the classes whose trade was the arts of expression. Lady Barb of course had never gone into it; but she knew that in her own class the business was not to express but to enjoy, not to represent but to be represented."

"Mrs Lemon's recognition of this river, I should say, was all it need have been; she held the Hudson existed for the purpose of supplying New Yorkers with poetical feelings, helping them to face comfortably occasions like the present, and in general, meet foreigners with confidence...."

"He believed, or tried to believe, the *salon* now possible in New York on condition of its being reserved entirely for adults; and in having taken a wife out of a country in which social traditions were rich and ancient he had done something toward qualifying his own house—so splendidly qualified in all strictly material respects—to be the scene of such an effort. A charming woman accustomed only to the best on each side, as Lady Beauchemin said, what mightn't she achieve by being at home—always to adults only—in an easy early inspiring comprehensive way and on the evening of the seven, when worldly engagements were least numerous? He laid this philosophy before Lady Barb in pursuance of a theory that if she disliked New York on a short acquaintance she couldn't fail to like it on a long. Jackson believed in the New York mind—not so much indeed in its literary, artistic, philosophic or political achievements as in its general quickness and nascent adaptability. He clung to this belief, for it was an indispensable neat block in the structure he was attempting to rear. The New York mind would throw its glamour over Lady Barb if she would only give it a chance; for it was thoroughly bright, responsive and sympathetic. If she would only set up by the turn of her hand a blest social centre, a temple of interesting talk in which this charming organ might expand and where she might inhale its fragrance in the most convenient and luxurious way, without, as it was, getting up from her chair; if she would only just try this graceful good-natured experiment—which would make every one like her so much too—he was sure all the wrinkles in the gilded scroll of his fate would be smoothed out. But Lady Barb didn't rise at all to his conception and hadn't the least curiosity about the New York mind. She thought it would be extremely disagreeable to have a lot of people tumbling in on Sunday evening without being invited, and altogether her husband's sketch of the Anglo-American salon seemed to her to suggest crude familiarity, high vociferation—she had already made a remark to him about 'screeching women'—and random extravagant laughter. She didn't tell him—for this somehow it wasn't in her power to express and, strangely enough, he never completely guessed it—that she was singularly deficient in any natural, or indeed, acquired understanding of what a salon might be. She had never seen or dreamed of one— and for the most part was incapable of imagining a thing she hadn't seen. She had seen great dinners and balls and meets and runs and races; she had seen garden-parties and bunches of people, mainly women—who, however, didn't screech— at dull stuffy teas, and distinguished companies collected in splendid castles; but all this gave her no clew to a train of conversation, to any idea of a social agreement that the interest of talk, its continuity, its accumulations from season to season shouldn't be lost. Conversation, in Lady Barb's experience, had never been continuous; in such a case it would surely have been a bore. It had been occasional and fragmentary, a trifle jerky, with allusions that were never explained; it had a dread of detail—it seldom pursued anything very far or kept hold of it very long."

1885. *Stories Revived*, adding to earlier tales *The Author of Beltraffio*, which opens with excess of the treading-on-eggs manner, too much to be borne for twenty-four volumes.

HENRY JAMES AND REMY DE GOURMONT

The pretence of extent of "people" interested in art and letters, *sic*: "It was the most complete presentation that had yet been made of the gospel of art; it was a kind of aesthetic war cry. 'People' had endeavoured to sail nearer 'to truth', etc."

He implies too much of art smeared on limited multitudes. One wonders if the eighties did in any great aggregate gush up to this extent. Doesn't he try to spread the special case out too wide?

The thinking is magnificently done from this passage up to page sixteen or twenty, stated with great concision. Compare it with *Madame Gervaisais* and we find Henry James much more interesting than the Goncourt when on the upper reaches. Compare his expressiveness, the expressiveness of his indirectness with that of constatation. The two methods are curiously mixed in the opening of *Beltraffio*. Such sentences as (page 30) "*He said the most interesting and inspiring things*" are, however, pure waste, pure "leaving the thing undone", unconcrete, unimagined; just simply bad writing or bad novelisting. As for his special case he does say a deal about the author or express a deal by him, but one is bothered by the fact that Pater, Burton, Hardy, Meredith were not, in mere history, bundled into one; that Burton had been to the East and the others had not; that no English novelist of that era would have taken the least notice of anything going on in foreign countries, presumably European, as does the supreme author of *Beltraffio*.

Doubtless he is in many ways the author Henry James would have liked to meet and more illustrative of certain English tones and limitations than any historical portrait might have been. Still Henry James does lay it on—more, I think, than the story absolutely requires. In *Beltraffio* he certainly presents (not that he does not comment to advantage) the two damn'd women appended to the gentlemanly hero of the tale. The most violent post-Strindbergian school would perhaps have called them bitches *tout bonnement*, but this word did not belong to Henry James' vocabulary and besides it is of too great an indistinctness. Author, same "bloody" (in the English sense) author with his passion for "form" appears in *Lesson of Master*, and most of H. J.'s stories of literary *milieux*. Perpetual Grandisonism or Grandisonizing of this author with the passion for form, all of 'em have it. *Ma ché!* There is, however, great intensity in these same "be-deared" and be-"poor-old"-ed pages. He has really got a main theme, a great theme, he chooses to do it in silver point rather than in the garish colours of,—well, of Cherbuliez, or the terms of a religious maniac with three-foot long carving knife.

Novel of the gilded pill, an aesthetic or artistic message, dogma, no better than a moral or ethic one, novel a cumbrous camouflage, substitute not for "that parlour game"* the polite essay, but for the impolite essay or conveyance of ideas; novel to do this should completely incarnate the abstraction.

Finish of *Beltraffio* not perhaps up to the rest of it. Not that one at all knows how else....

Gush on page 42† from both conversationalists. Still an adumbration of the search for the just word emerges on pages 43-44, real cut at barbarism and bigotry on the bottom of page 45 (of course not labelled by these monstrous and rhetorical brands, scorched on to their hides and rump sides). "Will it be a sin to make the most of that one too, so bad for the dear old novel?" Butler and James on the same side really chucking out the fake; Butler focused on Church of England; opposed to him the fakers booming the Bible "as literature" in a sort of last stand, a last ditch; seeing it pretty well had to go as history, cosmogony, etc., or the old tribal

---

* T. S. Eliot's phrase.
† Page numbers in New York edition.

Daddy-slap-'em-with-slab of the Jews as anything like an ideal:

"He told me more about his wife before we arrived at the gate of home, and if he be judged to have aired overmuch his grievance I'm afraid I must admit that he had some of the foibles as well as the gifts of the artistic temperament; adding, however, instantly that hitherto, to the best of my belief, he had rarely let this particular cat out of the bag. 'She thinks me immoral—that's the long and short of it', he said, as we paused outside a moment and his hand rested on one of the bars of his gate; while his conscious, expressive, perceptive eyes—the eyes of a foreigner, I had begun to account them, much more than of the usual Englishman—viewing me now evidently as quite a familiar friend, took part in the declaration. 'It's very strange when one thinks it all over, and there's a grand comicality in it that I should like to bring out. She's a very nice woman, extraordinarily well-behaved, upright and clever and with a tremendous lot of good sense about a good many matters. Yet her conception of a novel—she has explained it to me once or twice, and she doesn't do it badly as exposition—is a thing so false that it makes me blush. It's a thing so hollow, so dishonest, so lying, in which life is so blinked and blinded, so dodged and disfigured, that it makes my ears burn. It's two different ways of looking at the whole affair', he repeated, pushing open the gate. 'And they're irreconcilable!' he added with a sigh. We went forward to the house, but on the walk, halfway to the door, he stopped and said to me: 'If you're going into this kind of thing there's a fact you should know beforehand; it may save you some disappointment. There's a hatred of art, there's a hatred of literature—I mean of the genuine kinds. Oh, the shams—*those* they'll swallow by the bucket!' I looked up at the charming house, with its genial colour and crookedness, and I answered with a smile that those evil passions might exist, but that I should never have expected to find them there. 'Ah, it doesn't matter, after all', he a bit nervously laughed; which I was glad to hear, for I was reproaching myself with having worked him up".

Literature in the nineteenth and the beginning of the twentieth centuries was and is where science was in the days of Galileo and the Inquisition. Henry James not blinking it, neither can we. "Poor dears" and "dear olds" always a little too plentiful.

1885 (continued). *Pandora*, of the best. Let it pass as a sop to America's virginal charm; as counterweight to *Daisy Miller*, or to the lady of *The Portrait*. Henry James alert to the Teuton.

"The process of enquiry had already begun for him, in spite of his having as yet spoken to none of his fellow passengers; the case being that Vogelstein enquired not only with his tongue, but with his eyes—that is with his spectacles —with his ears, with his nose, with his palate, with all his senses and organs. He was a highly upright young man, whose only fault was that his sense of comedy, or of the humour of things, had never been specifically disengaged from his several other senses. He vaguely felt that something should be done about this, and in a general manner proposed to do it, for he was on his way to explore a society abounding in comic aspects. This consciousness of a missing measure gave him a certain mistrust of what might be said of him; and if circumspection is the essence of diplomacy our young aspirant promised well. His mind contained several millions of facts, packed too closely together for the light breeze of the imagination to draw through the mass. He was impatient to report himself to his superior in Washington, and the loss of time in an English port could only incommode him, inasmuch as the study of English institutions was no part of his mission. On the other hand the day was charming; the blue sea, in Southampton Water, pricked all over with light, had no movement but that of its infinite shimmer. Moreover, he was by no means sure that he should be happy in the United States, where doubtless he should find himself soon enough disembarked. He knew that this was not an important question and that happiness was an unscientific term, such as a man of his education should be ashamed to use even in the silence of his thoughts. Lost none the less in the inconsiderate crowd and feeling himself neither in his own country nor in that to which he was in a manner accredited, he was reduced to his mere personality; so that during the hour, to save his importance, he cultivated such ground as lay in sight for a judgment of this delay to which the German steamer was subjected in English waters. Mightn't it be proved, facts, figures and documents—or at least watch—in hand, considerably greater than the occasion demanded?

"Count Vogelstein was still young enough in diplomacy to think it necessary to have opinions. He had a good many, indeed, which had been formed without difficulty; they had been received ready-made from a line of ancestors who knew what they liked. This was of course—and under pressure, being candid, he would have admitted it—an unscientific way of furnishing one's mind. Our young man was a stiff conservative, a Junker of Junkers; he thought modern democracy a temporary phase and expected to find many arguments against it in the great Republic. In regard to these things it was a pleasure to him to feel that, with his complete training, he had been taught thoroughly to appreciate the nature of evidence. The ship was heavily laden with German emigrants, whose mission in the United States differed considerably from Count Otto's. They hung over the bulwarks, densely grouped; they leaned forward on their elbows for hours, their shoulders kept on a level with their ears: the men in furred caps, smoking long-bowled pipes, the women with babies hidden in remarkably ugly shawls. Some were yellow Germans and some were black, and all looked greasy and matted with the sea-damp. They were destined to swell still further the huge current of the Western democracy; and Count Vogelstein doubtless said to himself that they wouldn't improve its quality. Their numbers, however, were striking, and I know not what he thought of the nature of this particular evidence."

For further style in vignette:

"He could see for himself that Mr and Mrs Day had not at all her grand air. They were fat plain serious people who sat side by side on the deck for hours and looked straight before them. Mrs Day had a white face, large cheeks and small eyes; her forehead was surrounded with a multitude of little tight black curls; her lips moved as if she had always a lozenge in her mouth. She wore entwined about her head an article which Mrs Dangerfield spoke of as a 'nuby', a knitted pink scarf concealing her hair, encircling her neck and having among its convolutions a hole for her perfectly expressionless face. Her hands were folded on her stomach, and in her still, swathed figure her bead-like eyes, which occasionally changed their direction, alone represented life. Her husband had a stiff gray beard on his chin and a bare spacious upper lip, to which constant shaving had imparted a hard glaze. His eyebrows were thick and his nostrils wide, and when he was uncovered, in the saloon, it was visible that his grizzled hair was dense and perpendicular. He might have looked rather grim and truculent hadn't it been for the mild familiar accommodating gaze with which his large light-coloured pupils—the leisurely eyes of a silent man—appeared to consider surrounding objects. He was evidently more friendly than fierce, but he was more diffident than friendly. He liked to have you in sight, but wouldn't have pretended to understand you much or to classify you, and would have been sorry it should put you under an obligation. He and his wife spoke sometimes, but seldom talked, and there was something vague and patient about them as if they had become victims of a wrought spell. The spell, however, was of no sinister cast; it was the fascination of prosperity, the confidence of security, which sometimes makes people arrogant, but which had had such a different effect on this simple satisfied pair, in whom further development of every kind appeared to have been happily arrested".

Pandora's approach to her parents:

"These little offices were usually performed deftly, rapidly, with the minimum of words, and when their daughter drew near them, Mr and Mrs Day closed their eyes after the fashion of a pair of household dogs who expect to be scratched".

The tale is another synthesis of some of the million reasons why Germany will never conquer the world.

In describing *Pandora*'s success as "purely personal", Henry James has hit on the secret of the Quattrocento, 1450 to 1550, the vital part of the Renaissance. Aristocracy decays when it ceases to be selective, when the basis of selection is not personal. It is a critical acuteness, not a snobbism, which last is selection on some other principle than that of a personal quality. It is servility to rule-of-thumb criteria, and a dullness of perception, a timidity in acceptance. The whole force of the Renaissance was in the personality of its selection.

There is no faking the amount of perceptive energy concentrated in Henry James' vignettes in such phrases as that on the parents like domestic dogs waiting to be scratched, or in the ten thousand phrases of this sort which abound in his writings. If we were back in the time of Bruyère, we could easily make a whole book of "Characters" from

HENRY JAMES AND REMY DE GOURMONT

Henry James' vignettes.* The vein holds from beginning to end of his work; from this writing of the eighties to *The Ivory Tower*. As for example, Gussie Braddon:
"Rosanna waited facing her, noting her extraordinary perfection of neatness, of elegance, of arrangement, of which it couldn't be said whether they most handed over to you, as on some polished salver, the clear truth of her essential commonness or transposed it into an element that could please, that could even fascinate, as a supreme attestation of care. 'Take her as an advertisement of all the latest knowledges of how to "treat" every inch of the human surface and where to "get" every scrap of the personal envelope, so far as she *is* enveloped, and she does achieve an effect sublime in itself and thereby absolute in a wavering world'."

We note no inconsiderable progress in the actual writing, in *maestria*, when we reach the ultimate volumes.

1886. *Bostonians*. Other stories in this collection mostly rejected from collected edition.

Princess Casamassima, inferior continuation of *Roderick Hudson*. His original subject matter is beginning to go thin.

1888. *The Reverberator*, process of fantasia beginning.

Fantasia of Americans versus the "old aristocracy", *The American* with the sexes reversed. Possibly the theme shows as well in *Les Transatlantiques*, the two methods give one at least a certain pleasure of contrast.

1888. *Aspern Papers*, inferior. *Louisa Pallant*, a study in the maternal or abysmal relation, good James. *Modern Warning*, rejected from New York edition.

* Since writing the above I find that some such compilation has been attempted; had indeed been planned by the anthologist, and, in plan, approved by H. J.: *Pictures and Passages from Henry James*, selected by Ruth Head (Chatto and Windus, 1916), if not exactly the book to convince the rising generation of H. J.'s powers of survival, is at any rate a most charming tribute to our subject from one who had begun to read him in "the eighties".

HENRY JAMES AND REMY DE GOURMONT

1889. *A London Life. The Patagonia.*

The Patagonia, not a masterpiece. Slow in opening, excellent in parts, but the sense of the finale intrudes all along. It seems true but there is no alternative ending. One doubts whether a story is really constructed with any mastery when the end, for the purpose of making it a story, is so unescapable. The effect of reality is produced, of course, by the reality of the people in the opening scene; there is no doubt about that part being "to the life".

The Liar is superb in its way, perhaps the best of the allegories, of the plots invented purely to be an exposition of impression. It is magnificent in its presentation of the people, both the old man and the masterly Liar.

Mrs Temperly is another such excellent delineation and shows James as an excellent hater, but G. S. Street expresses a concentration of annoyance with a greater polish and suavity in method; and neither explains, theorizes, nor comments.

James never has Maupassant's reality by sequence of events. His (H. J.'s) people almost always convince, i.e. we believe implicitly that they exist. We also think that Henry James has made up some sort of story as an excuse for writing his impression of the people.

One sees the slight vacancy of the stories of this period, the short clear sentence, the dallying with *jeu d'esprit*, with epigram no better than, though not inferior to, the run of epigram in the nineties. It all explains James' need of opacity, his reaching out for a chiaroscuro to distinguish himself from his contemporaries and in which he could put the whole of his much more complex apperception.

Then comes, roughly, the period of cobwebs and of excessive cobwebs and of furniture, finally justified in *The Finer Grain*, a book of tales with no mis-fire, and the style so vindicated in the triumphs of the various books of Memoirs and *The American Scene*.

HENRY JAMES AND REMY DE GOURMONT

Fantasias: *Dominic Ferrand, Nona Vincent* (tales obviously aimed at the *Yellow Book*, but seem to have missed it, a detour in James' career). All artists who discover anything make such detours and must, in the course of things (as in the cobwebs), push certain experiments beyond the right curve of their art. This is not so much the doom as the function of all "revolutionary" or experimental art, and I think masterwork is usually the result of the return from such excess. One does not know, simply does not know, the true curve until one has pushed one's method beyond it. Until then it is merely a frontier, not a chosen route. It is an open question, and there is no dogmatic answer, whether an artist should write and rewrite the same story (à la Flaubert) or whether he should take a new canvas.

The Papers, a fantasia, diverting; *The Birthplace*, fairy-godmother element mentioned above, excellent; *Edmund Orme*, inferior; *Yellow Book* tale, not accepted by that periodical.

1889-93. Period of this entoilment in the *Yellow Book*, short sentences, the epigrammatic. He reacts from this into the allegorical. In general the work of this period is not up to the mark. *The Chaperon*, *The Real Thing*, fantasias of "wit". By fantasias I mean sketches in which the people are "real" or convince one of their verity, but where the story is utterly unconvincing, is not intended to convince, is merely a sort of exaggeration of the fitting situation or the situation which ought to result in order to display some type at its apogee. Thus the lady and gentleman models in *The Real Thing*, rather better than other stories in this volume. London society is finely ladled in *The Chaperon*, which is almost as a story, romanticism.

Greville Fane is a scandalous photograph from the life about which the great blagueur scandalously lies in his preface (New York edition). I have been too diverted comparing it with an original to give a sane view of its art.

1890. *The Tragic Muse*, uneven, full of good things but

HENRY JAMES AND REMY DE GOURMONT

showing Henry James in the didactic rôle a little too openly. He preaches, he also displays fine perception of the parochialism of the British political career. It is a readable novel with tracts interpolated. (Excellent and commendable tracts arguing certainly for the right thing, enjoyable, etc.) Excellent text-book for young men with ambitions, etc.

1892. *Lesson of the Master* (cobweb). *The Pupil*, a masterpiece, one of his best and keenest studies. *Brooksmith* of the best.

1893. *The Private Life*. Title story, waste verbiage at the start, ridiculous to put all this camouflage over something *au fond* merely an idea. Not life, not people, allegory, dated to *Yellow Book* era. Won't hold against *Candide*. H. J.'s tilting against the vacuity of the public figure is, naturally, pleasing, i.e. it is pleasing that he should tilt, but the amusement partakes of the nature of seeing coconuts hurled at an aunt sally.

There are other stories, good enough to be carried by H. J.'s best work, not detrimental, but not enough to have "made him": *Europe* (Hawthorny), *Paste*, *The Middle Years*, *Broken Wings*, etc. Part of the great man's work can perhaps only be criticized as "etc."

1895. *Terminations*, *Coxon Fund*, perhaps best of this lot, a disquisition, but entertaining, perhaps the germ of Galsworthy to be found in it (to no glory of either author) as perhaps a residuum of Dickens in Maisie's Mrs Wix. Verbalism, but delightful verbalism in Coxon affair, *sic*:

"Already, at hungry twenty-six, Gravener looked as blank and parliamentary as if he were fifty and popular",

or

"a deeply wronged, justly resentful, quite irreproachable and insufferable person", .

or (for the whole type)

"put such ignorance into her cleverness?"

Miss Anvoy's echo concerning "a crystal" is excellently

introduced, but is possibly in the nature of a sleight of hand trick (contemporary with *Lady Windermere's Fan*). Does H. J.'s "politics" remind one of Dizzy's scribbling, just a little? "Confidence, under the new Ministry, was understood to be reviving", etc.

Perhaps one covers the ground by saying that the James of this period is "light literature", entertaining if one have nothing better to do. Neither *Terminations* nor (1896) *Embarrassments* would have founded a reputation.

1896–7. Improvement through *Other House* and *Spoils of Poynton*. I leave the appreciation of these, to me, detestable works to Mr Hueffer. They seem to me full of a good deal of needless fuss, though I do not mean to deny any art that may be in them.

1897. The emergence in *What Maisie Knew*. Problem of the adolescent female. Carried on in:

1899. *The Awkward Age*, fairy godmother and spotless lamb and all the rest of it. Only real thing the impression of people, not observation or real knowledge. Action only to give reader the tone, symbolizing the tone of the people. Opening *tour de force*, a study in punks, a cheese *soufflé* of the leprous crust of society done to a turn and a niceness save where he puts on the *dolcissimo, vox humana*, stop. James was not the dispassionate observer. He started with the moral obsession; before he had worked clear of it he was entoiled in the obsession of social tone. He has pages of clear depiction, even of satire, but the sentimentalist is always lurking just round the corner. This softens his edges. He has not the clear hardness, the cold satiric justness that G. S. Street has displayed in treating situations, certain struggles between certain idiocies and certain vulgarities. This book is a *specialité* of local interest. It is an *étude* in ephemera. If it contained any revelation in 1899, it no longer contains it. His characters are reduced to the status of *voyeurs*, elaborate analysis of the much too special cases, a bundle of swine and asses who cannot mind their own business, who do not know enough to mind their own business. James' lamentable lack of the classics is perhaps responsible for his absorption in bagatelles.... He has no real series of backgrounds of *mœurs du passé*, only the "sweet dim faded lavender" tune and in opposition to modernity, plush nickel-plated, to the disparagement, naturally, of the latter.

Kipling's "Bigod, I-know-all-about-this" manner, is an annoyance, but one wonders if parts of Kipling by the sheer force of content, of tale to tell, will not outlast most of James' cobwebs. There is no substitute for narrative-sense, however many different and entrancing charms may be spread before us.

The Awkward Age might have been done, from one point of view, as satire, in one-fourth the space. On the other hand, James does give us the subtly graded atmospheres of his different houses most excellently. And indeed, this may be regarded as *his* subject.

If one were advocate instead of critic, one would definitely claim that these atmospheres, nuances, impressions of personal tone and quality *are his subject*; that in these he gets certain things that almost no one else had done before him. These timbres and tonalities are his stronghold, he is ignorant of nearly everything else. It is all very well to say that modern life is largely made up of velleities, atmospheres, timbres, nuances, etc., but if people really spent as much time fussing, to the extent of the Jamesian fuss about such normal, trifling, age-old affairs, as slight inclinations to adultery, slight disinclinations to marry, to refrain from marrying, etc., etc., life would scarcely be worth the bother of keeping on with it. It is also contendable that one must depict such mush in order to abolish it.*

---

* Most good prose arises, perhaps, from an instinct of negation; is the detailed, convincing analysis of something detestable;

HENRY JAMES AND REMY DE GOURMONT

The main feeling in *The Awkward Age* is satiric. The dashes of sentiment do not help the work as literature. The acute observer is often referred to:

Page 131. "The ingenious observer just now suggested might even have detected...."

Page 133. "And it might have been apparent still to our sharp spectator...."

of something which one wants to eliminate. Poetry is the assertion of a positive, i.e. of desire, and endures for a longer period. Poetic satire is only an assertion of this positive, inversely, i.e. as of an opposite hatred.

This is a highly untechnical, unimpressionist, in fact almost theological manner of statement; but is perhaps the root difference between the two arts of literature.

Most good poetry asserts something to be worth while, or damns a contrary; at any rate asserts emotional values. The best prose is, has been a presentation (complicated and elaborate as you like) of circumstances, of conditions, for the most part abominable or, at the mildest, amendable. This assertion of the more or less objectionable only becomes doctrinaire and rotten art when the narrator mis-states from dogmatic bias, and when he suggests some quack remedy (prohibition, Christianity, social theory of one sort or another), the only cure being that humanity should display more intelligence and goodwill than humanity is capable of displaying.

Poetry = Emotional synthesis, quite as real, quite as realist as any prose (or intellectual) analysis.

Neither prose nor drama can attain poetic intensity save by construction, almost by scenario; by so arranging the circumstance that some perfectly simple speech, perception, dogmatic statement appears in abnormal vigour. Thus when Frederic in *L'Education* observes Mme Arnoux's shoe-laces as she is descending the stair; or in Turgenev the quotation of a Russian proverb about the "heart of another", or "Nothing but death is irrevocable" toward the end of *Nichée de Gentilshommes*.

Page 310. "But the acute observer we are constantly taking for granted would perhaps have detected...."

Page 323. "A supposititious spectator would certainly have imagined...." (This also occurs in *Ivory Tower*, page 196.)

This scrutinous person wastes a great deal of time in pretending to conceal his contempt for Mrs Brook, Vanderbank, the other punks, and lays it on so *thick* when presenting his old sentimentalist Longdon, who at the one critical moment behaves *with a stupidity*, with a lack of delicacy, since we are dealing with these refinements. Of course neither this stupidity of his action nor the tone of the other characters would have anything to do with the question of *maestria*, if they *were* dispassionately or impartially rendered. The book is weak because all through it James is so manifestly carrying on a long *tenzone* so fiercely and loudly, a long argument *for* the old lavender. There is also the constant implication that Vanderbank ought to want Nanda, though why the devil he should be supposed to be even mildly under this obligation, is not made clear. A basis in the classics, castor oil, even Stevenson's *Virginibus Puerisque* might have helped matters. One's complaint is not that people of this sort don't exist, that they aren't like everything else a subject for literature, but that James doesn't anywhere in the book get down to bed-rock. It is too much as if he were depicting stage scenery not *as* stage scenery, but as nature.

All this critique is very possibly an exaggeration. Take it at half its strength; I do not intend to defend it.

Epigrammatic manner in opening, compare Kipling; compare Maupassant, superb ideas, verity, fantasia, fantasia group, reality, charming stories, poppycock. *Yellow Book* touches, in *The Real Thing*, general statements about their souls, near to bad writing, perfectly lucid.

Nona Vincent, he writes like an adolescent, might be a person of eighteen doing first story.

Page 201. "Public interest in spiritual life of the army." (*The Real Thing*.)

Page 201. German Invasion.

Loathsome prigs, stiff conventions, editor of cheap magazines ladled in Sir Wots-his-name.

1893. In the interim he had brought out *In the Cage*, excellent opening sentence, matter too much talked around and around, and *The Two Magics*. This last a Freudian affair which seems to me to have attracted undue interest, i.e. interest out of proportion to its importance as literature and *as part of* Henry James' own work, because of its subject matter. The obscenity of *The Turn of the Screw* has given it undue prominence. People now "drawn" by the obscene as were people of Milton's period by an equally disgusting bigotry; one unconscious on author's part; the other, a surgical treatment of a disease. Thus much for progress on part of authors if public has not progressed. The point of my remarks is that an extraneous criterion comes in. One must keep to the question of literature, not of irrelevancies. Galdos' *Lo Prohibido* does Freud long before the sex crank got to it. Kipling really does the psychic, ghosts, etc., to say nothing of his having the "sense of story".

1900. *The Soft Side*, collection containing: *The Abasement of the Northmores*, good; again the motif of the vacuity of the public man, the "figure"; he has tried it in *The Private Life*, which, however, falls into the allegorical. A rotten fall it is too, and Henry James at his worst in it, i.e. the allegorical *Fordham's Castle* appears in the collected edition only—it may belong to this period but is probably earlier, comedietta, excellently, perhaps flawlessly done. Here, as so often, the circumstances are mostly a description of the character, of the personal tone of the "sitters"; for his people are so much more, or so much more often, "sitters" than actors. Protagonists it may be. When they act, they are apt to stage-act, which reduces their action again to being a mere attempt at description. (*The Liar*, for example.) Compare Maupassant's *Toine* for treatment of case similar to *Fordham Castle*.

1902–5. *The Sacred Fount, Wings of a Dove, Golden Bowl* period.

Dove and *Bowl* certainly not models for other writers, a caviare not part of the canon (metaphors be hanged for the moment).

Henry James is certainly not a model for narrative novelists, for young writers of fiction; perhaps not even a subject of study till they have attained some sublimity of the critical sense or are at least ready to be constantly alert, constantly on guard.

I cannot see that he will harm a critic or a describer of places, a recorder of impressions, whether they be of people, places, music.

In *The Sacred Fount* he attains form, perfect form, his form. It is almost the only novel about which he says not a word in his prefaces. Whether or no this was intentional, it seems to be one work that he could afford to sit back, look at, and find completed. I don't in the least imply that he did so.

1903. *Better Sort*, mildish.

1903. *The Ambassadors*, rather clearer than the other work. Etude of Paris versus Woollett. Exhortation to the idle, well-to-do, to leave home.

1907. *The American Scene*, triumph of the author's long practice. A creation of America. A book no "serious American" will neglect. How many Americans make any attempt toward a realization of that country is of course beyond our power to compute. The desire to see the national face in a mirror may be in itself an exotic. I know of no such grave record, of no such attempt at faithful portrayal, as *The American Scene*. Thus America is to the careful observer; this volume and the American scenes in the fiction and memoirs, in *The Europeans, The Patagonia, Washington Square*, etc., bulk large in the very small amount of writing which can be counted as history of *mœurs contemporaines*, of national habit of our time and of the two or three generations preceding us. Newport, the standardized face, the Capitol, Independence Hall, the absence of penetralia, innocence, essential vagueness, etc., language "only definable as not *in intention* Yiddish", the tabernacle of Grant's ashes, the public collapse of the individual, the St Gaudens statue. There is nothing to be gained by making excerpts; the volume is large, but one should in time drift through it. I mean any American with pretences to an intellectual life should drift through it. It is not enough to have perused "The Constitution" and to have "heerd tell" of the national founders.

1910. *The Finer Grain*, collection of short stories without a slip. *The Velvet Glove, Mona Montravers, A Round of Visits* (the old New York versus the new), *Crapey Cornelia, The Bench of Desolation.*

It is by beginning on this collection, or perhaps taking it after such stories as *The Pupil* and *Brooksmith*, that the general literate reader will best come to James, must in brief be convinced of him and can tell whether or not the "marginal" James is for him. Whether or no the involutions of the *Golden Bowl* will titillate his arcane sensibilities. If the reader does not "get" *The Finer Grain* there is no sense in his trying the more elaborate *Wings of a Dove, Sacred Fount, Golden Bowl*. If, on the contrary, he does feel the peculiar, unclassic attraction of the author he may or may not enjoy the uncanonical books.

1911. *The Outcry*, a relapse. Connoisseurship fad again, inferior work.

1913. *A Small Boy and Others*, the beginning of the memoirs. Beginning of this volume disgusting. First three pages enough to put one off Henry James once and for all, damn badly written, atrocious vocabulary. Page 33, a few lines of good writing. Reader might start about here, any reader, that is, to whom New York of that period is of interest. New York of the fifties is significant, in so far as it is typical of what a hundred smaller American cities have been since. The tone of the work shows in excerpts:

"The special shade of its identity was thus that it was not conscious—really not conscious of anything in the world; or was conscious of so few possibilities at least, and these so immediate and so a matter of course, that it came almost to the same thing. That was the testimony that the slight subjects in question strike me as having borne to their surrounding medium—the fact that their unconsciousness could be so preserved...".

Or later, when dealing with a pre-Y.M.C.A. America.

"Infinitely queer and quaint, almost incongruously droll, the sense somehow begotten in ourselves, as very young persons, of our being surrounded by a slightly remote, yet dimly rich, outer and quite kindred circle of the tipsy. I remember how, once, as a very small boy, after meeting in the hall a most amiable and irreproachable gentleman, all but closely consanguineous, who had come to call on my mother, I anticipated his further entrance by slipping in to report to that parent that I thought *he* must be tipsy. And I was to recall perfectly afterwards the impression I so made on her—in which the general proposition that the gentlemen of a certain group or connection might on occasion be best described by the term I had used, sought to destroy the particular presumption that our visitor wouldn't, by his ordinary measure, show himself for one of these. He didn't to all appearance, for I was afterwards disappointed at the lapse of lurid evidence: that memory remained with me, as well as a considerable subsequent wonder at my having leaped to so baseless a view...."

"The grim little generalization remained, none the less, and I may speak of it—since I speak of everything—as still standing: the striking evidence that scarce aught but disaster *could*, in that so unformed and unseasoned society, overtake young men who were in the least exposed. Not to have been immediately launched in business of a rigorous sort was to *be* exposed—in the absence, I mean, of some fairly abnormal predisposition to virtue; since it was a world so simply constituted that whatever wasn't business, or exactly an office or a 'store', places in which people sat close and made money, was just simply pleasure, sought, and sought only, in places in which people got tipsy. There was clearly no mean, least of all the golden one, for it was just the ready, even when the moderate, possession of gold that determined, that hurried on disaster. There were whole sets and groups, there were 'sympathetic', though too susceptible, races, that seemed scarce to recognize or to find possible any practical application of moneyed, that is, of transmitted ease, however limited, but to go more or less rapidly to the bad with it—which meant even then going as often as possible to Paris...."

"The field was strictly covered, to my young eyes, I make out, by three classes, the busy, the tipsy, and Daniel Webster...."

"It has carried me far from my rather evident proposition that if we saw the 'natural' so happily embodied about us—and in female maturity, or comparative maturity, scarce less than in female adolescence—this was because the artificial, or in other words the complicated, was so little there to threaten it...."

On page 72 he quotes his father on "flagrant morality". In Chapter x we have a remarkable portrayal of a character by almost nothing save vacuums,

"timorous philistine in a world of dangers".

HENRY JAMES AND REMY DE GOURMONT

Our author notes the "finer civility" but does not see that it is a thing of no period. It is the property of a few individuals, personally transmitted. Henry James had a mania for setting these things in an era or a "faubourg", despite the continued testimony that the worst manners have constantly impinged upon the most brilliant societies; that decent detail of conduct is a personal talent.

The production of *Il Corteggiano* proves perhaps nothing more than the degree in which Castiglione's contemporaries "needed to be told".

On page 236 (*Small Boy and Others*) the phrase "presence without type".

On page 286, the people "who cultivated for years the highest instructional, social and moral possibilities of Geneva".

Page 283, "discussion of a work of art mainly hung in those days on that issue of the producible *name*".

Page 304, "For even in those days some Americans were rich and several sophisticated".

Page 313, the real give away of W. J. Page 341, Scarification of Ste-Beuve. Page 179, Crystal Palace. Page 214, Social relativity.

One is impatient for Henry James to do people.

A Little Tour in France. The disadvantage of giving impressions of real instead of imaginary places is that they conflict with other people's impressions. I do not see Angoulême via Balzac, nor do I feel Henry James' contacts with the places where our tracks have crossed, very remarkable. I dare say it is a good enough guide for people more meagrely furnished with associations or perceptions. Allow me my *piéton's* shrug for the man who has gone only by train.

HENRY JAMES AND REMY DE GOURMONT

Henry James is not very deep in ancient associations. The American's enjoyment of England in *The Passionate Pilgrim* is more searching than anything continental. Windy generality in *Tour in France*, and perhaps indication of how little Henry James' tentacles penetrated into any era before 1600, or perhaps before 1780.

Vignette bottom of pages 337–8 (*Passionate Pilgrim*) "full of glimpses and responses, of deserts and desolations". "His perceptions would be fine and his opinions pathetic." Commiseration of Searle versus detachment, in *Four Meetings*.

Of the posthumous work, *The Middle Years* is perhaps the most charming. *The Ivory Tower*, full of accumulated perceptions, swift illuminating phrases, perhaps part of a masterpiece. *The Sense of the Past*, less important. I leave my comment of *The Middle Years* as I wrote it, but have recast the analysis of notes to *The Ivory Tower*.

Flaubert is in six volumes, four or five of which every literate man must at one time or another assault. James is strewn over about forty—part of which must go into desuetude, has perhaps done so already.

I have not in these notes attempted the Paterine art of appreciation, e.g. as in taking the perhaps sole readable paragraph of Pico Mirandola and writing an empurpled descant.

The problem—discussion of which is about as "artistic" as a street map—is: can we conceive a five or six volume edition of James so selected as to hold its own internationally? My contention is for this possibility.

My notes are no more than a tentative suggestion, to wit: that some such compact edition might be, to advantage, tried on the less patient public. I have been, alas, no more fortunate than our subject in keeping out irrelevant, non-aesthetic, non-literary, non-technical vistas and strictures.

HENRY JAMES AND REMY DE GOURMONT

THE MIDDLE YEARS

The Middle Years is a tale of the great adventure; for, putting aside a few simple adventures, sentimental, phallic, Nimrodic, the remaining great adventure is precisely the approach to the Metropolis; for the provincial of our race the specific approach to London, and no subject surely could more heighten the pitch of writing than that the treated approach should be that of the greatest writer of our time and of our own particular language. We may, I think, set aside Thomas Hardy as of an age not our own; of perhaps Walter Scott's or of L'Abbé Prévost's, but remote from us and things familiarly under our hand; and we skip over the next few crops of writers as lacking in any comparative interest, interest in a writer being primarily in his degree of sensitization; and on this count we may throw out the whole Wells-Bennett period, for what interest can we take in instruments which must of nature miss two-thirds of the vibrations in any conceivable situation? In James the maximum sensibility compatible with efficient writing was present. Indeed, in reading these pages one can but despair over the inadequacy of one's own literary sensitization, one's so utterly inferior state of awareness; even allowing for what the author himself allows: his not really, perhaps, having felt at twenty-six, all that at seventy he more or less read into the memory of his feeling. The point is that with the exception of exceptional moments in Hueffer,* we find no trace of such degree of awareness in the next lot of writers, or until the first novels of Lewis † and Joyce, whose awareness is, without saying, of a nature greatly different in kind.

The section of reminiscences called *The Middle Years* is not the book for any reader to tackle who has not read a good

---

* F. Madox Ford, name changed by deed poll.
† Wyndham Lewis, author of *Tarr*.

deal of James, or who has not, in default of that reading, been endowed with a natural Jamesian sensibility (a case almost negligible by any likelihood); neither is it a book of memoirs, I mean one does not turn to it seeking information about Victorian worthies; any more than one did, when the old man himself was talking, want to be told anything; there are encyclopedias in sufficiency, and statistics, and human mines of information, boring sufficiency; one asked and asks only that the slow voice should continue—evaluating, or perhaps only tying up the strands of a sentence: "And how my old friend...*Howells*...", etc.

The effects of H. J.'s first breakfasts in Liverpool, or invited upstairs at Half Moon Street, are of infinitely more value than any anecdotes of the Laureate (even though H. J.'s inability not to see all through the Laureate is compensated by a quip melting one's personal objection to anything Tennyson touched, by making him merely an old gentleman whatsoever with a gleam of fun in his make-up).

All comers to the contrary, and the proportionate sale of his works, and statistics whatsoever to the contrary, only an American who has come abroad will ever draw *all* the succulence from Henry James' writings; the denizen of Manchester or Wellington may know what it feels like to reach London, the Londoner born will not be able quite to reconstruct even this part of the book; and if for intimacy H. J. might have stayed at the same hotel on the same day as one's grandfather; and if the same American names had part in one's own inceptions in London, one's own so wholly different and less padded inceptions; one has perhaps a purely personal, selfish, unliterary sense of intimacy: with, in my own case, the vast unbridgeable difference of settling-in and escape.

The essence of James is that he is always "settling-in", it is the ground-tone of his genius.

Apart from the state of James' sensibility on arrival

nothing else matters, the "mildness of the critical air", the fatuity of George Eliot's husband, the illustrational and accomplished lady, even the faculty for a portrait in a paragraph, not to be matched by contemporary effects in halfmetric, are indeed all subordinate to one's curiosity as to what Henry James knew, and what he did not know on landing. The portrait of the author on the cover showing him bearded, and looking rather like a cross between a bishop and a Cape Cod longshoreman, is an incident gratuitous, interesting, but in no way connected with the young man of the text.

The England of a still rather whiskered age, never looking inward, in short, the Victorian, is exquisitely embalmed, and "mounted", as is, I think, the term for microscopy. The book is just the right length as a volume, but one mourns there not being twenty more, for here is the unfinished work... not in *The Sense of the Past*, for there the pen was weary, as it had been in *The Outcry*, and the talent that was never most worth its own while when gone off on connoisseurship, was, conceivably, finished; but here in his depiction of his earlier self the verve returned in full vigour.

THE NOTES TO "THE IVORY TOWER"*

The great artists among men of letters have occasionally and by tradition burst into an *Ars Poetica* or an *Arte nuevo de hacer Comedias*, and it should come as no surprise that Henry James has left us some sort of treatise on novel-writing—no surprise, that is, to the discriminating reader who is *not*, for the most part, a writer of English novels. Various reviewers have hinted obscurely that some such treatise is either adumbrated or concealed in the Notes for *The Ivory Tower* and for *The Sense of the Past*; they have said, indeed, that novelists

---

* Recast from an article in Chas. Granville's magazine, *The Future*.

will "profit greatly", etc., but no one has set forth the gist or the generalities which are to be found in these notes.

Divested of its fine verbiage, of its clichés, of its provincialisms of American phrase, and of the special details relating to the particular book in his mind, the formula for building a novel (any novel, not merely any "psychological" novel); the things to have clearly in mind before starting to write it are enumerated in *The Ivory Tower* notes somewhat as follows:

1. Choice of names for characters; names that will "fit" their owners, and that will not "joggle" or be cacophonic when in juxtaposition on the page.

2. Exposition of one group of characters and of the "situation". (In *The Ivory Tower* this was to be done in three subdivisions. "Book I" was to give the "Immediate Facts".)

3. One character at least is hitched to his "characteristic". We are to have one character's impression on another.

4. (Book III.) Various reactions and interactions of characters.

5. The character, i.e. the main character, is "faced with the situation".

6. For *The Ivory Tower* and probably for any novel, there is now need to show clearly and definitely the "antecedents", i.e. anything that had happened before the story started. And we find Henry James making up his mind which characters have interacted before this story opens, and which things are to be due to fresh impacts of one character on another.

7. Particular consideration of the special case in hand. The working-free from incongruities inherent in the first vague preconceptions of the plot. Thus:

(*a*) The hinge of the thing is not to be the effect of A. on B. or of B. on A.; nor of A. on C. or of C. on B.; but is to be due to an effect all round, of A. and B. and C. working on each other.

(b) James' care not to repeat figures from earlier novels. Not a categoric prohibition, but a caution not to sail too near the wind in this matter.

(c) A care not to get too many "personally remarkable" people, and not enough stupid ones into the story.

(d) Care for the relative "weight" as well as the varied "tone" of the characters.

(We observe, in all this, the peculiarly American passion for "art"; for having a system in things, cf. Whistler.)

(e) Consideration how far one character "faces" the problem of another character's "character".

(This and section (d) continue the preoccupation with "moral values" shown in James' early criticism in *French Poets and Novelists*.)

8. Definite "joints"; or relations of one character to another finally fitted and settled.

This brings us again to point 5. The character, i.e. the main character definitely "faced" with the situation.

9. The consequences.

10. (a) Further consideration of the state of character C. before contact with B., etc.

(b) The effect of further characters on the mind, and thence on the action of A.

(c) Considerations of the effect of a fourth main character; of introducing a subsidiary character, and its effect, i.e. that of having an extra character for a particular function.

11. The great *coup* foreshadowed.

(In this case the mild Othello, more and more drifting consciously into the grip of the mild Iago—I use the terms "Othello" and "Iago" merely to avoid, if not "hero", at least "villain"; the sensitive temperament allowing the rapacious temperament to become effective.)

(a) The main character in perplexity as to how far he shall combat the drift of things.

(b) The opposed character's perception of this.

(These sub-sections are, of course, sub-sections for a psychological novel; one would have different but equivalent "joints" in a novel of action.)

(c) Effect of all this on third character. (In this case female, attracted to "man-of-action" quality.)

(d) A.'s general perception of these things and his weighing of values, a phase solely for the psychological novel.

(e) Weighing of how much A.'s perception of the relations between B. and C. is to be *dénouement*, and how much, more or less, known.

12. Main character's "solution" or vision of what course he will take.

13. The fourth character's "break into" things, or into a perception of things.

(a) Actions of an auxiliary character, of what would have been low life in old Spanish or Elizabethan drama. This character affects the main action (as sometimes a *gracioso* [servant, buffoon, Sancho Panza] affects the main action in a play, for example, of Lope de Vega).

(b) Caution not to let author's interest in fascinating auxiliary character run away with his whole plan and design.

(This kind of restraint is precisely what leaves a reader "wanting more"; which gives a novel the "feel" of being full of life; convinces the reader of an abundant energy, an abundant sense of life in an author.)

14. Effects of course of the action on fourth main character and on the others. The scale being kept by the relation here not being between main character and *one* antagonist, but with a group of three people, relations "different" though their "point" is the same; cf. a "main character" versus a Rosenkrantz and Guildenstern, or "attendant lords". James always has half an eye on play construction; the scene.

(a) The second auxiliary character brought out more definitely. (This is accidental. It might happen at any suitable point in a story wherever needed.)

(b) Act of this auxiliary person reaches through to main action.

15. We see the author determining just how bad a case he is going to make his villain.

(a) Further determination of his hero. (In this case an absolute non-producer, non-accumulator.)

(b) Care not to get an unmixed "bad" in his "villain", but to keep a right balance, a dependency, in this case, on the main character's weakness or easiness.

(c) Decision how the main *coup* or transfer shall slide through.

16. Effect upon C. Effect upon main character's relations to D., E. and F.

At this point, in the consideration of eight of the ten "books" of his novel, we see the author most intent on his composition or architecture, most anxious to get all the sections fitted in with the greatest economy, a sort of crux of his excitement and anxiety, a fullness of his perception that the thing must be so tightly packed that no sentence can afford to be out of place.

17. Climax. The *Deus* or, in this case, *Dea, ex machina*. Devices for prolonging climax. The fourth main character having been, as it were, held back for a sort of weight or balance here, and as a "resolution" of the tangles.

Finis.

18. Author's final considerations of time scheme, i.e. fitting the action into time not too great for unity, and great enough to allow for needed complexity. Slighter consideration of place scheme; where final scenes shall be laid, etc.

Here in a few paragraphs are the bare bones of the plan described in eighty of Henry James' pages. The detailed thoroughness of this plan, the complicated consciousness displayed in it, gives us the measure of this author's superiority, as conscious artist, over the "normal" British novelist, i.e.

over the sort of person who tells you that when he did his first book he "just sat down and wrote the first paragraph", and then found he "couldn't stop". This he tells you in a manner clearly implying that, from that humble beginning to the shining hour of the present, he has given the matter no further thought, and that his succeeding works were all knocked off with equal simplicity.

I give this outline with such fullness because it is a landmark in the history of the novel as written in English. It is inconceivable that Fielding or Richardson should have left, or that Thomas Hardy should leave, such testimony to a comprehension of the novel as a "form". The Notes are, on the other hand, quite distinct from the voluminous prefaces which so many French poets write before they have done anything else. James, we note, wrote no prefaces until there were twenty-four volumes of his novels and stories waiting to be collected and republished. The Notes are simply the accumulation of his craftsman's knowledge, they are, in all their length, the summary of the things he would have, as a matter of habit, in his mind before embarking on composition.

I take it rather as a sign of editorial woodenheadedness that these Notes are printed at the *end* of *The Ivory Tower*; if one have sense enough to suspect that the typical mentality of the elderly heavy reviewer has been shown, one will for oneself reverse the order; read the notes with interest and turn to the text already with the excitement of the sport or with the zest to see if, with this chance of creating the masterpiece so outlined, the distinguished author is going to make good. If on the other hand one reads the unfinished text, there is no escaping the boredom of re-reading in skeleton, with tentative and confusing names, the bare statement of what has been, in the text, more fully set before us.

The text is attestation of the rich, banked-up perception of the author. I dare say the snap and rattle of the fun, or much of it, will be only half perceptible to those who do not know both banks of the Atlantic; but enough remains to show the author at his best; despite the fact that occasionally he puts in the mouths of his characters sentences or phrases that no one but he himself could have used. I cannot attribute this to the unfinished state of the manuscript. These oversights are few, but they are the kind of slip which occurs in his earlier work. We note also that his novel is a descriptive novel, not a novel that simply depicts people speaking and moving. There is a constant dissertation going on, and in it is our major enjoyment.

The Notes to *The Sense of the Past* are not so fine a specimen of method, they are the plan not of a whole book, but only of the latter section. The editor is quite right to print them at the end of the volume.

Of the actual writing in the three posthumous books, far the most charming is to be found in *The Middle Years*...inn-rooms, breakfasts, butlers.... There is no need for its being "memoirs" at all; call the protagonist Mr Ponsonby or Mr Hampton, obliterate the known names of celebrities and half celebrities, and the whole thing becomes a James novel, and, so far as it goes, a mate to the best of them.

Retaining the name of the author, any faithful reader of James, or at any rate the attentive student, finds a good deal of amusement in deciphering the young James, his temperament as mellowed by recollection and here recorded forty years later, and then in contrasting it with the young James as revealed or even "betrayed" in his own early criticisms, *French Poets and Novelists*, a much cruder and more savagely puritanical and plainly New England product with, however, certain permanent traits of his character already in evidence, and with a critical faculty keen enough to hit on certain weaknesses in the authors analysed, often with profundity, and with often a "rightness" in his mistakes. I mean that apparent errors are at times only an excess of zeal, an overshooting of his mark, which was to make for an improvement, by him, of certain defects.

The prefaces are a special study belonging chronologically to the date of the New York edition with the Coburn photos, and the memory of his having travelled about with the photographer. I intended my notes as a study of H. J.'s art in the novel, not as a critique of his own criticism; though I seem to have neglected to say so. There is a marvellous passage on Ninevites in the Preface to *Lady Barberina*, and in another place he had already written his defence against charges which had been levelled at him and which I reiterate on p. 276, saying that if such people don't exist we ought at least, for the honour of the race, to pretend that they do.

II

REMY DE GOURMONT

A DISTINCTION

followed by notes

The mind of Rémy de Gourmont was less like the mind of Henry James than any contemporary mind I can think of. James' drawing of *mœurs contemporaines* was so circumstantial, so concerned with the setting, with detail, nuance, social aroma, that his transcripts were "out of date" almost before his books had gone into a second edition; out of date that is, in the sense that his interpretations of society could never serve as a guide to such supposititious utilitarian members of the next generation as might so desire to use them.

He has left his scene and his characters, unalterable as the little paper flowers permanently visible inside the lumpy glass paperweights. He was a great man of letters, a great artist in portrayal; he was concerned with mental temperatures, circumvolvulous social pressures, the clash of contending conventions, as Hogarth with the cut of contemporary coats.

On no occasion would any man of my generation have broached an intimate idea to H. J., or to Thomas Hardy, O.M., or, years since, to Swinburne, or even to Mr Yeats with any feeling that the said idea was likely to be received, grasped, comprehended. However much one may have admired Yeats' poetry; however much one may have been admonished by Henry James' prose works, one has never thought of agreeing with either.

You could, on the other hand, have said to Gourmont anything that came into your head; you could have sent him anything you had written with a reasonable assurance that he would have known what you were driving at. If this distinction is purely my own, and subjective, and even if it be wholly untrue, one will be very hard pressed to find any other man born in the "fifties" of whom it is even suggestible.

Gourmont prepared our era; behind him there stretches a limitless darkness; there *was* the counter-reformation, still extant in the English printer; there *was* the restoration of the Inquisition by the Catholic Roman Church, holy and apostolic, in the year of grace 1824; there was the Mephistopheles period, morals of the opera left over from the Spanish seventeenth-century plays of "capa y espada"; Don Juan for subject matter, etc.; there was the period of English Christian bigotry, Saml. Smiles, exhibition of 1851 ("Centennial of 1876"), machine-made building "ornament", etc., enduring in the people who did not read Saml. Butler; there was the Emerson-Tennysonian plus optimism period; there was the "aesthetic" era during which people "wrought" as the impeccable Beerbohm has noted; there was the period of funny symboliste trappings, "sin", satanism, rosy cross, heavy lilies, Jersey Lilies, etc.,

"Ch' hanno perduto il ben dell' intelletto";

all these periods had mislaid the light of the eighteenth century; though in the symbolistes Gourmont had his beginning.

In contradiction to, in wholly antipodal distinction from, Henry James, Gourmont was an artist of the nude. He was an intelligence almost more than an artist; when he portrays, he is concerned with hardly more than the permanent human elements. His people are only by accident of any particular era. He is poet, more by possessing a certain quality of mind than by virtue of having written fine poems; you could scarcely contend that he was a novelist.

He was intensely aware of the differences of emotional timbre; and as a man's message is precisely his *façon de voir*, his modality of apperception, this particular awareness was his "message".

Where James is concerned with the social tone of his subjects, with their entourage, with their *superstes* of dogmatized "form", ethic, etc., Gourmont is concerned with their modality and resonance in emotion.

Mauve, Fanette, Neobelle, La Vierge aux Plâtres, are all studies in different *permanent* kinds of people; they are not the results of environments or of "social causes", their circumstance is an accident and is on the whole scarcely alluded to. Gourmont differentiates his characters by the modes of their sensibility, not by sub-degrees of their state of civilization.

He recognizes the right of individuals to *feel* differently. Confucian, Epicurean, a considerer and entertainer of ideas, this complicated sensuous wisdom is almost the one ubiquitous element, the "self" which keeps his superficially heterogeneous work vaguely "unified".

The study of emotion does not follow a set chronological arc; it extends from the *Physique de l'Amour* to *Le Latin Mystique*; from the condensation of Fabre's knowledge of insects to

"Amas ut facias pulchram"

in the Sequaire of Goddeschalk (*Le Latin Mystique*).

He had passed the point where people take abstract statement of dogma for "enlightenment". An "idea" has little value apart from the modality of the mind which receives it. It is a railway from one state to another, and as dull as steel rails in a desert.

HENRY JAMES AND REMY DE GOURMONT

The emotions are equal before the aesthetic judgment. He does not grant the duality of body and soul, or at least suggests that this mediaeval duality is unsatisfactory; there is an interpenetration, an osmosis of body and soul, at least for hypothesis.

"My words are the unspoken words of my body."

And in all his exquisite treatment of all emotion he will satisfy many whom August Strindberg, for egregious example, will not. From the studies of insects to Christine evoked from the thoughts of Diomède, sex is not a monstrosity or an exclusively German study.* And the entire race is not bound to the habits of the *mantis* or of other insects equally melodramatic. Sex, in so far as it is not a purely physiological reproductive mechanism, lies in the domain of aesthetics, the junction of tactile and magnetic senses; as some people have accurate ears both for rhythm and for pitch, and as some are tone deaf, some impervious to rhythmic subtlety and variety, so in this other field of the senses some desire the trivial, some the processional, the stately, the master-work.

As some people are good judges of music, and insensible to painting and sculpture, so the fineness of one sense may entail no corresponding fineness in another, or at least no corresponding critical perception of differences.

Emotions to Henry James were more or less things that other people had and that one didn't go into; at any rate not in drawing rooms. The gods had not visited James, and the Muse, whom he so frequently mentions, appeared doubtless in corsage, the narrow waist, the sleeves puffed at the shoulders, *à la mode* 1890-2.

* "A German study, Hobson, A German study!" *Tarr.*

Gourmont is interested in hardly anything save emotions and the ideas that will go into them, or take life in emotional application. (Apperceptive rather than active.)

One reads *Les Chevaux de Diomède* (1897) as one would have listened to incense in the old Imperial court. There are many spirits incapable. Gourmont calls it a "romance of possible adventures"; it might be called equally an aroma, the fragrance of roses and poplars, the savour of wisdoms, not part of the canon of literature, a book like *Daphnis and Chloe* or like Marcel Schwob's *Livre de Monelle*; not a solidity like Flaubert; but a pervasion.

"My true life is in the unspoken words of my body."

In *Une Nuit au Luxembourg*, the characters talk at more length, and the movement is less convincing. *Diomède* was Gourmont's own favourite and we may take it as the best of his art, the most complete expression of his particular "façon d'apercevoir"; if, even in it, the characters do little but talk philosophy, or drift into philosophic expression out of a haze of images, they are for all that very real. It is the climax of his method of presenting characters differentiated by emotional timbre, a process which had begun in *Histoires Magiques* (1895); and in *D'un Pays Lointain* (published 1898, in reprint from periodicals of 1892-4).

Songe d'une Femme (1899) is a novel of modern life, Gourmont's sexual intelligence, as contrasted to Strindberg's sexual stupidity well in evidence. The work is untranslatable into English, but should be used before thirty by young men who have been during their undergraduate days too deeply inebriated with the *Vita Nuova*.

"Tout ce qui se passe dans la vie, c'est de la mauvaise littérature."

"La vraie terre natale est celle où on a eu sa première émotion forte."

HENRY JAMES AND REMY DE GOURMONT

"La virginité n'est pas une vertu, c'est un état; c'est une sous-division des couleurs."
Livres de chevet for those whom the Strindbergian school will always leave aloof.
"Les imbéciles ont choisi le beau comme les oiseaux choisissent ce qui est gras. La bêtise leur sert de cornes."

Cœur Virginal (1907) is a light novel, amusing, and accurate in its psychology.
I do not think it possible to overemphasize Gourmont's sense of beauty. The mist clings to the lacquer. His spirit was the spirit of Omakitsu; his *pays natal* was near to the peach-blossom-fountain of the untranslatable poem. If the life of Diomède is overdone and done badly in modern Paris, the wisdom of the book is not thereby invalidated. It may be that Paris has need of some more Spartan corrective, but for the descendants of witch-burners Diomède is a needful communication.

As Voltaire was a needed light in the eighteenth century, so in our time Fabre and Frazer have been essentials in the mental furnishings of any contemporary mind qualified to write of ethics or philosophy or that mixed molasses religion. *The Golden Bough* has supplied the data which Voltaire's incisions had shown to be lacking. It has been a positive succeeding his negative. It is not necessary perhaps to read Fabre and Frazer entire, but one must be aware of them; people unaware of them invalidate all their own writing by simple ignorance, and their work goes ultimately to the scrap heap.
Physique de L'Amour (1903) should be used as a text-book of biology. Between this biological basis in instinct, and the "Sequaire of Goddeschalk" in *Le Latin Mystique* (1892) stretch Gourmont's studies of amour and aesthetics. In Diomède we find an Epicurean receptivity, a certain aloof-

ness, an observation of contacts and auditions, in contrast to the Propertian attitude:

> "Ingenium nobis ipsa puella fecit",

this is perhaps balanced by

> "Sans vous, je crois bien que je n'aimerais plus beaucoup et que je n'aurais plus une extrême confiance ni dans la vie ni moi-même". (In *Lettres à l'Amazone*.)

But there is nothing more unsatisfactory than saying that Gourmont "had such and such ideas" or held "such and such views", the thing is that he held ideas, intuitions, perceptions in a certain personal exquisite manner. In a criticism of him, "criticism" being an over-violent word, in, let us say, an indication of him, one wants merely to show that one has oneself made certain dissociations; as here, between the aesthetic receptivity of tactile and magnetic values, of the perception of beauty in these relationships, and the conception of love, passion, emotion as an intellectual instigation; such as Propertius claims it; such as we find it declared in the King of Navarre's

> "De fine amor vient science et beauté";

and constantly in the troubadours.

(I cannot repeat too often that there was a profound psychological knowledge in mediaeval Provence, however Gothic its expression; that men, concentrated on certain validities, attaining an exact and diversified terminology, have there displayed considerable penetration; that this was carried into early Italian poetry; and faded from it when metaphors became decorative instead of interpretative; and that the age of Aquinas would not have tolerated sloppy expression of psychology concurrent with the exact expression of "mysticism". There is also great wisdom in Ovid. *Passons!*)

HENRY JAMES AND REMY DE GOURMONT

Gourmont's wisdom is not wholly unlike the wisdom which those ignorant of Latin may, if the gods favour their understanding, derive from Golding's *Metamorphoses*.

Barbarian ethics proceed by general taboos. Gourmont's essays collected into various volumes, *Promenades*, *Epilogues*, etc., are perhaps the best introduction to the ideas of our time that any unfortunate, suddenly emerging from Peru, Peoria, Oshkosh, Iceland, Kochin, or other out-of-the-way lost continent could desire. A set of Landor's collected works will go further towards civilizing a man than any university education now on the market. Montaigne condensed Renaissance awareness. Even so small a collection as Lionel Johnson's *Post Liminium* might save a man from utter barbarity.

But if, for example, a raw graduate were contemplating a burst into intellectual company, he would be less likely to utter unutterable *bêtises*, *gaffes*, etc., after reading Gourmont than before. One cannot of course create intelligence in a numbskull.

Needless to say, Gourmont's essays are of uneven value as the necessary subject matter is of uneven value. Taken together, proportionately placed in his work, they are a portrait of the civilized mind. I incline to think them the best portrait available, the best record that is, of the civilized mind from 1885–1915.

There are plenty of people who do not know what the civilized mind is like, just as there were plenty of mules in England who did not read Landor contemporaneously, or who did not in his day read Montaigne. Civilization is individual.

Gourmont arouses the senses of the imagination, preparing the mind for receptivities. His wisdom, if not of the senses, is at any rate viâ the senses. We base our "science" on perceptions, but our ethics have not yet attained this palpable basis.

In 1898, *Pays Lointain* (reprinted from magazine publication of 1892-4), Gourmont was beginning his method:
"Douze crimes pour l'honneur de l'infini".

He treats the special case, cases as special as any of James', but segregated on different demarcative lines. His style had attained the vividness of
"Sa vocation était de paraître malheureuse, de passer dans la vie comme une ombre gémissante, d'inspirer de la pitié, du doute et de l'inquiétude. Elle avait toujours l'air de porter des fleurs vers une tombe abandonnée". *La Femme en Noir.*

In *Histoires Magiques* (1894): *La Robe Blanche, Yeux d'eau, Marguerite Rouge, Sœur de Sylvie, Danaette,* are all of them special cases, already showing his perception of nevrosis, of hyperaesthesia. His mind is still running on tonal variations in *Les Litanies de la Rose.*

"Pourtant il y a des yeux au bout des doigts."
"Femmes, conservatrices des traditions milésiennes."

Epilogues (1895-8). Pleasant re-reading, a book to leave lying about, to look back into at odd half hours. A book of accumulations. Full of meat as a good walnut.

Heterogeneous as the following paragraphs:

"Ni la croyance en un seul Dieu, ni la morale ne sont les fondements vrais de la religion. Une religion, même le Christianisme, n'eut jamais sur les mœurs qu'une influence dilatoire, l'influence d'un bras levé; elle doit recommencer son prêche, non pas seulement avec chaque génération humaine, mais avec chaque phase d'une vie individuelle. N'apportant pas des vérités évidentes en soi, son enseignement oublié, elle ne laisse rien dans les âmes que l'effroi du peut-être et la honte d'être asservi à une peur ou à une espérance dont les chaînes fantômales entravent non pas nos actes mais nos désirs.

"L'essence d'une religion, c'est sa littérature. Or la littérature religieuse est morte." *Religions.*

"Je veux bien que l'on me protège contre des ennemis inconnus, l'escarpe ou le cambrioleur—mais contre moi-même, vices ou passions, non." *Madame Boulton.*

"Si le cosmopolitisme littéraire gagnait encore et qu'il réussît à éteindre ce que les différences de race ont allumé de haine de sang parmi les hommes, j'y verrais un gain pour la civilisation et pour l'humanité tout entière." *Cosmopolitisme.*

"Augier! Tous les lucratifs rêves de la bourgeoise économe; tous les soupirs des vierges confortables; toutes les réticences des consciences soignées; toutes les joies permises aux ventres prudents; toutes les veuleries des bourses craintives; tous les siphons conjugaux; toutes les envies de la robe montante contre les épaules nues; toutes les haines du waterproof contre la grâce et contre la beauté! Augier, crinoline, parapluie, bec-de-corbin, bonnet grec...." *Augier.*

"Dieu aime la mélodie grégorienne, mais avec modération. Il a soin de varier le programme quotidien des concerts célestes, dont le fond reste le plain-chant liturgique, par des auditions de Bach, Mozart, Haendel, Haydn, 'et même Gounod'. Dieu ignore Wagner, mais il aime la variété." *Le Dieu des Belges.*

"La propriété n'est pas sacrée; elle n'est qu'un fait acceptable comme nécessaire au développement de la liberté individuelle.

. . . . . .

"L'abominable loi des cinquantes ans—contre laquelle Proudhon lutta en vain si courageusement—commence à faire sentir sa tyrannie. La veuve de M. Dumas a fait interdire la reprise d'Antony. Motif: son bon plaisir. Des caprices d'héritiers peuvent d'un jour à l'autre nous priver pendant cinquante ans de toute une œuvre.

. . . . . .

"Demain les œuvres de Renan, de Taine, de Verlaine, de Villiers peuvent appartenir à un curé fanatique ou à une dévote stupide." *La Propriété Littéraire.*

"M. Desjardins, plus modeste, inaugure la morale artistique et murale, secondé par l'excellent M. Puvis de Chavannes qui n'y comprend rien, mais s'avoue tout de même bien content de figurer sur les murs." *U.P.A.M.*

"Les auteurs, 'avertis par le Public....' Il y a dans ces mots toute une esthétique, non seulement dramatique, mais démocratique. Plus d'insuccès. Plus de fours. Admirable invention par laquelle, sans doute, le peuple trouvera enfin l'art qui lui convient et les auteurs qu'il mérite." *Conscience Littéraire.*

"Le citoyen est une variété de l'homme; variété dégénérée ou primitive il est à l'homme ce que le chat de gouttière est au chat sauvage.

. . . . .

"Comme toutes les créations vraiment belles et noblement utiles, la sociologie fut l'œuvre d'un homme de génie, M. Herbert Spencer, et le principe de sa gloire.

. . . . .

"La saine Sociologie traite de l'évolution à travers les âges d'un groupe de métaphores, Famille, Patrie, Etat, Société, etc. Ces mots sont de ceux que l'on dit collectifs et qui n'ont en soi aucune signification, l'histoire les a employés de tous temps, mais la Sociologie, par d'astucieuses définitions précise leur néant tout en propageant leur culte.

"Car tout mot collectif, et d'abord ceux du vocabulaire sociologique sont l'objet d'un culte. A la Famille, à la Patrie, à l'Etat, à la Société, on sacrifie des citoyens mâles et des citoyens femelles; les mâles en plus grand nombre; ce n'est que par intermède, en temps de grève ou d'émeute, pour essayer un nouveau fusil que l'on perfore des femelles; elles offrent au coup une cible moins défiante et plus plaisante;

ce sont là d'inévitables petits incidents de la vie politique.
Le mâle est l'hostie ordinaire.

. . . . . .

"Le caractère fondamental du citoyen est donc le dévouement, la résignation et la stupidité; il exerce principalement ces qualités selon trois fonctions physiologiques, comme animal reproducteur, comme animal électoral, comme animal contribuable.

. . . . . .

"Devenu animal électoral, le citoyen n'est pas dépourvu de subtilité. Ayant flairé, il distingue hardiment entre un opportuniste et un radical. Son ingéniosité va jusqu'à la méfiance: le mot Liberté le fait aboyer, tel un chien perdu. A l'idée qu'on va le laisser seul dans les ténèbres de sa volonté, il pleure, il appelle sa mère, la République, son père, l'Etat.

. . . . . .

"Du fond de sa grange ou de son atelier, il entretient volontiers ceux qui le protègent contre lui-même.

. . . . . .

"Et puis songe: si tu te révoltais, il n'y aurait plus de lois, et quand tu voudrais mourir, comment ferais-tu, si le régistre n'était plus là pour accueillir ton nom?" *Paradoxes sur le Citoyen.*

"Si l'on est porté à souhaiter un déraillement, il faut parler, il faut écrire, il faut sourire, il faut s'abstenir—c'est le grand point de toute vie civique. Les actuelles organisations sociales ont cette tare fondamentale que l'abstention légale et silencieuse les rend inermes et ridicules. Il faut empoisonner l'Autorité, lentement, en jouant. C'est si charmant de jouer et si utile au bon fonctionnement humain! Il faut se moquer. Il faut passer, l'ironie dans les yeux, à travers les mailles des lois anti-libérales, et quand on promène à travers nos vignes, gens de France, l'idole gouvernementale, gardez-vous d'aucun acte vilain, des gros mots, des violences—rentrez chez vous, et mettez les volets. Sans avoir rien fait que de très simple et de très innocent vous vous réveillerez plus libres le lendemain." *Les Faiseurs de Statues.*

"Charmant Tzar, tu la verras chez toi, la Révolution, stupide comme le peuple et féroce comme la bourgeoisie; tu la verras, dépassant en animalité et en rapacité sanglante tout ce qu'on t'a permis de lire dans les tomes expurgés qui firent ton éducation." *Le Délire Russe.*

"Or un écrivain, un poète, un philosophe, un homme des régions intellectuelles n'a qu'une patrie: sa langue." *Querelles de Belgique.*

"Il faut encore, pour en revenir aux assassins, noter que le crime, sauf en des rares cas passionnels, est le moyen et non le but." *Crimes.*

"Le vers traditionnel est patriotique et national; le vers nouveau est anarchiste et sans patrie. Il semble que la rime riche fasse partie vraiment de la richesse nationale: on vole quelque chose à l'Etat en adoucissant la sonorité des ronrons: 'La France, Messieurs, manque de consonnes d'appui!' D'autre part, l'emploi de l'assonance a quelque chose de rétrograde qui froisse les vrais démocrates.

. . . . . .

"Il est amusant de voir des gens qui ne doivent leur état 'd'hommes modernes' qu'à la fauchaison brutale de toutes les traditions Françaises, protester aussi sottement contre des innovations non seulement logiques, mais inévitables. Ce qui donne quelque valeur à leur acrimonie, c'est qu'ils ignorent tout de cette question si complexe; de là leur liberté critique, n'ayant lu ni Gaston Paris, ni Darmesteter, ni aucun des écrivains récents qui étudièrent avec prudence tant de points obscurs de la phonétique et de la rythmique, ils tirent une autorité évidente de leur incompétence même."
Le Vers Libre et les Prochaines Elections.

Pèlerin du Silence (1896) contains: *Fleurs de Jadis* (1893),

HENRY JAMES AND REMY DE GOURMONT

Château Singulier (1894), *Livres des Litanies, Litanie de la Rose** (1892), *Théâtre Muet, Le Fantôme* (1893).

Livre des Masques (1896), not particularly important, though the preface contains a good reformulation, as, for example:

"Le crime capital pour un écrivain, c'est le conformisme, l'imitativité, la soumission aux règles et aux enseignements. L'œuvre d'un écrivain doit être non seulement le reflet, mais le reflet grossi de sa personnalité. La seule excuse qu'un homme ait d'écrire c'est de s'écrire lui-même, de dévoiler aux autres la sorte de monde qui se mire en son miroir individuel; Sa seule excuse est d'être original; il doit dire des choses non encore dites, et les dire en une forme non encore formulée. Il doit se créer sa propre esthétique—et nous devrons admettre autant d'esthétiques qu'il y a d'esprits originaux et les juger d'après ce qu'elles sont, et non d'après ce qu'elles ne sont pas.

. . . . . .

"L'esthétique est devenue elle aussi, un talent personnel." †
Préface.

"Comme tous les écrivains qui sont parvenus à comprendre la vie, c'est-à-dire son inutilité immédiate, M. Francis Poictevin, bien que né romancier, a promptement renoncé au roman.

. . . . . .

"Il est très difficile de persuader à de certains vieillards— vieux ou jeunes—qu'il n'y a pas de sujets; il n'y a en littérature qu'un sujet, celui qui écrit, et toute la littérature, c'est-à-dire toute la philosophie, peut surgir aussi bien à l'appel d'un chien écrasé qu'aux acclamations de Faust interpellant la Nature: 'Où te saisir, ô Nature infinie? Et vous, mamelles?'"
Francis Poictevin.

* Quoted in *Little Review*, Feb. 1918.
† Each of the senses has its own particular eunuchs.

This book is of the nineties, of temporary interest, judgment in mid-career, less interesting now that the complete works of the subjects are available, or have faded from interest. This sort of criticism is a duty imposed on a man by his intelligence. The doing it a duty, a price exacted for his possession of intelligence.

In places the careless phrase, phrases careless of sense, in places the thing *bien dit* as in his 'Verlaine'. Here and there a sharp sentence, as

"M. Moréas ne comprendra jamais combien il est ridicule d'appeler Racine le Sophocle de la Ferté Milon".

or:

"Parti de la chanson de Saint Léger, il en est, dit-on, arrivé au XVIIième siècle, et cela en moins de dix années; ce n'est pas si décourageant qu'on l'a cru. Et maintenant que les textes se font plus familiers, la route s'abrège; d'ici peu de haltes, M. Moréas campera sous le vieux chêne Hugo et, s'il persévère, nous le verrons atteindre le but de son voyage, qui est sans doute de se rejoindre lui-même". *Jean Moréas.*

This first *Livre des Masques* is of historical interest, as a list of men interesting at that time. It is work done in establishing good work, a necessary scaffolding, the debt to Gourmont, because of it, is ethical rather than artistic. It is a worthy thing to have done. One should not reproach flaws, even if it appears that the author wastes time in this criticism, although this particular sort of half energy probably wouldn't have been any use for more creative or even more formulative writing. It is not a carving of statues, but only holding a torch for the public; ancillary writing. Local and temporal, introducing some men now better known and some, thank Heaven, unknown or forgotten.

Deuxième Livre des Masques (1898), rather more important, longer essays, subjects apparently chosen more freely, leaves one perhaps more eager to read Alfred Vallette's *Le Vierge* than any other book mentioned.

"Etre nul arrêté dans son développement vers une nullité équilibrée".

We find typical Gourmont in the essay on Rictus:

"Ici c'est l'idée de la résignation qui trouble le Pauvre; comme tant d'autres, il la confond avec l'idée bouddhiste de non-activité. Cela n'a pas d'autre importance en un temps où l'on confond tout, et où un cerveau capable d'associer et de dissocier logiquement les idées doit être considéré comme une production miraculeuse de la Nature.

. . . . . .

"Or l'art ne joue pas; il est grave, même quand il rit, même quand il danse. Il faut encore comprendre qu'en art tout ce qui n'est pas nécessaire est inutile; et tout ce qui est inutile est mauvais". *Jehan Rictus.*

He almost convinces one of Ephraim Mikhail's poetry, by his skilful leading up to quotation of:

"Mais le ciel gris est plein de tristesse caline
Ineffablement douce aux cœurs chargés d'ennuis".

The essay on the Goncourt is important, and we find in it typical dissociation:

"Avec de la patience, on atteint quelquefois l'exactitude, et avec de la conscience, la véracité; ce sont les qualités fondamentales de l'histoire.

. . . . . .

"Quand on a goûté à ce vin on ne veut plus boire l'ordinaire vinasse des bas littérateurs. Si les Goncourt étaient devenus populaires, si la notion du style pouvait pénétrer dans les cerveaux moyens! On dit que le peuple d'Athènes avait cette notion.

. . . . . .

"Et surtout quel mémorable désintéressement! En tout autre temps nul n'aurait songé à louer Edmond de Goncourt pour ce dédain de l'argent et de la basse popularité, car l'amour est exclusif et celui qui aime l'art n'aime que l'art: mais après les exemples de toutes les avidités qui nous ont été donnés depuis vingt ans par les boursiers des lettres, par la coulisse de la littérature, il est juste et nécessaire de glorifier, en face de ceux qui vivent pour l'argent, ceux qui vécurent pour l'idée et pour l'art.

. . . . .

"La place des Goncourt dans l'histoire littéraire de ce siècle sera peut-être même aussi grande que celle de Flaubert, et ils la devront à leur souci si nouveau, si scandaleux, en une littérature alors encore toute rhétoricienne, de la 'non-imitation'; cela a révolutionné le monde de l'écriture. Flaubert devait beaucoup à Chateaubriand: il serait difficile de nommer le maître des Goncourt. Ils conquirent pour eux, ensuite pour tous les talents, le droit à la personnalité stricte, le droit pour un écrivain de s'avouer tel quel, et rien qu'ainsi, sans s'inquiéter des modèles, des règles, de tout le pédantisme universitaire et cénaculaire, le droit de se mettre face-à-face avec la vie, avec la sensation, avec le rêve, avec l'idée, de créer sa phrase—et même, dans les limites du génie de la langue, sa syntaxe". *Les Goncourt.*

One is rather glad M. Hello is dead. Ghil is mentionable, and the introductory note on Félix Fénéon is of interest.

Small periodicals are praised in the notes on Dujardins and Alfred Vallette.

"Il n'y a rien de plus utile que ces revues spéciales dont le public élu parmi les vrais fidèles admet les discussions minutieuses, les admirations franches." *Edouard Dujardins.*

"Il arrive dans l'ordre littéraire qu'une revue fondée avec quinze louis a plus d'influence sur la marche des idées et, par conséquent, sur la marche du monde (et peut-être sur

la rotation des planètes) que les orgueilleux recueils de capitaux académiques et de dissertations commerciales."
Alfred Vallette.

Promenades Philosophiques (1905-8). One cannot brief such work as the *Promenades*. The sole result is a series of aphorisms, excellent perhaps, but without cohesion; a dozen or so will show an intelligence, but convey neither style nor personality of the author:

"Sans doute la religion n'est pas vraie, mais l'anti-religion n'est pas vraie non plus: la vérité réside dans un état parfait d'indifférence.

. . . . . .

"Peu importe qu'on me sollicite par des écrits ou par des paroles; le mal ne commence qu'au moment où on m'y plie par la force". *Autre Point de Vue.*

"L'argent est le signe de la liberté. Maudire l'argent, c'est maudire la liberté, c'est maudire la vie qui est nulle si elle n'est libre". *L'Argent.*

"Quand on voudra définir la philosophie du XIXième siècle, on s'apercevra qu'il n'a fait que de la théologie.

. . . . . .

"Apprendre pour apprendre est peut-être aussi grossier que manger pour manger.

. . . . . .

"C'est singulier en littérature, quand la forme n'est pas nouvelle, le fond ne l'est pas non plus.

. . . . . .

"Le nu de l'art contemporain est un nu d'hydrothérapie.

. . . . . .

"L'art doit être à la mode ou créer la mode.

. . . . . .

HENRY JAMES AND REMY DE GOURMONT

"Les pacifistes, de braves gens à genoux, près d'une balance et priant le ciel qu'elle s'incline, non pas selon les lois de la pesanteur, mais selon leurs vœux.

. . . . . .

"La propriété est nécessaire, mais il ne l'est pas qu'elle reste toujours dans les mêmes mains.

. . . . . .

"Il y a une simulation de l'intelligence comme il y a une simulation de la vertu.

. . . . . .

"Le roman historique. Il y a aussi la peinture historique, l'architecture historique, et, à la mi-carême, le costume historique.

. . . . . .

"Etre impersonnel c'est être personnel selon un mode particulier: Voyez Flaubert. On dirait en jargon: l'objectif est une des formes du subjectif.

. . . . . .

"La maternité, c'est beau, tant qu'on n'y fait pas attention. C'est vulgaire dès qu'on admire.

. . . . . .

"L'excuse du christianisme, ça a été son impuissance sur la réalité. Il a corrompu l'esprit bien plus que la vie.

"Je ne garantis pas qu'aucune de ces notes ne se trouve déjà dans un de mes écrits, ou qu'elle ne figurera pas dans un écrit futur. On les retrouvera peut-être même dans des écrits qui ne seront pas les miens." *Des Pas sur le Sable.*

Those interested in the subject will take *Le Problème du Style* (1902) entire; the general position may perhaps be indicated very vaguely by the following quotations:

"Quant à la peur de se gâter le style, c'est bon pour un Bembo, qui use d'une langue factice. Le style peut se fatiguer comme l'homme même; il vieillira de même que l'intelligence et la sensibilité dont il est le signe; mais pas plus que l'individu, il ne changera de personnalité, à moins d'un cataclysme psychologique. Le régime alimentaire, le séjour à la campagne ou à Paris, les occupations sentimentales et leurs suites, les maladies ont bien plus d'influence sur un style vrai que les mauvaises lectures. Le style est un produit physiologique, et l'un des plus constants; quoique dans la dépendance des diverses fonctions vitales.

. . . .

"Les Etats-Unis tomberaient en langueur, sans les voyages en Europe de leur aristocratie, sans la diversité extrême des climats, des sols et par conséquent des races en évolution dans ce vaste empire. Les échanges entre peuples sont aussi nécessaires à la révigoration de chaque peuple que le commerce social à l'exaltation de l'énergie individuelle. On n'a pas pris garde à cette nécessité quand on parle avec regret de l'influence des littératures étrangères sur notre littérature.

. . . .

"Aujourd'hui l'influence d'Euripide pourrait encore déterminer en un esprit original d'intéressantes œuvres; l'imitateur de Racine dépasserait à peine le comique involontaire. L'étude de Racine ne deviendra profitable que dans plusieurs siècles et seulement à condition que, complètement oublié, il semble entièrement nouveau, entièrement étranger, tel que le sont devenus pour le public d'aujourd'hui Adenès li Rois ou Jean de Meung. Euripide était nouveau au XVIIième siècle. Théocrite l'était alors que Chénier le transposait. 'Quand je fais des vers, insinuait Racine, je songe toujours à dire ce qui ne s'est point encore dit dans notre langue.' André Chénier a voulu exprimer cela aussi dans une phrase maladroite; et s'il ne l'a dit il l'a fait. Horace a bafoué les serviles imitateurs; il n'imitait pas les Grecs, il les étudiait.

. . . .

HENRY JAMES AND REMY DE GOURMONT

"'Le style est l'homme même' est un propos de naturaliste, qui sait que le chant des oiseaux est déterminé par la forme de leur bec, l'attache de leur langue, le diamètre de leur gorge, la capacité de leurs poumons.

. . . . . .

"Le style, c'est de sentir, de voir, de penser, et rien plus.

. . . . . .

"Le style est une spécialisation de la sensibilité.

. . . . . .

"Une idée n'est qu'une sensation défraîchie, une image effacée.

. . . . .

"La vie est un dépouillement. Le but de l'activité propre d'un homme est de nettoyer sa personnalité, de la laver de toutes les souillures qu'y déposa l'éducation, de la dégager de toutes les empreintes qu'y laissèrent nos admirations adolescentes.

. . . . . .

"Depuis un siècle et demi, les connaissances scientifiques ont augmenté énormément; l'esprit scientifique a rétrogradé; il n'y a plus de contact immédiat entre ceux qui lisent et ceux qui créent la science, et (je cite pour la seconde fois la réflexion capitale de Buffon): 'On n'acquiert aucune connaissance transmissible, qu'en voyant par soi-même': Les ouvrages de seconde main amusent l'intelligence et ne stimulent pas son activité.

. . . .

"Rien ne pousse à la concision comme l'abondance des idées." *Le Problème du Style*, 1902.

Christianity lends itself to fanaticism. Barbarian ethics proceed by general taboos. The relation of two individuals is so complex that no third person can pass judgment upon it. Civilization is individual. The truth is the individual. The light of the Renaissance shines in Varchi when he declines to pass judgment on Lorenzaccio.

One might make an index of, but one cannot write an essay upon, the dozen volumes of Gourmont's collected discussions. There was weariness towards the end of his life. It shows in even the leisurely charm of *Lettres à l'Amazone*. There was a final flash in his drawing of M. Croquant.

The list of his chief works published by the *Mercure de France*, 26 Rue de Condé, Paris, is as follows:

Sixtine.
Le Pèlerin du Silence.
Les Chevaux de Diomède.
D'un Pays Lointain.
Le Songe d'une Femme.
Lilith, suivi de Théodat.
Une Nuit au Luxembourg.
Un Cœur Virginal.
Couleurs, suivi de Choses Anciennes.
Histoires Magiques.
Lettres d'un Satyre.
Le Chat de Misère.
Simone.

CRITIQUE

Le Latin Mystique.
Le Livre des Masques (Iier et IIième).
La Culture des Idées.
Le Chemin de Velours.
Le Problème du Style.
Physique de l'Amour.
Epilogues.
Esthétique de la Langue Française.
Promenades Littéraires.

HENRY JAMES AND REMY DE GOURMONT

Promenades Philosophiques.
Dialogue des Amateurs sur les Choses du Temps.
Nouveaux Dialogues des Amateurs sur les Choses du Temps.
Dante, Béatrice et la Poésie Amoureuse.
Pendant l'Orage.

Gourmont's readiness to co-operate in my first plans for establishing some sort of periodical to maintain communications between New York, London and Paris, was graciously shown in the following (post-mark June 13, 1915):

Dimanche.

Cher Monsieur:

J'ai lu avec plaisir votre longue lettre, qui m'expose si clairement la nécessité d'une revue unissant les efforts des Américains, des Anglais, et des Français. Pour cela, je vous servirai autant qu'il sera en mon pouvoir. Je ne crois pas que je puisse beaucoup. J'ai une mauvaise santé et je suis extrêmement fatigué; je ne pourrai vous donner que des choses très courtes, des indications d'idées plutôt que des pages accomplies, mais je ferai de mon mieux. J'espère que vous réussirez à mettre debout cette petite affaire littéraire et que vous trouverez parmi nous des concours utiles. Evidemment si nous pourrions amener les Américains à mieux sentir la vraie littérature française et surtout à ne pas la confondre avec tant d'œuvres courantes si médiocres, cela serait un résultat très heureux. Sont-ils capables d'assez de liberté d'esprit pour lire, sans être choqués, mes livres par exemple? Il est bien douteux et il faudrait pour cela un long travail de préparation. Mais pourquoi ne pas l'entreprendre? En tous les pays, il y a un noyau de bons esprits, d'esprits libres, il faut leur donner quelque chose qui les change de la fadeur des magazines, quelque chose qui leur donne confiance en eux-mêmes et leur soit un point d'appui. Comme vous le dites, il faudra pour commencer les amener à respecter l'individualisme français, le sens de la liberté que quelques-

HENRY JAMES AND REMY DE GOURMONT

uns d'entre nous possèdent à un si haut point. Ils comprennent cela en théologie. Pourquoi ne le comprendraient-ils pas en art, en poésie, en littérature, en philosophie. Il faut leur faire voir—s'ils ne le voient pas déjà—que l'individualisme français peut, quand il le faut, se plier aux plus dures disciplines.
   Conquérir l'Américain n'est pas sans doute votre seul but. Le but du *Mercure* a été de permettre à ceux qui en valent la peine d'écrire franchement ce qu'ils pensent—seul plaisir d'un écrivain. Cela doit aussi être le vôtre.
Votre bien dévoué,
REMY DE GOURMONT.

"The aim of the *Mercure* has been to permit any man, who is worth it, to write down his thought frankly—this is a writer's sole pleasure. And this aim should be yours."
   "Are they capable of enough mental liberty to read my books, for example, without being horrified? I think this very doubtful, and it will need long preparation. But why not try it? There are in all countries knots of intelligent people, open-minded; one must give something to relieve them from the staleness of magazines, something which will give them confidence in themselves and serve as a rallying point. As you say, one must begin by getting them to respect French individualism; the sense of liberty which some of us have in so great degree. They understand this in theology, why should they not understand it in art, poetry, literature?"
   If only my great correspondent could have seen letters I received about this time from English alleged intellectuals!!!!!!! The incredible stupidity, the ingrained refusal of thought!!!!! Of which more anon, if I can bring myself to it. Or let it pass? Let us say simply that Gourmont's words form an interesting contrast with the methods employed by the British literary episcopacy to keep one from writing what one thinks, or to punish one (financially) for having done so.

Perhaps as a warning to young writers who cannot afford the loss, one would be justified in printing the following:

50 *a* Albemarle Street, London, W.
22 October, 1914.

Dear Mr Pound,
Many thanks for your letter of the other day. I am afraid that I must say frankly that I do not think I can open the columns of the Q. R.—at any rate, at present—to any one associated publicly with such a publication as *Blast*. It stamps a man too disadvantageously.

Yours truly,
G. W. PROTHERO.

Of course, having accepted your paper on the *Noh*, I could not refrain from publishing it. But other things would be in a different category.

I need scarcely say that *The Quarterly Review* is one of the most profitable periodicals in England, and one of one's best "connections", or sources of income. It has, of course, a tradition.

"It is not that Mr Keats (if that be his real name, for we almost doubt that any man in his senses would put his real name to such a rhapsody)"—

wrote their Gifford of Keats' *Endymion*. My only comment is that the *Quarterly* has done it again. Their Mr A. Waugh is a lineal descendant of Gifford, by way of mentality. A century has not taught them manners. In the eighteen forties they were still defending the review of Keats. And more recently Waugh has lifted up his senile slobber against Mr Eliot. It is indeed time that the functions of both English and American literature were taken over by younger and better men.

As for their laying the birch on my pocket. I compute that my support of Lewis and Brzeska has cost me at the lowest estimate about £20 per year, from one source alone since that regrettable occurrence, since I dared to discern a great sculptor and a great painter in the midst of England's artistic desolation. ("European and Asiatic papers please copy.")

Young men, desirous of finding before all things smooth berths and elderly consolations, are cautioned to behave more circumspectly.

The generation that preceded us does not care much whether we understand French individualism, or the difference between the good and bad in French literature. Nor is it conceivable that any of them would write to a foreigner: "indications of ideas, rather than work accomplished, but I will send you my best".

Gourmont's next communication to me was an inquiry about Gaudier-Brzeska's sculpture.

A STRAY DOCUMENT

The "Don'ts" in the following reprint had a plain utilitarian purpose in that they were intended as a rejection slip to be used by a trade paper. They are aimed at the faults most prevalent of poetry as we found it 1905–1912.

Naturally the second clause in the Imagist triad was the first to be avoided. That really did require a little thought and consciousness, and was promptly followed by various more wordy formulae designed to avoid the trouble.

It is not to be expected that a great number of people in any age will be able to maintain an interesting tenseness in verbal manifestation, any more than we are likely to be beset by a large herd of great draughtsmen or an overwhelming swarm of composers capable of great melodic invention.

A RETROSPECT

In the spring or early summer of 1912, "H. D.", Richard Aldington and myself decided that we were agreed upon the three principles following:

1. Direct treatment of the "thing" whether subjective or objective.

2. To use absolutely no word that does not contribute to the presentation.

3. As regarding rhythm: to compose in the sequence of the musical phrase, not in sequence of a metronome.

Upon many points of taste and of predilection we differed, but agreeing upon these three positions we thought we had as much right to a group name as a number of French "schools" proclaimed by Mr Flint in the August number of Harold Munro's magazine for 1911.

This school was later "joined" or "followed" by numerous people who, whatever their merits, do not show any signs of agreeing with the second specification. *Vers libre* has become as prolix and as verbose as any of the flaccid varieties of verse that preceded it. It has brought in faults of its own. The actual language and phrasing in it is often as bad as that of our elders, without having even the excuse that the words are shoveled in to fill a metric pattern or to complete the noise of a rhyme-sound. Whether or no the phrases followed by the followers are musical must be left to the reader's decision. At times I can find a marked metre in *"vers libres"*, as stale and hackneyed as any pseudo-Swinburnian, at times the writers seem to follow no musical structure whatever. But it is, on the whole, good that the field should be ploughed. A few excellent poems have come from the new method, thereby is it justified.

Criticism is not a circumscription or a set of prohibitions. It offers fixed points of departure. It may startle a dull reader into alertness. That little of it which is good is to be found mostly in stray phrases; an older artist helping a younger in great measure by rules of thumb or cautions gained by experience.

A FEW DON'TS*

An "Image" is that which presents an intellectual and emotional complex in an instant of time. I use the term "complex" rather in the technical sense employed by the newer psychologists, such as Hart, though we might not agree absolutely in our application.

It is the presentation of such a "complex" instantaneously which gives that sense of sudden liberation; that sense of freedom from time limits and space limits; that sense of sudden growth, which we experience in the presence of the greatest works of art.

* *Poetry* for March, 1913.

A STRAY DOCUMENT

It is better to present one Image in a lifetime than to produce voluminous works.

All this, however, some may consider open to debate. The immediate necessity is to tabulate A LIST OF DON'TS for those beginning to write verses. I can not put all of them into Mosaic negative.

To begin with, consider the three propositions (demanding direct treatment, economy of words, and the sequence of the musical phrase), not as dogma—never consider anything as dogma—but as the result of long contemplation, which, even if it is someone else's contemplation, may be worth consideration.

Pay no attention to the criticism of men who have never themselves written a notable work. Consider the discrepancies between the actual writing of the Greek poets and dramatists, and the theories of the Graeco-Roman grammarians, concocted to explain their metres.

Language

Use no superfluous word, no adjective, which does not reveal something.

Don't use such an expression as "dim lands *of peace*". It dulls the image. It mixes an abstraction with the concrete. It comes from the writer's not realizing that the natural object is always the *adequate* symbol.

Go in fear of abstractions. Do not re-tell in mediocre verse what has already been done in good prose. Don't think any intelligent person is going to be deceived when you try to shirk all the difficulties of the unspeakably difficult art of good prose by chopping your composition into line lengths.

What the expert is tired of to-day the public will be tired of to-morrow.

Don't imagine that the art of poetry is any simpler than the art of music, or that you can please the expert before you have spent at least as much effort on the art of verse as the average piano teacher spends on the art of music.

Be influenced by as many great artists as you can, but have the decency either to acknowledge the debt outright, or to try to conceal it.

Don't allow "influence" to mean merely that you mop up the particular decorative vocabulary of some one or two poets whom you happen to admire. A Turkish war correspondent was recently caught red-handed babbling in his dispatches of "dove-gray" hills, or else it was "pearl-pale" I can not remember.

Use either no ornament or good ornament.

Rhythm and Rhyme

Let the candidate fill his mind with the finest cadences he can discover, preferably in a foreign language* so that the meaning of the words may be less likely to divert his attention from the movement; e.g., Saxon charms, Hebridean Folk Songs, the verse of Dante, and the lyrics of Shakespeare—if he can dissociate the vocabulary from the cadence. Let him dissect the lyrics of Goethe coldly into their component sound values, syllables long and short, stressed and unstressed, into vowels and consonants.

It is not necessary that a poem should rely on its music, but if it does rely on its music that music must be such as will delight the expert.

Let the neophyte know assonance and alliteration, rhyme immediate and delayed, simple and polyphonic, as a musician would expect to know harmony and counterpoint and all the minutiae of his craft. No time is too great to give to these matters or to any one of them, even if the artist seldom have need of them.

* This is for rhythm, his vocabulary must of course be found in his native tongue.

A STRAY DOCUMENT

Don't imagine that a thing will "go" in verse just because it's too dull to go in prose.

Don't be "viewy"—leave that to the writers of pretty little philosophic essays. Don't be descriptive; remember that the painter can describe a landscape much better than you can, and that he has to know a deal more about it.

When Shakespeare talks of the "Dawn in russet mantle clad" he presents something which the painter does not present. There is in this line of his nothing that one can call description; he presents.

Consider the way of the scientists rather than the way of an advertising agent for a new soap.

The scientist does not expect to be acclaimed as a great scientist until he has *discovered* something. He begins by learning what has been discovered already. He goes from that point onward. He does not bank on being a charming fellow personally. He does not expect his friends to applaud the results of his freshman class work. Freshmen in poetry are unfortunately not confined to a definite and recognizable class room. They are "all over the shop". Is it any wonder "the public is indifferent to poetry?"

Don't chop your stuff into separate *iambs*. Don't make each line stop dead at the end, and then begin every next line with a heave. Let the beginning of the next line catch the rise of the rhythm wave, unless you want a definite longish pause.

In short, behave as a musician, a good musician, when dealing with that phase of your art which has exact parallels in music. The same laws govern, and you are bound by no others.

Naturally, your rhythmic structure should not destroy the shape of your words, or their natural sound, or their meaning. It is improbable that, at the start, you will be able to get a rhythm-structure strong enough to affect them very much, though you may fall a victim to all sorts of false stopping due to line ends and caesurae.

A STRAY DOCUMENT

The musician can rely on pitch and the volume of the orchestra. You can not. The term harmony is misapplied to poetry; it refers to simultaneous sounds of different pitch. There is, however, in the best verse a sort of residue of sound which remains in the ear of the hearer and acts more or less as an organ-base.

A rhyme must have in it some slight element of surprise if it is to give pleasure; it need not be bizarre or curious, but it must be well used if used at all.

Vide further Vildrac and Duhamel's notes on rhyme in *Technique Poétique*.

That part of your poetry which strikes upon the imaginative *eye* of the reader will lose nothing by translation into a foreign tongue; that which appeals to the ear can reach only those who take it in the original.

Consider the definiteness of Dante's presentation as compared with Milton's rhetoric. Read as much of Wordsworth as does not seem too unutterably dull.

If you want the gist of the matter go to Sappho, Catullus, Villon, Heine when he is in the vein, Gautier when he is not too frigid; or, if you have not the tongues, seek out the leisurely Chaucer. Good prose will do you no harm, and there is good discipline to be had by trying to write it.

Translation is likewise good training, if you find that your original matter "wobbles" when you try to rewrite it. The meaning of the poem to be translated can not "wobble".

If you are using a symmetrical form, don't put in what you want to say and then fill up the remaining vacuums with slush.

Don't mess up the perception of one sense by trying to define it in terms of another. This is usually only the result of being too lazy to find the exact word. To this clause there are possibly exceptions.

The first three simple proscriptions will throw out nine-tenths of all the bad poetry now accepted as standard and classic; and will prevent you from many a crime of production.

"...*Mais d'abord il faut être un poète*", as MM. Duhamel and Vildrac have said at the end of their little book, *Notes sur la Technique Poétique*.

. . . . .

Since March, 1913, Ford Madox Hueffer has pointed out that Wordsworth was so intent on the ordinary or plain word that he never thought of hunting for *le mot juste*.

John Butler Yeats has handled or man-handled Wordsworth and the Victorians, and the criticism, contained in letters to his son, is now printed and available.

7

CAVALCANTI

MEDIAEVALISM

I

"Safe may'st thou go my canzon whither thee pleaseth
Thou art so fair attired"

Apart from the welcome given to or withheld from a fine performance, it seems to me that the vogue of Guido's canzone, *Donna mi Prega*, was due to causes not instantly apparent to the modern reader. I mean that it shows traces of a tone of thought no longer considered dangerous, but that may have appeared about as soothing to the Florentine of A.D. 1290 as conversation about Tom Paine, Marx, Lenin and Bucharin would to-day in a Methodist bankers' board meeting in Memphis, Tenn.

The teaching of Aristotle had been banned in the University of Paris in 1213. This prejudice had been worn down during the century, but Guido shows, I think, no regard for anyone's prejudice. We may trace his ideas to Averroes, Avicenna; he does not definitely proclaim any heresy, but he shows leanings toward not only the proof by reason, but toward the proof by experiment. I do not think that he swallowed Aquinas. It may be impossible to prove that he had heard of Roger Bacon, but the whole canzone is easier to understand if we suppose, or at least one finds, a considerable interest in the speculation, that he had read Grosseteste on the Generation of Light.

CAVALCANTI

In all of which he shows himself much more "modern" than his young friend Dante Alighieri, *qui était diablement dans les idées reçues*, and whose shock is probably recorded in the passage of *Inferno* x where he finds Guido's father and father-in-law paying for their mental exertions. In general, one may conclude that the conversation in the Cavalcanti-Uberti family was more stimulating than that in Tuscan bourgeois and ecclesiastical circles of the period.

My conclusions are based on the whole text of Guido, or at least the serious part of the text, excluding rhymed letters, skits and simple pastorals; the canzone by itself does not conclusively prove my assertions.

II

The mediaeval Italian poets brought into poetry something which had not been or not been in any so marked and developed degree in the poetry of the troubadours. It is still more important for anyone wishing to have well-balanced critical appreciation of poetry in general to understand that this quality, or this assertion of value, has not been in poetry *since*; and that the English "philosophical" and other "philosophical" poets have not produced a comparable *Ersatz*.

The Greek aesthetic would seem to consist wholly in plastic, or in plastic moving toward coitus, and limited by incest, which is the sole Greek taboo. This new thing in mediaeval work that concerns us has nothing to do with Christianity, which people both praise and blame for utterly irrelevant and unhistorical reasons. Erotic sentimentality we can find in Greek and Roman poets, and one may observe that the main trend of Provençal and Tuscan poets is not toward erotic sentimentality.

But they are not pagans, they are called pagans, and the troubadours are also accused of being Manichaeans, obviously because of a muddle somewhere. They are opposed to a form of stupidity not limited to Europe, that is, idiotic asceticism and a belief that the body is evil. This more or less masochistic and hell-breeding belief is always accompanied by bad and niggled sculpture (Angoulême or Bengal); Gandhi to-day is incapable of making the dissociation that it is not the body but its diseases and infirmities which are evil. The same statement is true of mind: the infections of mind being no less hideous than those of physique. In fact, a man's toothache annoys himself, but a fool annoys the whole company. Even for epidemics, a few cranks may spread wider malefaction than anything short of plague universal. This invention of hells for one's enemies, and messy confusion in sculpture, is always symptomatic of supineness, bad hygiene, bad physique (possibly envy); even the diseases of mind, they do not try to cure as such, but devise hells to punish, not to heal, the individual sufferer.

Against these European Hindoos we find the "mediaeval clean line" as distinct from mediaeval niggle. Byzantium gives us perhaps the best architecture, or at least the best inner structure, that we know, I mean for proportions, for ornament flat on the walls, and not bulging and bumping and indulging in bulbous excrescence. The lines for example of the Byzantine heritage in Sicily, from which the best "Romanesque", developing to St Hilaire in Poictiers; or if the term Romanesque has become too ambiguous through loose usage, let me say that there are mediaeval churches such as the cathedral at San Leo, or San Zeno in Verona, and others of similar form which are simply the Byzantine minus riches. It is the bare wall that the Constantinopolitan would have had money enough to cover with gold mosaic.

Perhaps out of a sand-swept country, the need of interior harmony. That is conjecture. Against this clean architecture, we find the niggly Angoulême, the architectural ornament of bigotry, superstition, and mess.

What is the difference between Provence and Hellas?

There is, let us grant, a line in Propertius about *ingenium nobis fecit*. But the subject is not greatly developed. I mean that Propertius remains mostly inside the classic world and the classic aesthetic, plastic to coitus. Plastic plus immediate satisfaction.

The whole break of Provence with this world, and indeed the central theme of the troubadours, is the dogma that there is some proportion between the fine thing held in the mind, and the inferior thing ready for instant consumption.

Their freedom is not an attack on Christian prudery, because prudery is not a peculiarly Christian excrescence. There is plenty of prudery in Virgil, and also in Ovid, where rumour would less lead one to expect it.

I am labouring all this because I want to establish a distinction as to the Tuscan aesthetic. The term metaphysic might be used if it were not so appallingly associated in people's minds with unsupportable conjecture and devastated terms of abstraction.

The Tuscan demands harmony in something more than the plastic. He declines to limit his aesthetic to the impact of light on the eye. It would be misleading to reduce his aesthetic to terms of music, or to distort the analysis of it by analogies to the art of sonority. Man shares plastic with the statue, sound does not require a human being to produce it. The bird, the phonograph, sing. Sound can be exteriorized as completely as plastic. There is the residue of perception, perception of something which requires a human being to produce it. Which even may require a certain individual to produce it. This really complicates the aesthetic. You deal with an interactive force: the *virtu* in short.

And dealing with it is not anti-life. It is not maiming, it is not curtailment. The senses at first seem to project for a few yards beyond the body. Effect of a decent climate where a man leaves his nerve-set open, or allows it to tune in to its ambience, rather than struggling, as a northern race has to, for self-preservation to guard the body from assaults of weather.

He declines, after a time, to limit reception to his solar plexus. The whole thing has nothing to do with taboos and bigotries. It is more than the simple athleticism of the *mens sana in corpore sano*. The conception of the body as perfected instrument of the increasing intelligence pervades. The lack of this concept invalidates the whole of monastic thought. Dogmatic asceticism is obviously not essential to the perceptions of Guido's ballate.

Whether it is necessary to modernize or nordicize our terminology and call this "the aesthetic or interactive vasomotor magnetism in relation to the consciousness", I leave to the reader's own taste and sense of proportion. I am inclined to think that a habit of mind which insists upon, or even tends toward, such terminology somewhat takes the bloom off the peach.

Out of these fine perceptions, or subsequent to them, people say that the Quattrocento, or the sculpture of the Quattrocento, discovered "personality". All of which is perhaps rather vague. We might say: The best Egyptian sculpture is magnificent plastic; but its force comes from a non-plastic idea, i.e. the god is inside the statue.

I am not considering the merits of the matter, much less those merits as seen by a modern aesthetic purist. I am using historic method. The god is inside the stone, *vacuos exercet aera morsus*. The force is arrested, but there is never any question about its latency, about the force being the essential, and the rest "accidental" in the philosophic technical sense. The shape occurs.

There is hardly any debate about the Greek classical sculpture, to them it is the plastic that matters. In the case of the statue of the Etruscan Apollo at Villa Giulia (Rome) the "god is inside", but the psychology is merely that of an Hallowe'en pumpkin. It is a weak derivation of fear motive, strong in

CAVALCANTI

Mexican masks, but here reduced to the simple briskness of small boy amused at startling his grandma. This is a long way from Greek statues, in which "the face don't matter".

This sculpture with something inside, revives in the Quattrocento portrait bust. But the antecedents are in verbal manifestation.

Nobody can absorb the *poeti dei primi secoli* and then the paintings of the Uffizi without seeing the relation between them, Daniel, Ventadorn, Guido, Sellaio, Botticelli, Ambrogio Praedis, Nic. del Cossa.

All these are clean, all without hell-obsession.

Certain virtues are established, and the neglect of them by later writers and artists is an impoverishment of their art. The stupidity of Rubens, the asinine nature of French court life from Henry IV to the end of it, the insistence on two dimensional treatment of life by certain modernists, do not constitute a progress. A dogma builds on vacuum, and is ultimately killed or modified by, or accommodated to knowledge, but values stay, and ignorant neglect of them answers no purpose.

Loss of values is due usually to lumping and to lack of dissociation. The disproved is thrown out, and the associated, or contemporarily established, goes temporarily with it.

"Durch Rafael ist das Madonnenideal Fleisch geworden", says Herr Springer, with perhaps an unintentional rhyme. Certainly the metamorphosis into carnal tissue becomes frequent and general somewhere about 1527. The people are corpus, corpuscular, but not in the strict sense "animate", it is no longer the body of air clothed in the body of fire; it no longer radiates, light no longer moves from the eye, there is a great deal of meat, shock absorbing, perhaps—at any rate absorbent. It has not even Greek marmoreal plastic to restrain it. The dinner scene is more frequently introduced, we have the characters in definite act of absorption; later they will be but stuffing for expensive upholsteries.

CAVALCANTI

Long before that a change had begun in the poetry. The difference between Guido and Petrarch is not a mere difference in degree, it is a difference in kind.

There are certain things Petrarch does not know, cannot know. I am not postulating him as "to blame" for anything, or even finding analogy for his tone in post-Peruginian painting.

Leave all question of any art save poetry. In that art the gulf between Petrarch's capacity and Guido's is the great gulf, not of degree, but of kind. In Guido the "figure", the strong metamorphic or "picturesque" expression is there with purpose to convey or to interpret a definite meaning. In Petrarch it is ornament, the prettiest ornament he could find, but not an irreplaceable ornament, or one that he couldn't have used just about as well somewhere else. In fact he very often does use it, and them, somewhere, and nearly everywhere, else, all over the place.

We appear to have lost the radiant world where one thought cuts through another with clean edge, a world of moving energies "*mezzo oscuro rade*", "*risplende in sè perpetuale effecto*", magnetisms that take form, that are seen, or that border the visible, the matter of Dante's *paradiso*, the glass under water, the form that seems a form seen in a mirror, these realities perceptible to the sense, interacting, "*a lui si tiri*" untouched by the two maladies, the Hebrew disease, the Hindoo disease, fanaticisms and excess that produce Savonarola, asceticisms that produce fakirs, St Clement of Alexandria, with his prohibition of bathing by women. The envy of dullards who, not having "*intelletto*", blame the lack of it on innocent muscles. For after asceticism, that is anti-flesh, we get the asceticism that is anti-intelligence, that praises stupidity as "simplicity", the cult of *naïveté*. To many people the term "mediaeval" connotes only the two diseases. We must avoid these unnecessary idea-clots. Between those diseases, existed the Mediterranean sanity.

The "*section d'or*", if that is what it meant, that gave the churches like St Hilaire, San Zeno, the Duomo di Modena, the clear lines and proportions. Not the pagan worship of strength, nor the Greek perception of visual non-animate plastic, or plastic in which the being animate was not the main and principal quality, but this "harmony in the sentience" or harmony *of* the sentient, where the thought has its demarcation, the substance its *virtu*, where stupid men have not reduced all "energy" to unbounded undistinguished abstraction.

For the modern scientist energy has no borders, it is a shapeless "mass" of force; even his capacity to differentiate it to a degree never dreamed by the ancients has not led him to think of its shape or even its loci. The rose that his magnet makes in the iron filings, does not lead him to think of the force in botanic terms, or wish to visualize that force as floral and extant (*ex stare*).

A mediaeval "natural philosopher" would find this modern world full of enchantments, not only the light in the electric bulb, but the thought of the current hidden in air and in wire would give him a mind full of forms, "*Fuor di color*" or having their hyper-colours. The mediaeval philosopher would probably have been unable to think the electric world, and *not* think of it as a world of forms. Perhaps algebra has queered our geometry. Even Bose with his plant experiments seems intent on the plant's capacity to feel—not on the plant idea, for the plant brain is obviously filled with, or is one idea, an *idée fixe*, a persistent notion of pattern from which only cataclysm or a Burbank can shake it. Or possibly this will fall under the eye of a contemporary scientist of genius who will answer: But, damn you, that is exactly what we do feel; or under the eye of a painter who will answer: Confound you, you *ought* to find just that in my painting.

CAVALCANTI

DONNA MI PREGA

(*Dedicace*—To Thomas Campion his ghost, and to the ghost of Henry Lawes, as prayer for the revival of music)

BECAUSE a lady asks me, I would tell
Of an affect that comes often and is fell
And is so overweening: Love by name.
E'en its deniers can now hear the truth,
I for the nonce to them that know it call,
Having no hope at all
                     that man who is base in heart
Can bear his part of wit
                 into the light of it,
And save they know't aright from nature's source
I have no will to prove Love's course
                     or say
Where he takes rest; who maketh him to be;
Or what his active *virtu* is, or what his force;
Nay, nor his very essence or his mode;
What his placation; why he is in verb,
Or if a man have might
                 To show him visible to men's sight.

IN memory's locus taketh he his state   *Place*
Formed there in manner as a mist of light   *La ove*
Upon a dusk that is come from Mars and stays.   *e*
Love is created, hath a sensate name,   *chi lo*
His modus takes from soul, from heart his will;   *fa*
From form seen doth he start, that, understood,   *creare*
Taketh in latent intellect—
As in a subject ready—
               place and abode,
Yet in that place it ever is unstill,

CAVALCANTI

Spreading its rays, it tendeth never down
By quality, but is its own effect unendingly
Not to delight, but in an ardour of thought
That the base likeness of it kindleth not.

Virtù
e
potenza

IT is not *virtu*, but perfection's source
Lying within perfection postulate
Not by the reason, but 'tis felt, I say.
Beyond salvation, holdeth its judging force,
Maintains intention reason's peer and mate;
Poor in discernment, being thus weakness' friend,
Often his power meeteth with death in the end
Be he withstayed
     or from true course
          bewrayed
E'en though he meet not with hate
         or villeiny
Save that perfection fails, be it but a little;
Nor can man say he hath his life by chance
Or that he hath not stablished seigniory
Or loseth power, e'en lost to memory.

Essenza
e
movimento

HE comes to be and is when will's so great
It twists itself from out all natural measure;
Leisure's adornment puts he then never on,
Never thereafter, but moves changing state,
Moves changing colour, or to laugh or weep
Or wries the face with fear and little stays,
Yea, resteth little
     yet is found the most
Where folk of worth be host.
And his strange property sets sighs to move
And wills man look into unformèd space
Rousing there thirst
     that breaketh into flame.

CAVALCANTI

None can imagine love
                that knows not love;
Love doth not move, but draweth all to him;
Nor doth he turn
          for a whim
                  to find delight
Nor to seek out, surely,
                great knowledge or slight.

LOOK drawn from like,   *Piacimento*
        delight maketh certain in seeming
Nor can in covert cower,
                beauty so near,
Not yet wild-cruel as darts,
So hath man craft from fear
                in such his desire
To follow a noble spirit,
                edge, that is, and point to the dart,
Though from her face indiscernible;
He, caught, falleth
                plumb on to the spike of the targe.
Who well proceedeth, form not seeth,
                following his own emanation.
There, beyond colour, essence set apart,
In midst of darkness light light giveth forth
Beyond all falsity, worthy of faith, alone
That in him solely is compassion born.

SAFE may'st thou go my canzon whither thee pleaseth
    Thou art so fair attired that every man and each
Shall praise thy speech
So he have sense or glow with reason's fire,
To stand with other
              hast thou no desire.

CAVALCANTI

PARTIAL EXPLANATION

A commentary is a piece of writing in which we expose and seek to excuse our ignorance of the subject. The less we know, the longer our explanations.

The following canzone was known as "the philosophic canzone"; the stir that it caused, over and above the stir aroused by any beautiful work, may be attributed in part to the state of philosophic opinion in and about A.D. 1290. Guido is called a "natural philosopher", I think an "atheist", and certainly an "Epicurean", not that anyone had then any clear idea or has now any very definite notion of what Epicurus taught. But a natural philosopher was a much less safe person than a "moral philosopher".

It is not so much what Guido says in the poem, as the familiarity that he shows with dangerous thinking: *natural demonstration* and the proof by experience or (?) experiment. If after-dinner talk of the Uberti and Cavalcanti was any warrant for Guido's tone it is small wonder that Dante who was, as a young man, *bien pensant*, and probably quite content with the orthodoxy of Guinicello, thought it necessary to lodge the tough-minded seniors of these tribes in the Tenth Canto of his *Inferno*, where indeed, the elder Cavalcanti might seem to be expecting his son.

My own sympathies extend even to the disrespect for Virgilio, but that point may seem irrelevant.

From this poem and from passages elsewhere it would seem that Guido had derived certain notions from the Aristotelian commentators, the "*filosofica famiglia*" Ibn Sina, for the *spiriti*, *spiriti* of the eyes, of the senses; Ibn Rachd, *che il gran comento feo*, for the demand for intelligence on the part of the recipient; Albertus Magnus, for the proof by experience; and possibly Grosseteste, *De Luce et de Incohatione Formarum*, although this will need proving.

CAVALCANTI

At any rate for any serious thought in Guido's time we must suppose the Arabian background: the concentric spheres of the heavens, Ibn Baja's itinerary of the soul going to God, Averroes's specifications for the degrees of comprehension; and we may perhaps consider Guido as one of that "tenuous line who from Albertus Magnus to the renaissance" meant the freedom of thought, the contempt, or at least a moderated respect, for stupid authority.

He is possibly against Sigier and for Albertus, he wants no proof that contradicts the "*rationes naturales*", he is not jamming down a dogma unsupported by nature. His truth is not against "*natural dimostramento*" or based on authority. It is a truth for elect recipients, not a truth universally spreadable or acceptable. The "*dove.sta memoria*" is Platonism. The "*non razionale ma che si sente*" is for experiment, it is against the tyranny of the syllogism, blinding and obscurantist. The tone of his mind is infinitely more "modern" than Dante's. "*Fuor di salute, giudichar mantiene*", his position, here as on the rest of these cardinal points, shows him to be "very dangerous" to the peace of the mediaeval mind, if immobility may be considered as "peace".

And all this is done with the suavity of a song, with the neatness of scalpel-cut. Guido is eclectic, he swallows none of his authors whole. There is no open "atheism", indeed no direct attack on any church dogma, but there is probably a sense of briskness; I mean it would not have been comforting to lovers of quiet.

If part of this is conjecture, I think one can, at any rate, scarcely exaggerate the gulf between Guido's state of mind and that of Dante in the same epoch, or between it and Dante's willingness to take on any sort of holy and orthodox furniture. Dante's "heresies" are due to feeling, annoyance with Popes and so forth, rather than to intellectual hunger, or to his feeling cramped in the Aquinian universe.

I may be wrong, but I cannot believe that Guido "swallowed" Aquinas. It is perhaps by merest accident, but we find nowhere in his poems any implication of a belief in a geocentric or theocentric material universe.

"BUT THE POEM IS VERY OBSCURE."

The poem is extremely clear in a number of places, the philosophic terms are used with a complete precision of technique. I am aware that I have distorted "*accidente*" into "affect" but I have done so in order not to lose the tone of my opening line by introducing an English word of *double entente*.

For the rest, there are certain enigmas, and the celebrated commentators have done nothing to solve them. These which face us to-day are precisely the same ones which faced Del Garbo in 1302 or 1320 or Di Giunta in 1527.

Considering the clarity and precision of the text where it is clear, I am loth to think that these obscure points indicate merely a loose usage or *remplissage*, on the part of the author.

Textual research brings us to a definite limit of knowledge about certain MS. readings. The earliest known copyists found certain passages either illegible or incomprehensible: as for example, *la gire, largir*, or *laire simiglglianza*.

Frate Egidio (Colonna, Romano, il beato, degli Agostiniani) goes round it. He begins his commentary with a graceful description of a notable lady, who must have begun life "of Paphos and the Isles" but has attained a safe anonymity. She is seated on an anonymous mountain, by an anonymous fountain, whence she sends forth her ministers: Solomon and Ovidius Naso. However, *il beato* casts no satisfactory light on the phrase "*laire simiglglianza*". Dino del Garbo is, in the modern sense, a much more serious character. He quotes a good deal of Aristotle, explains the preceding line as if it read: "*E si non ha diletto*", or "*quando non ha diletto*" but slurs over the *la gir* or *largir*. The manuscripts do not help us.

CAVALCANTI

La gire means "turn there", and *largir* is "to give away freely", "to give likeness freely"? Or is *simiglglianza* the subject? For purpose of translation one has, as Rossetti remarks, to cut through various knots, and make arbitrary decisions. I have perforce, here as elsewhere, selected one of the possible meanings, or at least attempted to do so, but without any wish to insist upon it, or to conceal either the depths of my ignorance, or my width of uncertainty. Gilson* summarizes Grosseteste's ideas on light as follows:

"*La lumière est une substance corporelle très subtile et qui se rapproche de l'incorporel. Ses propriétés caractéristiques sont de s'engendrer elle-même perpétuellement et de se diffuser sphériquement autour d'un point d'une manière instantanée. Donnons-nous un point lumineux, il s'engendre instantanément autour de ce point comme centre une sphère lumineuse immense. La diffusion de la lumière ne peut être contrariée que par deux raisons: ou bien elle rencontre une obscurité qui l'arrête, ou bien elle finit par atteindre la limite extrême de sa raréfaction, et la propagation de la lumière prend fin par là même. Cette substance extrêmement ténue est aussi l'étoffe dont toutes choses sont faites; elle est la première forme corporelle et ce que certains nomment la corporéité*".

This French summary is most able, and most lucid. It is far more suggestive of the canzone, *Donna mi Prega*, than the original Latin of Grosseteste,† but my suggestion is not that Guido is a mere dilettante poetaster dragging in philosophic terms or caught by a verbal similarity (e.g. as Lorenzo Medici, dabbling in Platonism in his rhymed account of talk

* Etienne Gilson, *Philosophie du Moyen Age*, Payot, Paris, 1925.
† L. Baur, *Die philosophischen Werke des Robert Grosseteste*, Münster, 1912, *Beiträge z. Gesch. Phil. d. Mittelalt*. Latin text and German commentary, vols. IX and XVIII, 4–6.

with Ficino). For *"risplende in sè perpetuale effecto"* we find the Latin approximation (*De Luce*, the Baur edition):

p. 51, *Lux enim per se in omnem partem se ipsam diffundit....
...a puncto lucis sphaera lucis quamvis magna...generetur....*

p. 52, *Lux prima forma in materia creata, seipsam seipsam... multiplicans* (? *multiplicans = largir*).

p. 56, *aer quoque ex se corpus spirituale vel spiritum corporalem generans.*

p. 58, *Forma autem, ut pote simplicissima unitatis obtinet locum,* as bearing on the *"formato"* or *"non formato loco"*.

p. 73, *aut transitus radii ad rem visam est rectus per medium diaphani unius generis...aut transitus...modi spiritualis, per quam ipsum est speculum...transitus...per...plura diaphana....*

p. 91, reference to Plato...*anima substantia seipsam movens.*

p. 345, *formam lucis in aere vel in corpore...transparente... nec lucis essentiam ibi esse...conceditur...nomine formae habitus consentitur....*

p. 347, *aeternae rationes rerum causatarum,* from Timaeus.

Grosseteste derives from Arabic treatises on perspective. It is too much to say that Guido had, perforce, read the Bishop of Lincoln, but certainly that is the *sort* of thing he had read.

His definition of "*l'accidente*", i.e. the whole poem, is a scholastic definition in form, it is as clear and definite as the prose treatises of the period, it shows an equal acuteness of thought. It seems to me quite possible that the whole of it is a sort of metaphor on the generation of light, or that at any rate greater familiarity with the philosophy of the period would elucidate the remaining tangles, particularly if one search for the part of philosophy that was in a state of activity in the years 1270-1290. One cannot absolutely rule out the possibility of Guido's having seen some scraps of MS. by Roger Bacon, although that is, perhaps, unlikely.

Considering the quality of Guido's mind as manifest in

indisputable passages it would, I think, be the greatest possible error to imagine that any part of the poem is decoration or stuffing. "*Talento di voler*" looks weak, but may not even that be due to an *idée fixe* on our part—"*di voler provare*" meaning, perhaps, technically, "try to prove", and the whole phrase, "I have no inclination to attempt proof" rather than "wish to will to prove"? If not, the *talento* is dragged in for the rhyme, and we must count it a blemish.

It may not be amiss, as illustrating the contemporary situation of philosophic thought in the British desert, and the recognition of one serious mind by another, to recall an incident of fifteen years past. When the late T. E. Hulme was trying to be a philosopher in that milieu, and fussing about Sorel and Bergson and getting them translated into English, I spoke to him one day of the difference between Guido's precise interpretive metaphor, and the Petrarchan fustian and ornament, pointing out that Guido thought in accurate terms; that the phrases correspond to definite sensations undergone; in fact, very much what I had said in my early preface to the Sonnets and Ballate.

Hulme took some time over it in silence, and then finally said: "That is very interesting"; and after a pause: "That is more interesting than anything anyone ever said to me. It is more interesting than anything I ever read in a book".

I was talking of certain passages in the Sonnets and Ballate, and not of this canzone, but the point should hold as well for the canzone.

What we need now is not so much a commentator as a lexicon. It is the precise sense of certain terms as *understood at that particular epoch* that one would like to have set before one.

For example does "*intenzion*" mean intention (a matter of will)? does it mean intuition, intuitive perception, or does the line hold the same meaning as that in Yeats's Countess Cathleen, *intenzion* being intention, and *ragione* meaning not reason, but "being right"?

At such points the commentators either branch off and give their own theories about the cosmos in general, or they restate with vague verbosity what Guido has said with greater pre- and con- cision.

As the philosophy of the time has been completely scrapped, there are very few specialists who can help us. I should be glad to hear from anyone who has more definite knowledge. Up to the present I have found out what I have found out by concentration on the text, and not by reading commentators, and I strongly suspect that is the road the next man will have to follow.

There are certain definite impasses, for definite palaeographical reasons. The copyists simply did not know, and we are unlikely to find any more or anterior manuscripts.

The other dimension of the poem is its lyricism, in the strictest sense of the term. It is made for song not for rhetorical declamation; on which count Dante twice mentions it in *De Vulgari Eloquio*, II, 12. First in connection with his own: "*Donne ch' avete intelletto d' amore*"; and secondly in comparison with his "*Poscia ch' Amor del tutto m' ha lasciato*".

CAVALCANTI

THE CANZONE

As it appears in the manuscript "Ld", Laurenziano 46-40, folio 32 verso, with a few errors corrected. Accents added from the Giuntine edition.

                                                                               Edizione Giuntina 1527.

DONNA mi priegha
                perch' i volglio dire   *io*
  D' un accidente   *uno*
          che sovente
                é fero
Ed é sí altero
      ch' é chiamato amore   *Amore*

SICCHE chi l negha   *Si chì lo*
       possa il ver sentire
Ond a 'l presente   *Ed a'l*
     chonoscente
        chero
Perch i no spero   *io nò*
     ch om di basso chore   *c' huom*

ATAL ragione portj chonoscenza   *raggio ne*
  Chè senza
      natural dimostramento
Non o talento   *hó*
     di voler provare   *Ld mostrare*
Laove nascie e chì lo fá criare   *Là dove ei posa, è*

EQUAL è sua virtu e sua potenza   *sia...vertute, è potenza*
  L' essenza
     e poi ciaschun suo movimento
E 'l piacimento   *MS. per*
     che 'l fá dire amare
E se hom per veder lo puó mostrare:—   *huomo*

363

Edizione Giuntina 1527.

IN quella parte
dove sta memoria *memora*
Prende suo stato *MS. su*
sí formato
chome
Diafan dal lume
d' una schuritade *oscuritate*

LA qual da Marte *Loqual*
viene e fá dimora
Elgli é creato
e a sensato *ed há*
nome
D' alma chostume
di chor volontade *è di cor*

VIEN da veduta forma ches' intende *chè s' Giuntine and Ld*
Che 'l prende *Chè prende*
nel possibile intelletto
Chome in subgetto
locho e dimoranza
E in quella parte mai non a possanza *há posanza*
MS. Ca *pesança*

PERCHÈ da qualitatde non disciende
Risplende *MS. risprende*
in sé perpetuale effecto
Non a diletto *há*
mà consideranza
Perche non pote laire simiglglianza:— *Si, ch' ei non puote largir simiglianza*

CAVALCANTI

N ON é virtute
                mà da questa vene   *dà quella*
    Perfezione   *Perchè perfettion si*
        ches si pone
                tale
Non razionale
            mà che si sente dicho   *omits s*

F UOR di salute
            giudichar mantene
E l antenzione   *Chè là intenzion*
        per ragione   *per ragion*
                vale
Discerne male   *MS. Diserue*
            in chui é vizio amicho

D I sua virtu seghue ispesso morte   *sua potenza...*
  Se forte   *spesso*
            la virtú fosse impedita
La quale aita
            la contrara via   *contraria*
Nonche opposito natural sia   *Non perchè opposta naturale*

M À quanto che da ben perfett e torte   *buon perfetto tort' é*
  Per sorte   *MS. forte*
            non po dir om ch abbi vita   *puó...c'*
Che stabilita   *haggia*
        non a singnioria   *há*
A simil puó valer quant uom l obblia:—   *valor quando s'oblia*

CAVALCANTI

LESSER é quando
             lo volere a tanto
  Ch oltre misura
             di natura
                    torna
Poi non si addorna
             di riposo maj

MOVE changiando
             cholr riso in pianto
E lla fighura
       con paura
             storna
Pocho soggiorna
             anchor di lui vedraj

CHE n gente di valore il piu si trova
  La nova
             qualità move a sospirj
E vol ch om mirj
             in un formato locho
Destandos' ira la qual manda focho

INMAGINAR nol puo hom che nol prova
  E non si mova
   MS. Ca Ne mova perch' a llui si tirj
                 gia
  E non si aggirj
             per trovarvi giocho
  E certamente gran saver nè pocho:—

Margin notes:
Edizione Giuntina 1527.
MS. omits é
é
oltra

s' adorna

core, è riso, è pianto

i sospiri

MS. Ld Destandositj loqual

puote
Gid non

giri
Nè certamente

366

CAVALCANTI

Da ssimil tragge
    complessione e sghuardj
 Che fá parere
   lo piacere
     piu certo
Non puó choverto
   star quand é si giunto

Non giá selvagge
    la biltá son dardj
Ch a tal volere
  per temere
    sperto
Hom seghue merto
   spirito che punto

E non si puó chonosciere per lo viso
 Chompriso
    biancho in tale obbietto chade
E chi ben aude
   forma non si vede
Perchè lo mena chi dallui procede

Fuor di cholore essere diviso
 Asciso
   mezzo schuro luce rade
Fuor d' ongni fraude
   dice dengno in fede
Chè solo da chostui nasce merzede :—

Tu puoj sichuramente gir chanzone
  Dove ti piace ch i t o sí ornata
  Ch assa lodata
    sará tua ragione
Dalle persone
   ch anno intendimento
Di star con l' altre tu non aj talento :—

Edizione Giuntina 1527.
Di MS. comprenssione sguardo. omits *e*

omits *piu*

le...*dardo*
Chè *tal*

esperto
Consegue
ch' é

, *bianco,*
vade
Ca *informa*
dà *lei*

d' *essere*
Assiso
in *mezzo oscuro luci*

di

ch' io t' hó si *adornata*
assai

CAVALCANTI

THE OTHER DIMENSION

The danger of a canzone composed entirely in hendecasyllabics is that of going heavy. Dante avoids it in *Donne ch' Avete* without using inner rhymes. Here Guido employs them.

The canzone of Guido's which Dante takes as a model of "construction" is not the *Donna mi Prega*, but *Poiche di Doglia*, of which only the first strophe is preserved, and this strophe for some obscure reason (or from simple habits of imitation) all editors insist on printing as a ballata, beginning with Di Giunta and ending, curiously enough, with Rivalta. Apart from Dante's clear reference to it, one should be able to observe its formation.

The reader will not arrive at a just appreciation of the canzone unless he be aware that there are three kinds of melopœia, that is to say, poems made to speak, to chant, and to sing. This canzone, Guido's poetry in general, and the poems of mediaeval Provence and Tuscany in general, were all made to be sung. Relative estimates of value inside these periods must take count of the cantabile values.

Modern professors with lifted eyebrows patronizing Dante's judgments in such matters appear to me rather like hypothetical persons who having taken an elementary course in phonetics or physics and having heard their wives' sisters play Chaminade, bring out: "Bach's opinions on the fugue which our later criticism has superseded...".

The canzone was to poets of this period what the fugue was to musicians in Bach's time. It is a highly specialized form, having its own self-imposed limits. I trust I have managed to print the *Donna mi Prega* in such a way that its articulations strike the eye without need of a rhyme table. The strophe is here seen to consist of four parts, the second

CAVALCANTI

lobe equal to the first as required by the rules of the canzone; and the fourth happening to equal the third, which is not required by the rules as Dante explains them.

Each strophe is articulated by 14 terminal and 12 inner rhyme sounds, which means that 52 out of every 154 syllables are bound into pattern. The strophe reverses the proportions of the sonnet, as the short lobes precede the longer. This reversal is obviously of advantage to the strophe *as part of* a longer composition.

At this point we divagate for fuller ultimate reference. The prestige of the sonnet in English is a relic of insular ignorance. The sonnet was not a great poetic *invention*. The sonnet occurred automatically when some chap got stuck in the effort to make a canzone. His "genius" consisted in the recognition of the fact that he had come to the end of his subject matter.

It should not be necessary for me now to quote the whole of the *De Vulgari Eloquio*. That notable opusculum is available in many and cheap editions. My own brief study of Arnaut Daniel may throw a further light on earlier phases of the canzone in the *lingua materna*.

As to the use of canzoni in English, whether for composition or in translation: it is not that there aren't rhymes in English; or enough rhymes or even enough two-syllable rhymes, but that the English two-syllable rhymes are of the wrong timbre and weight. They have extra consonants at the end, as in *flowing* and *going*; or they go squashy; or they fluff up as in *snowy* and *goeth*. They are not *rime agute*; they do not offer readily the qualities and contrasts that Dante has discussed so ably in *De Eloquio*.

Even so, it is not that one "cannot" use them but that they demand, at times, sacrifice of values that had not come into being and were therefore not missed in Limoges, A.D. 1200. Against which we have our concealed rhymes and our semi-submerged alliteration. (*En passant*, the alliteration

CAVALCANTI

in Guido's canzone is almost as marked as the rhyming though it enters as free component.)

It is not that one language cannot be made to do what another has done, but that it is not always expeditious to approach the same goal by the same alley. I do not think rhyme-aesthetic, *any* rhyme-aesthetic, can ever do as much damage to English verse as that done by latinization, in Milton's time and before. The rhyme pattern is, after all, a matter of chiselling, and a question of the *lima amorosa*, whereas latinization is a matter of compost, and in the very substance of the speech. By latinization I mean here the attempt to use an uninflected language as if it were an inflected one, i.e. as if each word had a little label or postscript telling the reader at once what part it takes in the sentence, and specifying its several relations. Not only does such usage—with remnants of Latin order—ruin the word order in English, but it shows a fundamental miscomprehension of the organism of the language, and fundamental stupidity of this kind is bound to spread its effects through the whole fibre of a man's writing.

HENDECASYLLABLES

Another prevalent error is that of dealing with Italian hendecasyllables as if they were English "iambic pentameter". One is told in college that Italian verse is not accentual but syllabic but I can't remember anyone's having ever presented the Anglo-American reader with a lucid discrimination between the two systems of measurement.

Some day I shall erect a monument to the books one reads in country hotels. Their titles and their authors evade one. One is not there "on business", one does not take notes and make excerpts. Let me, however, record here, that once in Sicily I came upon a century-old Italian school-book containing intelligent remarks upon metric. It was probably G. Biagioli's *Tractato d'Armonia di Verso Italiano* (Palermo,

1836), with references to the *Elementi di Poesia* of G. Gherardini. The author did not "lay down rules", he merely observed that Dante's hendecasyllables were composed of combinations of rhythm units of various shapes and sizes and that these pieces were put together in lines so as to make, roughly, eleven syllables in all. I say "roughly" because of the liberties allowed in elision. I had discovered this fact for myself in Indiana twenty years before and in my own work had made use of the knowledge continually, but I wish to salute Messrs Biagioli and Gherardini.

This system represented versification when it was in a healthy state, when *motz* had not been divorced from *son* and before the sonnet had got in its dirty work.

Historically the sonnet, the "little tune", had already in Guido's day become a danger to composition. It marks an ending or at least a decline of metric invention. It marks the beginning of the divorce of words and music. Sonnets with good musical setting are rare. The spur to the musician is slight. The monotony of the 14 even lines as compared to the constantly varying strophes of Ventadour or of Arnaut; the vocal heaviness of the hendecasyllable unrelieved by a shorter turn are all blanketing impediments for the music. This is not to say that the unrelieved hendecasyllable is impossible, and Dante, seeking the difficult, is quite right to set the canzone in unrelieved hendecasyllables as the grand bogey of technical mastery.

Guido, as we here observe, and as Dante had observed before us:

rithimorum repercussionem frequenter videtur assumptum.

He keeps the sound sharp and light in the throat by the rhymes inside the long line. Even some of the best Provençals, using a strophe of half his length, are unable to keep this cantabile virtue. All of which is probably a matter for specialists who will not be content with any general statement but will want to compare sound by sound the actual examples of mastersong that *totam artem comprehendunt*.

But one owes it to the general reader to jab his curiosity as to the degree of sonorous art, one might almost say of concrete or material sonority, required in this exposition of a general theme in the case of the *Donna mi Prega*; and of its relativity to the sonnet.

Of the great songs one remembers, that is songs sung with music, from *Ierusalem Mirabilis* to *Le Pauvre Laboureur*, and from that to Debussy's settings of Charles d'Orléans, does one remember a sonnet? And if so, how many?

The canzone, any canzone, is obviously in intention a *capolavoro*, a consummation of métier. Perhaps no poet has left half a dozen, or shall we say that Dante and Arnaut Daniel alone have left a half dozen each, that anyone can remember? If I exaggerate, I do not exaggerate very greatly.

Of Guido this one survives undisputed. There is one inferior canzone ascribed to him; there is a strophe of another (*Poiche di Doglia*); and there is, I should be inclined to sustain, a *chance* of his having written the first strophe, though certainly not the entire, canzone to Fortune.*

Apart from *Donna mi Prega*, Guido's reputation rests largely on the ballate, more or less his own field. That is to say, for purposes of song he chose a lighter and freer form, *not* the sonnet. In the ballata the first lobe is not immediately re-echoed. Tradition is that the ballata is made from popular dance-song, a scrap of folk-song caught up for the beauty of its tune, or for some felicity, and then made into an art-form, more emotional and more emotive than the form of the Italian canzone.

* 1934. Whole question of authenticity of the other canzoni thrown wide open again by examination of manuscript I. ix. 18 in Comunale di Siena. For further details, see my *Guido Cavalcanti: Rime*, Genova, anno X.

Note that by A.D. 1290 the sonnet is already ceasing to be lyric, it is already the epistle without a tune, it is in a state of becoming, and tends already to oratorical *pronunciamento*.

The strophes of canzoni are perforce symmetrical as the musical composition is only one-fifth or one-sixth the length of the verbal composition and has to be repeated. I don't believe we can prove complete absence of modulation; or that in case of canzon in tenzone one should assume impossibility of answer to tonic from dominant. Neither do we know what happened to the tune of the sestina while the recurrence scheme was performing its evolution; the six units of the tune may, and in the case of Arnaut's *Oncle ed Ongla* could very well, have followed some permutation of modes or key. The aesthetic of the carry-through of one rhyme scheme from strophe to strophe is of Provençal not of Tuscan composition.

We know something of twelfth-century music, or have at least some grounds for particular conjecture, graphs, that is, of pitch sequence for some two hundred melodies; we are without any such comparable guide for "Dante and his Circle". I know of no manuscript containing music of that particular period; the one "item" in the Siena *Archivio* is not a fragment of melody, but two lines of police record: Casella jugged for being out after curfew.

But considering the finesse of some of the Limousin melodies there is nothing to prevent our conjecture that the decadence of verbal mastery in Italian poetry may have paced a parallel decline in the melodic component. This would apply to the perfection of the single line or the "snatch" of song; to the close fit of word and melody, but not, presumably, to the whole form of the music. One may summarize the phases of development of the canzon as follows:

1. Strophe with few terminal sounds, no more than four

sounds, repeated throughout the poem, meaning that the same rhyme would occur 18 or 24 times in the poem, or even more. After a century or so this grew monotonous, and we have

2. Use of *rimas escarsas* which may mean either the hunting up of less usual terminal sounds, or the spacing out of the rhymes. In Arnaut's *L'Aura Amara*, we have 14 different rhyme sounds only 3 of which repeat inside the strophe, 11 of them repeat only from one strophe to the rest, that is occur only 6 or 7 times in the poem.

3. Abandonment of the carry-through in *Can Chai la Fueilla*. Here in Guido's canzone eight different sounds form the pattern inside the strophe; five occur four times, and three twice.

To be well done this patterning must lighten, not clog the movement, either of sense or sound.

As to the atrocities of my translation, all that can be said in excuse is that they are, I hope, for the most part intentional, and committed with the aim of driving the reader's perception further into the original than it would without them have penetrated. The melodic structure is properly indicated —and for the first time—by my disposition of the Italian text, but even that firm indication of the rhyme and the articulation of the strophe does not stress *all* the properties of Guido's triumph in sheer musicality.

One must strive almost at any cost to avoid a sort of mealy mumbling almost universally tolerated in English. If English verse undulates the average ear tolerates it, or even welcomes it, though the undulation be but as a wobble of bread-dough, utterly noncantabile, even when not wholly unspeakable.

I have not given an English "equivalent" for the *Donna mi Prega*; at the utmost I have provided the reader, unfamiliar with old Italian, an instrument that may assist him in gauging some of the qualities of the original.

All this is not so unconnected with our own time as it might seem. Those writers to whom *vers libre* was a mere "runnin' dahn th' road", videlicet escape, and who were impelled thereto by no inner need of, or curiosity concerning, the quantitative element in metric, having come to the end of that lurch, lurch back not into experiment with the canzone or any other unexplored form, but into the stock and trade sonnet.

THE VOCABULARY

In accordance with the views exposed in the preceding pages, and recognizing the justness of Karl Vossler's remarks about our "schwankenden Kenntnis", but being dubious of the sense in which he applies the term, or the justness of applying it to the "nicht weniger schwankenden psychologischen Terminologie Cavalcantis" I have spent a certain amount of time trying to deal with the vocabulary used in the canzone, and elsewhere in Guido.

The following pages have appeared or may appear elsewhere in discussion of Luigi Valli's theories *re* secret conspiracies, mystic brotherhoods, widely distributed (and uniform) cipher in "all" or some poems of the period, etc. I do not believe that much, if anything, that Valli says can be applied to the *Donna mi Prega*. Some of it, perhaps a good deal of it, may possibly apply to the sonnets; at any rate Valli deserves thanks for disturbing a too facile acceptance of cut and dried acceptances. In one or two cases where I think him wrong, I certainly owe him a quickened curiosity, and a better guess than I should have made without the irritant of his volume.*

I now set down simply citations and passages from works accessible to Cavalcanti (or contemporaneous or slightly later), where technical philosophical terms occur in a sense compatible

* Luigi Valli, "Il Linguaggio Segreto di Dante". Roma, "Optima," 1928.

with, or casting light on the usage of the same or similar terms in his writing. In the case of the canzone itself the reader may, if still interested, compare the clarity and profundity of the literal sense of the poem, with the, to me at least, far less satisfactory and coherent exposition by Signor Valli.

If he have a long memory he may even recall that I cited Avicenna and Averroes as, probably, the main origins of Guido's philosophical location, and indicated his possible acquaintance with Grosseteste. As to my further digging:

1. Where various MSS. and most editions read *destando s' ira*, I had left the reading of MS. Ld, *destandositj*, in order to indicate the uncertainty of the reading. I was looking for some possible equivalent of the Latin *sitis*. This is not necessary, as *Ira* makes sense, but it does not mean Wrath. It is a very good illustration of the way words shift in meaning through careless usage. Dr Walther Echstein of Vienna having given me a clue, a list of more or less forgotten technical and theological lexicons, I find in that of Johannes Tytz (pub. 1619) that *Ire, Ira* "according to Aristotle" (by which Tytz obviously means some Latin translation of Aristotle) is *accensio sanguinis circum cor*; which can be translated with the varying shades: "enflaming, inflammation, or enkindling of the blood about the heart". Tytz continues citing other writers by abbreviation: "Ioan. Damas. vaporatione fellis, vel perturbatione fiens (?splenis). Hugo. irrationabilis perturbatio mentis. Aug. ulciscendi libido. Casid. immoderatus animi motus, concitatus ad poenam seu vindictam. Gers. ira est duplex, non est peccatum imo magis poena". That is to say that in the norm of use *Ire* meant the commotion. It is only its excesses that meant "Wrath". "Species Irae excesse effectu nominatae sunt, furor, insania, rancor. Non puram passionem, imo quamdam actionem qua deordinatur homo, et quantum ad Deum et quantum ad proximum."

The six daughters of Ire are: "rixa, timor mentis, contumelia, clamor, indignatio, blasphemia". This also lights a line in one of the sonnets. "Che ciascun' altra in ver di lei chiamo ira." I made a dull translation of it eighteen years ago, because I was interested in the other lines of the sonnet and that one seemed merely a blank. The *Ira* is, as we see, not wrath. And the line means: "So that by comparison with her, any other woman seems merely a senseless confusion".

2. *Chiamo* and *Dico* appear in Guido's Canzone and the Sonnets. They look at first, second and third sight like padding. A plunge into the prose philosophers of the period shows that they are used as "*I define*", or "*for this I should use the term*". And that they thus in verse give an air of leisure and precision; are not cotton wool but an elegance.

3. I guessed right in stressing the difference between *Amore* (noun) and *Amare* (verb) in the first strophe. The philosophical difference is that a noun is a significant sound which makes no discrimination as to time. "Nomen est vox significativa, ad placitum, sine tempore, cuius nulla pars est significativa separate." The verb locates in time. "Verbum logice consideratum est quod consignificat tempus" (Albertus Magnus).

The reader will see that the English version of St John loses this philosophical or metaphysical shade in reading: "the word became flesh", for "verbum caro", etc.

4. Perhaps the strongest justification of collateral research is to be found when we come to the passage which the best editors have up to now read (with various spellings):

"che prende—nel possibile intelletto
   come 'n subietto".

There is no metrical or palaeographic objection to this reading which occurs in several very early codices. But I find in Avicenna's *Metaphysices Compendium* (trad. Nematallah Carame; pub. Pont. Inst. Orient. Stud. 1926) that when one thing enters or exists in another as a wooden peg in a wall this thing is not *accidens* in a "subject". Therefore if the phrase reads *che prende* Guido is either using very careless language or means that his image of the seen form busts up or melts when it enters the possible (or receptive) intellect.

Lib. I, Cap. 3, III. "Quando autem etc. non sicut palus et

murus, sed utraque in altera diffusa secundum totam suam essentiam...etc. Omnis autem essentia cuius subsistentia est in subiecto est accidens."

So that turning to Codex Ce, Chigiana L.V. 176 which contains the Del Garbo exegesis of the canzone we find *che 'l prende*; it is slightly rougher metrically, but it is presumably the correct reading as neither from the character of the excellent old MSS. nor from Del Garbo's prose have we any reason to think that either he or the scribe inserted the extra pronoun. The single letter would show both that Guido read Avicenna (or someone who agreed with that dissociation of ideas) and more important for our literary purpose that his language is speech of precision.

The MSS. Ce, Mm, Rh, Lh, Lb and La

Michele Barbi suspects that Ce shows the writing of Boccaccio "in his old age when his hand was no longer steady". This might well be. Boccaccio was a friend of the Garbo family as we know by his sonnet on the death of Dino's son. Dino had a wide reputation as physician, he attended Mussato and we have record of the bracing effect of his presence in the sick room.

The reading *che 'l* persists in MSS. Mm, Rh, Lh, in the text given with Garbo's commentary in Lb and finally in La from which we can calculate the probable duration of the mediaeval tradition or at least the interest in, and knowledge of, Avicenna, etc. The Medicean scholar who transcribed La was presumably the last copyist to understand the text placed before him. This single detail gives much greater authority to La than one would otherwise have accorded it.

Avicenna is, *en passant*, one of the most attractive authors of the period, I recommend to Signor Valli's attention the *seicento* edition of the *De Almahad* which contains the paragraph beginning "Amplius in coitu phantasia".

5. The rashness of hasty conclusion is again indicatable from another line where the change of a single letter would shift our whole series of guesses concerning Guido's philosophical leanings. There is absolutely no certainty whatsoever in the present state

of our knowledge, and I think "scientific" certainty will probably remain out of the question. The importance of the matter will never outweigh the difficulties or the value of living men's time.

In my text I gave *laire simiglglianza*; other writers gave *largir* or some variant, there are more than a dozen readings of this passage, which indicates that the copyists were puzzled, and in the end had to put down something whether they understood it or not. Reading "*largir*" one can at a pinch cast out guesses regarding Grosseteste or about some treatise on light and maximum of diffusion. But supposing that the illegible or incomprehensible word were not the *largir* or *la ire* or *la gire*, but that the copyist had dropped an *r* from the *pote* that precedes it; we should have *porte l'aire*. The reading does not occur in any MSS. But the single letter would throw the passage into "pneumatic philosophy". There is plenty of pneumatism in Guido's sonnets.

The study of terms of abuse has been neglected. For centuries if you disliked a man you called him a Manichaean, as in some circles to-day you would call him a Bolshevic to damage his earning capacity. But suppose the term Epicurean in 1290 had not become merely a term of abuse, a pejorative likely to damage the slandered object. Suppose that some germ of the admittedly uncertain sense of Epicureanism still existed, and that tradition is correct and has even a shade of precise meaning when it calls Guido Epicurean, one is within one's rights in wondering whether this pneumatism comes *via* Epicurus.

Salvadori says that the doctrine comes originally out of Egypt, and Fr. Fiorentino that it comes *via* Democritus; it exists in both Stoic and Epicurean forms.

One cannot insist on the reading *porte*, but it does indicate the kind of possibility one must consider before plumping it down that Guido belonged to such or such gang of mystics.

With the general precision of terminology in an age when highbrows had very little save terminology to occupy their attention, we have no right to suppose that the meaning of Epicureanism had been filed down to mean merely "exaggerated and lazy hedonism".

CAVALCANTI

According to the pneumatici the likeness of things, or a sort of emanation of them was carried upon the *pneuma*, or special air, and entered the hearts, etc. If Guido's sonnet:

"Per gli occhi fiere un spirito sottile"

is not as thoroughgoing a bit of pneumatism as one could desire, it is at any rate a more complete exposition of its modus than I am likely to get into a couple of lines. If I muddle the question it is at least one that has to be considered. As is also the then opinion, or ten dozen opinions regarding hypostasis; "lumen est colorum hypostasis" says one writer out of agreement, it would appear, with subsequent science.

The serious author (I was about to write: Confound it, the serious author) must really look into these details before blandly, or energumenicly assuring us that the canzone expresses some one particular dogma, let alone that dogma in cipher.

I don't think I began translating it with any preconceived notion of what I should find; but if ever poem seemed to me a struggle for clear definition, that poem is the *Donna mi Prega*. Nor do I see where a code cipher could be slipped into it. Valli would indubitably leap on the first word, *Donna*, but there is nothing to prove the contention that even if Guido is writing to a fellow lodge member he is writing in cipher. There is the *bianco* in the last strophe, which Valli might connect with his Augustinian "dealbatio". But we are still far from heresy, let alone such an one as he postulates, a violent and dangerous heresy which would land the lot of them "nel rogo", indeed the odour of roast heretic is far more prevalent in Valli's conjecture than in the pages of contemporary chronicle.

Taking the analysis from another angle. Or let us say, looking for its Christian affiliation: of Augustine I find nothing but the agreement with Augustine's sequence of

"esse, species rei, et ordo"

corresponding to Persons of the Trinity, and, in the human spirit to

"memory, intelligence and will".

CAVALCANTI

This sequence is followed in the *Donna mi Prega*. But it is probably too general to serve as indication of anything in particular. One can merely observe that there is in this connection no contradiction between the two authors.

There is certainly more meat for us in Avicenna's passage, already noticed.

"Deinceps, si recipiens in sui constitutivo non indiget eo quod in ipso recipitur, tunc hoc vocamus recepti subjectum; si autem eo indiget, tunc non subjectum ipsum vocaremus sed forsitan hylen ("YΛH) vocabimus. Omnis essentia quae non sit in subiecto est substantia. Omnis autem essentia cuius subsistentia est in subiecto est accidens" (*Metaphysices Compendium*, Tr. I, Cap. III, 3, p. 6; Bishop Carame's translation, Pont. Inst. Orient. Stud. 1926).

Albertus Magnus also offers: "Secundum autem accidens memorabilia sunt quaecumque sunt cum phantasia, sicut sunt intellecta intellectus possibilis quae ex phantasmatibus iterum applicantur, quando ex intellectis anima reflectitur in rem prius per sensum acceptam". But his tone of mind is not quite in keeping with Guido's thought.

There is, as I had indicated, a mare's nest in "*intenzione*"; in some theologians it is a matter of will, with the meaning "intention". But from Alfarabi into Averroes, and from them into Albertus there is a first and a second *intentio*, which are modes of perception. Duns Scotus's "voluntas super intellectu" seems to have no bearing on the poem. The whole poem is alive with Eriugenian vigour.

Occam, after Guido's death, has written: "terminus conceptus est intentio seu passio animae aliquid naturaliter significans vel consignificans, nata esse pars propositionibus mentalis". That is no use as "source" but it might serve as determining verbal usage *circa* 1328.

At times and with some texts before me, "natural dimostramento", would seem to imply almost biological proof. In postulating Guido as "the great logician", which Boccaccio says that he was, I do not want to exaggerate, or cast him in the fifteenth century in place of the thirteenth.

However, if Guido and his correspondents are a gang (secret) of Nonconformists, aching to reform mother church, plotting and corresponding in hyper-heretical cipher, the most indigestible morsel for Signor Valli is Egidio Colonna, il beato. Colonna is a very dead author, possibly no Anglo-Saxon has seen his name save in some brief passage or footnote to the effect that he wrote a comment on Guido, and seen it but to be bored. Some old geezer has written a commentary. He is indeed a very dead author, my sincere commiseration goes out to anyone who has to read his appallingly prolix work on the education of princes. (Dante in *Convito*, IV, 24, l. 97 disposed of an Egidio Eremita.) The researcher's first jolt comes, or at least my first jolt came in discovering how many editions of his work were printed between the years 1500 and 1600; my second in finding (Fr. Fiorentino's *Manual of Philosophy*) that the Frate Egidio was chief among the immediate disciples of Aquinas. "Tra i seguaci di questa prima età spetta il primo luogo ad Egidio Colonna." So that when the editor of the *Parnaso* mentions Egidio's commentary in evidence of Guido's position, it was for that age very much what it would be if we found to-day a commentary by William James on some lyrist whose work had filled less than a hundred pages.

Are we to conclude that the eminent Thomist was gulled, or that he was a heretic ramping in secret and concealing the poet's meaning?

In either case Signor Valli should look at Egidio's exegesis. It begins aptly for his purpose with the secret fountain, obviously the source or font of tradition, the lady sends out her messengers, the first of whom is King Solomon, excellent for the mystic theory, but the second is Ovidius Naso, and while you and I, gentle reader, might grant that Ovid had in him more divine wisdom than all the Fathers of the Church put together, would Signor Valli at this point join our party?

Of course if Valli can seriously find his ascetic cipher in the ballata beginning:

"In un boschetto trovai pastorella"

he might even find it in Ovid's eclogue that begins with the words: "Aestus erat". But would the Frate Egidio? Would the eminent Aristotelian have chosen just these three men, Solomon, Ovid and Guido, as messengers from our lady of Paphos, or from the Divina Sapienza? Was Ovid also singing the yearning of the passive intellect for the active, and if so did he suspect it?

There are still other difficulties before Signor Valli, but perhaps I have mentioned enough. And perhaps Guido was enamoured as Dante has remarked of a certain Madonna Primavera, who, as Dante does not remark, had set the dance in Langue d'Oc and in Lemosi.

And even if Dante's admiration for Virgil's "style" is a cryptogram meaning not Virgil's style but his "maniera di simboleggiare" (Valli); might not Guido's disrespect of Virgil free him from charge of simboligization?

By all of which I do not mean Valli is necessarily wrong in his main contention. He is merely a very bad advocate, trusting to conviction rather than to clear-headed observation and logic. If he will throw out his suppositions, and his inept evidence and stick to the unsolved enigmas one can give him many passages on which the, by him, hated positivisti could gain no foothold whatever.

Arnaut would be perhaps better ground for him than Guido. What for example is "Mantle of Indigo"? Is "doma", in "cils di doma", an equivalent to the Italian word *domma*, meaning dogma?

If Arnaut says "I love her more than god does her of the dogma", does he speak of a secret doctrine more precious to its followers than the orthodox? Does the illegible "di noigandres" boggle a Greek "ennoia" or "dianoia"? At least it is open ground, and if Valli chose to assert these things no one could bring proof against him. Coming to Guido, he could find various inexplicable passages: "Morte" would indeed fit his cipher in several places; as in

"che Morte 'l porta in man tagliato in croce".

The
"beyond life's compass thrown,

. . . . .

melted of bronze or carven in tree or stone",
"Fatto di pietra o di rame o di legno",
would serve him. What is the magic river "filled full of lamias" that Guido sends to Pinella in return for her caravan? Who is "del tondo sesto" and why the "sixth round"?

It would be as myopic to reject Valli's theory as impossible, as it would be to think Valli had proved his case, or even approached a proof, or considered the limits and definition of what he says he is proving.

There are places where attempted application of his code would turn a good poem into a mere piece of priggishness and vain theory, in no way accounting for its manifest lyric impulse, or for the emotional force in its cadence. Here the code theory will, naturally, be as unwelcome and annoying, as it is welcome when he tries to turn a bad poem into a subject of historic interest, or to at least an amusing riddle. Valli must try to imagine what sort of mysticism his adepts and neophytes practised, and what its effect would have been, for certainly neither Frederick II nor Cavalcanti were openly famed as ascetics. Frederick has been accused of nearly everything, even, recently, of orthodoxy (to the great distress of his admirers), but never yet of timidity.

If Guido is concealing anything it is certainly not the spirit of complete personal independence, nor yet of open defiance of piety—for whoever be the heroine of the sonnet "Una figura..." its blasphemous intention is open to the simplest capacity. If sect existed, Guido's pastorellas, as distinct from Donne, may as well imply contempt for the sect as for anything else in the neighbourhood.

A really good mind throws out not only the *idées reçues* of its time, but the fancy snobbism of the "elect"; Rabelais was no more bluffed by the pagan authors so modish in his day, than he was by the ecclesiastics.

In sum, Valli cannot offer us merely two alternatives, he must offer us something like thirty. He can take the *Convito*, and play with it as he likes, but he must leave the *De Vulgari Eloquio*, which, if not an aesthetic treatise in modern mode, is most certainly a technical treatise, on the way to hammer sounds into lines, and as such still valid. Whatever Dante's symboligating propensities, he was positivist on his craft, in this he was a *fabbro*, and one respecting the craft and the worker. Italian poetry would have gained by following his traces, and our own would be less a mess if Chaucer had so closely considered technique instead of uselessly treating the Astrolabe.

In no case can the answer be simple, and in any case the learned Valli might do well to recognize the still extant folk-ways of the Latins; having offered him so many subjects for meditation I offer him still another though he may not see the connection: I was once engaged in trying to get a Northumbrian intellectual out of jail *emprès Ponthoise*, and in so doing I fell into converse with the Corsican cop on duty, and at the end of eight or ten minutes he drew from his pocket two poems written in Anagram, so that the letters beginning the lines in the one read "PIERRE ET MARIE", and in the other "LUCILE ET PIERRE", and after I read through them he added, as excuse, or as explanation, "Ça plaît beaucoup aux dames".

There is still perfectly solid ground for arguing that the language of Guido is secret only as the language of any technical science is secret for those who have not the necessary preparation. The "tondo sesto" may be the "tondo di Sesto" ("Empirico").

THE CANZONE: FURTHER NOTES

It is "impossible" to argue every opinion on every passage of the canzone, or in any case it would conduce to an endless volume. Without disputing Valli's opinion or anyone else's opinion, I shall now simply tabulate some few bits of information or

CAVALCANTI

tradition that, as I see it, should be considered before coming to a conclusion, regardless as to whether they confirm my own views or anyone's views. In none of the immediately following notes do I mean to imply anything, or to lead the reader to think that, say Del Garbo's opinion, or anyone else's opinion is conclusive.

STROPHE I

(I give the words, and omit line numbers)

Donna.

Del Garbo, egregio medicine doctor and as such presumably acquainted with Averroes. (MS. Ce, Chig. L, 176.) *Sic:* "Causa aūt (ait or aiunt) movês (the circumflex means *n*) ad hoc ē mulier ut dn̄a (donna) que i pm̄ rogavit... attribuit nom̄ donna... mulieri digne... e in etate puerile iq̄ua cognitio nô perfecta nô attribuit. hc nom̄ donna. Iterum et attribuit muliere digne", etc. Del Garbo is not looking for or admitting any cryptogram, he is concerned with its being a woman old enough to possess knowledge, and of good family. The question noble blood, etc., was then, as we know from Dante, a subject of interest and debate.

Accidente.

(See quotation from Avicenna on p. 378.)

For Del Garbo it is "passio" (affect), distinct from the extrinsic, an "accidente" and the dogmas are mainly concerned with substances, original creations, the Trinity, etc., also with original sin.

From the rest of the list it would seem that the time spirit among the students in Paris, 1279, was drifting much more to general *non curanza* and scepticism than to mystic conjurations. Something that Renan translates as "raison naturelle" had appeared in one of Gregory IX's denunciations of Frederick II.

Natural dimostramento.

After the repeated, somewhat frenetic attacks on Averroism, by Albert, Aquinas, etc., and repeated condemnations, Etienne Tempier, in 1277, condemns among other propositions: "Quod

CAVALCANTI

naturalis philosophus simpliciter debet negare mundi novitatem, quia nititur causis et rationibus naturalibus: *fidelis* autem potest negare mundi æternitatem quia nititur causis supernaturalibus".

The bishop *versus* the quarter; Aquinas foams at the mouth about people who discuss these things with kids, instead of publishing formal answers to him; there is question whether the accursed by Gm. de Tocco are Goliardiae, "qui Averrois erant communiter sectantes", or whether it ought to read Garlandiae (data in Renan's *Averroès*).

In any case the poet is obstreperous. His work is no guarantee of tranquillity and mental sleep.

I do not want to lengthen the list of commentators who re-state Guido's propositions less accurately than he has. Still if one is to speculate on where his propositions lead, I should say he even exceeds the last remark in this paragraph of condemnation of Tempier's, which is: "philosophus debet captivare intellectum in obsequium fidei". Guido certainly in "non razionale, ma che si sente" allows more importance to feeling than the bishop would have approved.

BUT I doubt if it can be proved that Guido has emitted a provably heretical proposition, i.e. one definitely bashing in any specific dogma. He defines.

Del Garbo (Ce) *sic*: "et ĉ -i- sine nāli dem̂ostratiôe q̄ī velit dicere q̄/ eo q̄ dicet extræt ex pr̂icipi^s_j fac̄ naturaī et nô solū extract ex principij fac̄ nāl (illegible word...? uno) ex principi^o_j fac̄ moral et astrologie et ô (audieret huic) sermonis dz c̄c̄ îteligês". The interesting contribution, despite the illegibility, is the "astrologie". And the main contention would seem to be that he "extracts", sets apart the natural fact from "principles", i.e. dogma. And "not only the natural fact, but the moral and astrological fact". Del Garbo died, I believe, Sept. 30th, A.D. 1327. The passage would seem to back up what I have already said regarding Guido's general attitude. Del Garbo would seem to have noticed the same implications that I did. (The MS. Ce reads erroneously "posa" for "nasce", l. 10, and "amore" for "amare", l. 13, with later correction above the line. Garbo is misled by these readings in his comment.) I think we might consider Del Garbo's comment as that of the objective critic, Averroist, natural philosopher, really looking at Guido's words (i.e. the MS. as it lay before him even in its one or two textual errors); and that we might consider Egidio as seeking the theological rather than philosophical verity, i.e. lecturing on what Guido "ought to have meant". I do not want to force this view. *Vide infra*, end of note on "intelletto".

Amare.

In distinction to *amore*, vide p. 377.

STROPHE II

Memoria. Vide p. 381.

Diafan. Vide pp. 359–60. Cf. *Paradiso* x, 69.

Marte.

Da Marte: I suppose as "impulse". At any rate there is a Neoplatonic gradation of the assumption of faculties as the mind descends into matter through the seven spheres, *via* the gate of Cancer: in Saturn, reason; in Jupiter, practical and moral; in Mars, the "spirited"; in Venus, the sensuous. Cf. Dante's *voi ch' intendendo il terzo ciel movete.* Macrobius, *In Somnium Scipionis*; and Plotinus, *Ennead.*

Del Garbo animadverts on the "luxurious" nature of those in whose horoscope Mars is in the house of Venus, Taurus, Libra, etc.

S' intende.

Cf. Spinoza: The intellectual love of a thing consists in the understanding of its perfections. The *forma s' intende* so that the *amore* (accidens) takes *state*.

Che 'l prende. Vide p. 378.

Possibile intelletto and *Come in subjecto.* Vide p. 378.

There is no **safety**: until several specialists have been on this topic for a decade each, no one has any right to present opinions as if they were proved.

Albertus says memory. Renan has a note (*Averroès et l'Aver-*

roïsme, p. 126) on Denis, combating Averroes regarding "intellect passif". Sic: "L'intellect passif n'est alors que la faculté de recevoir les PHANTASMATA". This is exactly what I think is NOT in Guido Cavalcanti. The terms *intellectus possibilis*, POSSIBLE, and the *Passive* intellect belong to two different schools, two different sets of terminology. In dealing with Guido Cavalcanti we should stick to such authors as use "possibile intelletto". Or if the "passif" equals the "possible" then the *l* before *prende* goes out.

Unless a term is left meaning one particular thing, and unless all attempt to unify different things, however small the difference, is clearly abandoned, all metaphysical thought degenerates into a soup. A soft terminology is merely an endless series of indefinite middles.

Del Garbo explains: "et sic dyaphani qñ lumine îformat ita informat^v memoria ex spc$^\wedge$ rei ex^a_qcatur amor". In addition to which I note the following in Renan, speaking of Zimara on Averroes: "L'intellect actif n'est ni Dieu lui-même...ni une simple faculté de l'âme...mais une substance supérieure à l'âme, séparable, incorruptible" (Renan, *Averroès*, p. 376). Cf. debate of Guido Cavalcanti with Orlandi, Sonnet XVI and Orlandi's reply.

Guido is, I think, "safe" in confining himself to a discussion of an "accidens", which probably lay outside the scope of the dogma. I mean that he can remain scientific without treading on the toes of theology (save of course by implication and general frame of mind). And the "che si sente" would even justify my use of the term "affect" in translation.

Cf. also Carlini's translation of Aristotle's *Metaphysics* (XI (K) 1. 1059 a, 29): "Che se diversa è la scienza che studia le sostanze, e...quella che studia gli accidenti? E quale delle due è la sapienza? Poiché una di esse procederà dimostrativamente, quella intorno agli accidenti; l'altra, quella delle sostanze, riguarderà, invece, i primi principii".

Locho, dimoranza.

("Proprio loco", in Orlandi's sonnet.)

CAVALCANTI

Risplende in sé. Vide p. 360.

Largir simiglianza: simiglianza. (p. 379.)

The pseudo Dionysius mentions that the order of angels called Dominions is "elevated above dissimilarity"..

Largir simiglianza: Largir.

Renan (*Averroès et l'Averroïsme*) cites a passage of Albertus (*De apprehensione*, pars v, vol. 21 of the works): "Possibilis speculativa recipiens cum eis lumen suscipit agentis, cui de die in diem fit similior; et quum acceperit possibilis omnia speculata seu intellecta, habet lumen agentis ut formam sibi adhaerentem.... Ex possibili et agente compositus est intellectus adeptus, et divinus dicitur, et tunc homo perfectus est. Et fit per hunc intellectum homo Deo quodam modo similis, eo quod potest sic operari divina, et LARGIRI sibi et aliis intellectus divinos, et accipere omnia intellecta quodam modo, et est hoc illud scire quod omnes appetunt, in quo felicitas consistit contemplativa".

I do not think this indicates that Guido was in any way taking Albertus as model. Renan prefaces the citation with a phrase that would suit Signor Valli: "L'intellect agent s'unit au possible", it continues "si comme la lumière au diaphane".

I do not, in the canzone, smell "ittisâl", Sufi doctrine of union.

In one receipt for "contemplation" I find that it properly should imply contemplation of divine things, from which *Amore* is omitted. It seems possible that Guido is claiming rank for *Amor*. In any case my thesis would be that he, familiar with the most lively philosophic thought of the time, is treating his topic rather more efficiently than the contemporary prose lecturers. Using the citation from Albertus solely as lexicography, the meaning of the passage enclosing "largir simiglianza" would yield: Radiates splendour in itself, itself's perpetual effect,...as it cannot confer its likeness (on anything else).

Or, one might interpret: glows throughout the possible intellect, which it has completely transfused, but does not penetrate into lower strata.

Pesanza for *Possanza* seems to me simply the duller, even stupider word, a dead instead of an active word: simpliste reading. Ld and Ce both clearly read *possanza*. Di Giunta: *posanza*. The ignorant connection of weight and descent would easily account for ignorant changing to *pesanza* as precursor of *discende*. Colonna reads *posanza* and comments on *inquietudine*. Frachetta makes out a sort of case for *pesanza*, less poetical to our sense. He was perhaps more anxious to display his "knowledge" of Aristotle than an understanding of Guido. However, the intellectual concept was not supposed to be subject to whatever the Middle Ages called what we now call gravity.

The error *chei* in the last line of the strophe would, however, naturally occur from someone *understanding* "largir simiglianza", and looking, too hastily, for an object upon which the *simiglianza* was to be conferred. ("Si chei non puote.")

Ld and Ce *ought* to be independent if the dissimilarity of "Perche non pote" (Ld) and "Si che non puote" (Ce, Del Garbo) is any indication. Rivalta in fact derives them from Mart. and Ba of his main middle group. His reasons for preferring *pesanza* are not clear to me.

STROPHE III

Virtute.

Del Garbo in discussing the opening lines of this strophe formulates the alternative: "ut virtus, aut procedens ex virtute".

Antenzione. Vide p. 361.

Discerne male.

The interpreter with too great a thirst for metaphysics, and metaphysical interpretations, must not rush over this phrase. It blocks several too abstract, too deadly intellectual decodings. If the *Amor* is limited to *amor sapientiae* why drag in this phrase and why also drag in the *che si sente*?

Opposito natural.

Merely to note the repetition of *natural* at this point and refer it to anything that has been said regarding *natural dimostramento* (Strophe I).

STROPHE IV

L'esser é quando.
 Time relation established. If the "*possibil*" *intelletto* is merely faculty for receiving phantasmata, the *amor* here should presumably pass from latent possibility into "being" (? active existence). Cf. also the lines in Orlandi's sonnet:

"Sustanza, o accidente, o ei memora?
 E cagion d' occhi, o è voler di core?"

Formato locho.
 In my translation I followed the reading "non formato". I do not think it can be held as the correct one. Rivalta chooses "non fermato" which I distinctly disbelieve in, despite the emendation above the lines in the Roman, Del Garbo MS. (Ce). Rivalta argues from his favourite "Mart". Ba, with the Colonna comment, gives very visibly "un formato".

This occurs also in the highly respectable Mb and in Ld. Di Giunta's editing of the canzone was extremely careful, as may be indicated still further by the list of variants known to him.

The point would also dispose of the canard that MS. Ma was in any way connected with Di Giunta's edition despite certain similarities in its other readings. Neither can I believe that its calligraphy indicates any such antiquity. If it represents any state of Di Giunta's opinion, even copied by a later hand, it does not represent his final opinion whereby the *non fermato* is relegated to rejected variants. "Non formato" is useful for immediate effect, i.e. of the single line, but does not cohere in the general exposition. The "formato locho" is the tract or locus marked out in the "possibile intelletto", and is buttressed by the rest of Orlandi's line "ov' ei dimora". I do not think Egidio is sound in thinking the "formato *locho*" is a single image. Determined locus or habitat would be nearer the mark. This is not absolutely what Egidio Colonna specifies when he says: "riguardar l' imagine ...laquale è nella fantasia...laquale è formata e figurata di diverse figure...e diverse imagine".

Colonna has read "che prende" not "che 'l prende" and obscured our Avicennian "accident" diffused throughout the "subject". To keep all the distinctions the "formato *locho*" would have, I should say, to be the "fantasia" itself, already pervaded by the *accidente*, which *comes from* the seen form.

As to "form"; you may here add the whole of mediaeval philosophy by way of footnote. Form, Gestalt, "every spiritual form sets in movement the bodies in which (or among which) it finds itself". Aquinas's attack on Averroes in which he has to twist the meaning of the term almost 180 degrees off its course, etc. "Veduta forma" must, however, be extrinsic and perceived, if we are to leave any shred of verbal meaning in any term whatsoever.

As parallel to the "qual è suo *proprio* luogo?" in the second line of Orlandi's sonnet of enquiry, Albertus Magnus (I think it is in the *Sex principiis*) has: "non omnis situs est proprie et principaliter dicta positio".

Destandosi ira.

I think we can accept this reading as correct, for *ira, vide* p. 376. We have Ba, Ma, Rivalta against a dispersed set of readings.

Immaginar.

Still meaning at that time, I should think, to form an image. Taking this line by itself, perhaps a rash procedure, you can isolate a general negation of image-making faculty in those not "chonoscenti".

STROPHE V

Da simil.

Possibly far-fetched to drag in supposedly Epicurean attraction of likes, or to say that this widely held doctrine is here any special indication of Guido Cavalcanti's position, save in so far as it would rule out certain forms of mysticisms which teach attraction of opposites. A very slight flimsy aid in any sort of discussion.

Non giá selvagge.

Ce gives: "Mon gia selnagg? la belta suo dardo".

Mb: "Non go (or ga) selvagge, la (or lo) bilta f̄q̄. dardi" with several dots around whatever I take or mistake for the *q*.

In Ce the *o* over the terminal *i* of *selnaggi* may also be intended for an *e*. At any rate I do not pretend to understand this strophe, or to know whether *punto* is noun or verb, or whether *selvaggie* or *o* is the verb in that line, or whether the verb is *son* supposing that word is not *suo*.

The reading of Ld is clearly: "Non gia selvagge la bilta son dardj".

Rivalta: "selvaggio le beltà son dardo".

Di Giunta: "selvagge le bilta son dardo".

La: "suo dardo" (followed, I think, by Lc).

Le seems to have: "suo tardo".

Lm: "son dardo".

Ba is clearly: "la bilta son dardo" (or else I cannot read my own handwriting in my copy of Ba).

With which, as the general meaning is fairly clear, whichever phrase is correct, I cheerfully abandon the line to that ultimate judge, Tom Tiddler.

Punto.

Colonna, reading *che punto*, takes it to mean *stimulo*.

Bianco.

I think my translation is forced. I doubt very much if *bianco* can here have the highly particularized meaning of the "bull's eye" or centre of the target. The reader must choose for himself among mediaeval doctrines of colour, of diaphana, of all colours united in the white, of (I think less likely) ideas of katharsis, and balance this or bring it into relation with the "ultra-violet" or whatever interpretation one is to give to the "outside of colour" three lines further on; "colores fiant ex complexione ignis cum corpore dyaphano". My final opinion is that *compriso bianco* means understood as a whole. Cf. *Paradiso* VIII, 112 and X, 42.

Frachetta and the "Aldine".

Frachetta was a cultivated man who made a serious attempt to understand the canzone *via* Aristotle, we may take him as indicative of the state of aesthetics in 1585. There is nothing to indicate that he tried to place himself in 1290. His general interpretation of this passage (*cade*, etc.) is that it is simple negation of the question asked in l. 14: "Et se huom per veder lo puo mostrare?" The visual sense perceives colour, the mind perceives the proportion; Love is not colour, nor an object having colour.

The idea that Frachetta mistook the Giuntine edition for an Aldine could not have been put forward by anyone who had read F. with care. Thanks to Mr Adrian Stokes I have been able to locate the Aldine text; not of Guido's complete poems but of this canzone. Aldus printed it at the end of his second or third edition of Petrarch with the canzoni of Dante and Cino cited by Petrarch in "Lasso me, ch' io non so in qual parte pieghi".

Pico's remarks on Guido in the commentary on G. Benivieni, end of cap. 2, add nothing to our esteem of Pico.

Aude.

With the well-known alternative *vade*, Cd gives yet another turn with "Et che bene ha diforma nô se vede". Here, as in the case of the *dardo*, all one can say is that no one has yet improved on Di Giunta during the four disposable centuries.

Asciso.

I have no doubt regarding this reading. It means cut off. Contrast this with the "formam adhaerentem" of Albertus (*vide* note on *largir*) and connect with note on *rade*.

Rade.

The fifth meaning given to *radere* in the *Vocabolario della Crusca* is *andar resente*, and the example "Quella torre è dritta, e perpendicolare, e ci mostra (il senso) quella pietra nel cadere venirla radendo senza piegar pur un capello da questa o da quella parte". I take it that the *Amor* moves with the light in darkness, never touching it and never a hair's breadth from it.

Frachetta takes *radere* to mean merely cut off or blot out. This would let one in for the dark night of the soul, instead of leaving us the clean though highly complicated image. I think both

Guido and Arnaut exploit Latin. Guido was not slave to use of the article, which has now become such a bore in French and Italian. "Quoi! paroles en liberté!" exclaims a disgusted state examiner. I also think Guido is avoiding *radiare* and the "delle tenebre radiare luce". In Dante the "primum mobile" might be said *radere* the fixed heaven (*abscissum*).

Envoi. There is a diverting parallel to the coda in the 1602 edition of Colonna's commentary:

> "Va spositione mia sicuramente
> A gente di valor, a cui ti mando,
> Di star con nessun' huomo ti comando
> Il qual vuol usar l' occhio per la mente".

This is very possibly Thomism, in extreme gibe at observing Averroists and Roger-Baconians? Or perhaps it is only general exuberance at getting to the end of his job (not necessarily scribbled down by the learned commentator in person).

GUIDO'S RELATIONS

The critic, normally a bore and a nuisance, can justify his existence in one or more minor and subordinate ways: he may dig out and focus attention upon matter of interest that would otherwise have passed without notice; he may, in the rare cases when he has any really general knowledge or "perception of relations" (swift or other) locate his finds with regard to other literary inventions; he may, thirdly, or as you might say, conversely and as part and supplement of his first activity, construct cloacae to carry off the waste matter, which stagnates about the real work, and which is continuously being heaped up and caused to stagnate by academic bodies, obese publishing houses, and combinations of both, such as the Oxford Press. (We note their particular infamy in a recent re-issue of Palgrave.)

Since Dante's unfinished brochure on the common tongue Italy may have had no general literary criticism, the brochure is somewhat "special" and of interest mainly to practitioners of the art of writing. Lorenzo Valla somewhat altered the course of history by his close inspection of Latin usage. His prefaces have here and there a burst of magnificence, and the spirit of the Elegantiae should benefit any writer's lungs. As he wrote about an ancient idiom, Italian and English writers alike have, when they have heard his name at all, supposed that he had no "message" and, in the case of the Britons, they returned, we may suppose, to Pater's remarks on Pico. (Based on what the weary peruser of some few other parts of Pico's output, might pettishly denounce as Pico's one remarkable paragraph.)

The study called "comparative literature" was invented in Germany but has seldom if ever aspired to the study of "comparative values in letters".

The literature of the Mediterranean races continued in a steady descending curve of renaissance-ism. There are minor upward fluctuations. The best period of Italian poetry ends in the year 1321. So far as I know one excellent Italian tennis-player and no known Italian writer has thought of considering the local literature in relation to rest of the world.

Leopardo read, and imitated Shakespeare. The Prince of Monte Nevoso has been able to build his unique contemporary position because of barbarian contacts, whether consciously, and *via* visual stimulus from any printed pages, or simply because he was aware of, let us say, the existence of Wagner and Browning. Il Nostro Gabriele started something new in Italian. Hating barbarism, teutonism, never mentioning the existence of the ultimate Britons, unsurrounded by any sort of society or milieu, he ends as a solitary, superficially eccentric, but with a surprisingly sound standard of values, values, that is, as to the relative worth of a few perfect lines of writing, as contrasted to a great deal of flub-dub and "action".

The only living author who has ever taken a city or held up the diplomatic crapule at the point of machine-guns, he is in a position to speak with more authority than a batch of neurasthenic incompetents or of writers who never having swerved from their jobs, might be, or are, supposed by the scientists and the populace to be incapable of action. Like other serious characters who have taken seventy years to live and to learn to live, he has passed through periods wherein he lived (or wrote) we should not quite say "less ably", but with less immediately demonstrable result.

This period "nel mezzo", this passage of the "selva oscura" takes men in different ways, so different indeed that comparison is more likely to bring ridicule on the comparer than to focus attention on the analogy—often admittedly far-fetched.

In many cases the complete man makes a "very promising start", and then flounders or appears to flounder for ten years, or for twenty or thirty (cf. Henry James's middle period) to end, if he survive, with some sort of demonstration, discovery, or other justification of his having gone by the route he has (apparently) stumbled on.

When I "translated" Guido eighteen years ago I did *not* see Guido at all. I saw that Rossetti had made a remarkable translation of the *Vita Nuova*, in some places improving (or at least enriching) the original; that he was indubitably the man "sent", or "chosen", for that particular job, and that there was something in Guido that escaped him or that was, at any rate, absent from his translations. A *robustezza*, a masculinity. I had a great enthusiasm (perfectly justified) but I did not clearly see exterior demarcations—Euclid inside his cube, with no premonition of Cartesian axes.

My perception was not obfuscated by Guido's Italian,

difficult as it then was for me to read. I was obfuscated by the Victorian language.

If I hadn't been, I very possibly couldn't have done the job at all. I should have seen the too great multiplicity of problems contained in the one problem before me.

I don't mean that I didn't see dull spots in the sonnets. I saw that Rossetti had taken most of the best sonnets, that one couldn't make a complete edition of Guido simply by taking Rossetti's translations and filling in the gaps, it would have been too dreary a job. Even though I saw that Rossetti had made better English poems than I was likely to make by (in intention) sticking closer to the direction of the original. I began by meaning merely to give prose translation so that the reader ignorant of Italian could see what the melodic original meant. It is, however, an illusion to suppose that more than one person in every 300,000 has the patience or the intelligence to read a foreign tongue for its sound, or even to read what are known to be the masterworks of foreign melody, in order to learn the qualities of that melody, or to see where one's own falls short.

What obfuscated me was not the Italian but the crust of dead English, the sediment present in my own available vocabulary—which I, let us hope, got rid of a few years later. You can't go round this sort of thing. It takes six or eight years to get educated in one's art, and another ten to get rid of that education.

Neither can anyone learn English, one can only learn a series of Englishes. Rossetti made his own language. I hadn't in 1910 made a language, I don't mean a language to use, but even a language to think in.

It is stupid to overlook the lingual inventions of precurrent authors, even when they were fools or flapdoodles or Tennysons. It is sometimes advisable to sort out these languages and inventions, and to know what and why they are.

Keats, out of Elizabethans, Swinburne out of a larger set

CAVALCANTI

of Elizabethans and a mixed bag (Greeks, *und so weiter*), Rossetti out of Sheets, Kelly, and Co. plus early Italians (written and painted); and so forth, including *King Wenceslas*, ballads and carols.

Let me not discourage a possible reader, or spoil anyone's naïve enjoyment, by saying that my early versions of Guido are bogged in Dante Gabriel and in Algernon. It is true, but let us pass by it in silence. Where both Rossetti and I went off the rails was in taking an English sonnet as the equivalent for a sonnet in Italian. I don't mean in overlooking the mild difference in the rhyme scheme. The mistake is "quite natural", very few mistakes are "unnatural". Rime looks very important. Take the rimes off a good sonnet, and there is a vacuum. And besides the movement of *some* Italian sonnets *is* very like that in some sonnets in English. The feminine rhyme goes by the board...again for obvious reasons. It had gone by the board, quite often, in Provençal. The French made an ecclesiastical law about using it 50/50.

As a bad analogy, imagine a Giotto or Simone Martini fresco, "translated" into oils by "Sir Joshua", or Sir Frederick Leighton. Something is lost, something is somewhat denatured.

Suppose, however, we have a Cimabue done in oil, not by Holbein, but by some contemporary of Holbein who can't paint as well as Cimabue.

There are about seven reasons why the analogy is incorrect, and six more to suppose it inverted, but it may serve to free the reader's mind from preconceived notions about the English of "Elizabeth" and her British garden of songbirds.—And to consider language as a medium of expression.

(Breton forgives Flaubert on hearing that Father Gustave was trying only to give "l'impression de la couleur jaune" (*Nadja*, p. 12).)

Dr Schelling has lectured about the Italianate Englishman of Shakespeare's day. I find two Shakespeare plots within

CAVALCANTI

ten pages of each other in a forgotten history of Bologna, printed in 1596. We have heard of the effects of the travelling Italian theatre companies, *commedia dell' arte*, etc. What happens when you idly attempt to translate early Italian into English, unclogged by the Victorian era, freed from sonnet obsession, but trying merely to sing and to leave out the dull bits in the Italian, or the bits you don't understand?

I offer you a poem that "don't matter", it is attributed to Guido in Codex Barberiniano Lat. 3953. Alacci prints it as Guido's; Simone Occhi in 1740 says that Alacci is a fool or words to that effect and a careless man without principles, and proceeds to print the poem with those of Cino Pistoia. Whoever wrote it, it is, indubitably, not a *capo lavoro*.

"Madonna la vostra belta enfolio
Si li mei ochi che menan lo core   MS. *oghi*
A la bataglia ove l' ancise amore
Che del vostro placer armato uscio;   *usio*

Si che nel primo asalto che asalio
Passo dentro la mente e fa signore,
E prese l' alma che fuzia di fore
Planzendo di dolor che vi sentio.

Però vedete che vostra beltate
Mosse la folia und e il cor morto
Et a me ne convien clamar pietate,

Non per campar, ma per aver conforto
Ne la morte crudel che far min fate
Et o rason sel non vinzesse il torto."

Is it worth an editor's while to include it among dubious attributions? It is not very attractive: until one starts playing with the simplest English equivalent.

"Lady thy beauty doth so mad mine eyes,
Driving my heart to strife wherein he dies."

CAVALCANTI

Sing it of course, don't try to speak it. It thoroughly falsifies the movement of the Italian, it is an opening quite good enough for Herrick or Campion. It will help you to understand just why Herrick, and Campion, and possibly Donne are still with us.

The next line is rather a cliché; the line after more or less lacking in interest. We pull up on:

> "Whereby thou seest how fair thy beauty is
> To compass doom".

That would be very nice, but it is hardly translation.

Take these scraps, and the almost impossible conclusion, a tag of Provençal rhythm, and make them into a plenum. It will help you to understand some of M. de Schloezer's remarks about Stravinsky's trend toward melody. And you will also see what the best Elizabethan lyricists did, as well as what they didn't.

My two lines take the opening and two and a half of the Italian, English more concise; and the octave gets too light for the sestet. Lighten the sestet.

> "So unto Pity must I cry
> Not for safety, but to die.
> Cruel Death is now mine ease
> If that he thine envoy is."

We are preserving one value of early Italian work, the cantabile; and we are losing another, that is the specific weight. And if we notice it we fall on a root difference between early Italian, "The philosophic school coming out of Bologna", and the Elizabethan lyric. For in these two couplets, and in attacking this sonnet, I have let go the fervour and the intensity, which were all I, rather blindly, had to carry through my attempt of twenty years gone.

And I think that if anyone now lay, or if we assume that they mostly *then* (in the expansive days) laid, aside care for specific statement of emotion, a dogmatic statement, made with the seriousness of someone to whom it mattered whether he had three souls, one in the head, one in the heart, one possibly in his abdomen, or lungs, or wherever Plato, or Galen had located it; if the anima is still breath, if the stopped heart is a dead heart, and if it is all serious, much more serious than it would have been to Herrick, the imaginary investigator will see more or less how the Elizabethan modes came into being.

Let him try it for himself, on any Tuscan author of that time, taking the words, not thinking greatly of their significance, not balking at clichés, but being greatly intent on the melody, on the single uninterrupted flow of syllables—as open as possible, that can be sung prettily, that are not very interesting if spoken, that don't even work into a period or an even metre if spoken.

And the mastery, a minor mastery, will lie in keeping this line unbroken, as unbroken in sound as a line in one of Miro's latest drawings is on paper; and giving it perfect balance, with no breaks, no bits sticking ineptly out, and no losses to the force of individual phrases.

> "Whereby thou seest how fair thy beauty is
> To compass doom."

Very possibly too regularly "iambic" to fit in the finished poem.

There is opposition, not only between what M. de Schloezer distinguishes as musical and poetic lyricism, but in the writing itself there is a distinction between poetic lyricism, the emotional force of the verbal movement, and melopœic lyricism, the letting the words flow on a melodic current, realized or not, realizable or not, if the line is supposed to be sung on a sequence of notes of different pitch.

But by taking these Italian sonnets, which are not metrically the equivalent of the English sonnet, by sacrificing, or losing, or simply not feeling and understanding their cogency, their sobriety, and by seeking simply that far from quickly or so-easily-as-it-looks attainable thing, the perfect melody, careless of exactitude of idea, or careless as to which profound and fundamental idea you, at that moment, utter, perhaps in precise enough phrases, by cutting away the apparently non-functioning phrases (whose appearance deceives) you find yourself in the English *seicento* song-books.

Death has become melodious; sorrow is as serious as the nightingale's, tombstones are shelves for the reception of rose-leaves. And there is, quite often, a Mozartian perfection of melody, a wisdom, almost perhaps an ultimate wisdom, deplorably lacking in guts. My phrase is, shall we say, vulgar. Exactly, because it fails in precision. Guts in surgery refers to a very limited range of internal furnishings. A thirteenth-century exactitude in search for the exact organ best illustrating the lack, would have saved me that plunge. We must turn again to the Latins. When the late T. Roosevelt was interviewed in France on his return from the jungle, he used a phrase which was translated (the publication of the interview rather annoyed him). The French at the point I mention ran: "Ils ont voulu me briser les *reins*, mais je les ai solides".

And now the reader may, if he like, return to the problem of the "eyes that lead the heart to battle where him love kills". This was not felt as an inversion. It was 1280, Italian was still in the state that German is to-day. How can you have "PROSE" in a country where the chambermaid comes into your room and exclaims: "Schön ist das Hemd!"

Continue: "who armed with thy delight, is come forth so that at the first assault he assails, he passes inward to the mind, and lords it there, and catches the breath (soul) that was fleeing, lamenting the grief I feel.

"Whereby thou seest how thy beauty moves the madness, whence is the heart dead (stopped) and I must cry on Pity, not to be saved but to have ease of the cruel death thou puttest on me. And I am right (?) save the wrong him conquereth".

Whether the reader will accept this little problem in melopœia as substitute for the cross-word puzzle I am unable to predict. I leave it on the supposition that the philosopher should try almost everything once.

As second exercise, we may try the sonnet by Guido Orlando which is supposed to have invited Cavalcanti's *Donna mi Prega.*

> "Say what is Love, whence doth he start ?
> Through what be his courses bent ?
> Memory, substance, accident ?
> A chance of eye or will of heart ?
>
> Whence he state or madness leadeth ?
> Burns he with consuming pain ?
> Tell me, friend, on what he feedeth ?
> How, where, and o'er whom doth he reign ?
>
> Say what is Love, hath he a face ?
> True form or vain similitude ?
> Is the Love life, or is he death ?
>
> Thou shouldst know for rumour saith:
> Servant should know his master's mood—
> Oft art thou ta'en in his dwelling-place."

I give the Italian to show that there is no deception, I have invented nothing, I have given a *verbal* weight about equal to that of the original, and arrived at this equality by dropping a couple of syllables per line. The great past-master of pastiche has, it might seem, passed this way before me. A line or two of this, a few more from Lorenzo Medici, and he has concocted one of the finest gems in our language.

> "Onde si move e donde nasce Amore
>   qual è suo proprio luogo, ov' ei dimora?

> Sustanza, o accidente, o ei memora?
> E cagion d' occhi, o è voler di cuore?
>
> Da che procede suo stato o furore?
> Come fuoco si sente che divora?
> Di che si nutre domand' io ancora,
> Come, e quando, e di cui si fa signore?
>
> Che cosa è, dico, amor? ae figura?
> A per se forma o pur somiglia altrui?
> E vita questo amore ovvero e morte?
>
> Chi 'l serve dee saver di sua natura:
> Io ne domando voi, Guido, di lui:
> Odo che molto usate in la sua corte."

We are not in a realm of proofs, I suggest, simply, the way in which early Italian poetry has been utilized in England. The Italian of Petrarch and his successors is of no interest to the practising writer or to the student of comparative dynamics in language, the collectors of bric-à-brac are outside our domain.

There is no question of giving Guido in an English contemporary to himself, the ultimate Britons were at that date unbreeched, painted in woad, and grunting in an idiom far more difficult for us to master than the Langue d'Oc of the Plantagenets or the Lingua di Si.

If, however, we reach back to pre-Elizabethan English, of a period when the writers were still intent on clarity and explicitness, still preferring them to magniloquence and the thundering phrase, our trial, or mine at least, results in:

> "Who is she that comes, makying turn every man's eye
> And makying the air to tremble with a bright clearenesse
> That leadeth with her Love, in such nearness
> No man may proffer of speech more than a sigh?
>
> Ah God, what she is like when her owne eye turneth, is
> Fit for Amor to speake, for I cannot at all;

Such is her modesty, I would call
Every woman else but an useless uneasiness.

No one could ever tell all of her pleasauntness
In that every high noble vertu leaneth to herward,
So Beauty sheweth her forth as her Godhede;

Never before so high was our mind led,
Nor have we so much of heal as will afford
That our mind may take her immediate in its embrace".

The objections to such a method are: the doubt as to whether one has the right to take a serious poem and turn it into a mere exercise in quaintness; the "misrepresentation" not of the poem's antiquity, but of the proportionate feel of that antiquity, by which I mean that Guido's thirteenth-century language is to twentieth-century Italian sense much less archaic than any fourteenth-, fifteenth-, or early sixteenth-century English is for us. It is even doubtful whether my bungling version of twenty years back isn't more "faithful", in the sense at least that it tried to preserve the fervour of the original. And as this fervour simply does not occur in English poetry in those centuries there is no ready-made verbal pigment for its objectification.

In the long run the translator is in all probability impotent to do *all* of the work for the linguistically lazy reader. He can show where the treasure lies, he can guide the reader in choice of what tongue is to be studied, and he can very materially assist the hurried student who has a smattering of a language and the energy to read the original text alongside the metrical gloze.

This refers to "interpretive translation". The "other sort", I mean in cases where the "translator" is definitely making a new poem, falls simply in the domain of original writing, or if it does not it must be censured according to equal standards, and praised with some sort of just deduction, assessable only in the particular case.